ROYALTIES

VICTORIAN LITERATURE AND CULTURE SERIES

Karen Chase, Jerome J. McGann, *and* Herbert Tucker, *Editors*

ROYALTIES

The Queen and
Victorian Writers

————⦿————

Gail Turley Houston

UNIVERSITY PRESS OF VIRGINIA
Charlottesville and London

The University Press of Virginia
© 1999 by the Rector and Visitors of the University of Virginia
All rights reserved
Printed in the United States of America

First published 1999

∞ The paper used in this publication meets the minimum requirements of the
American National Standard for Information Sciences—Permanence of Paper
for Printed Library Materials, ANSI z39.48-1984.

Library of Congress Cataloging-in-Publication Data
Houston, Gail Turley, 1950–
Royalties : the queen and Victorian writers / Gail Turley Houston.
p.   cm. — (Victorian literature and culture series)
Includes bibliographical references and index.
ISBN 0-8139-1893-6 (cloth : alk. paper)
1. English literature—19th century—History and criticism.   2. Politics and
literature—Great Britain—History—19th century.   3. Women and
literature—Great Britain—History—19th century.   4. Victoria, Queen of
Great Britain, 1819–1901—Influence.   5. Great Britain—History—Victoria,
1837–1901.   6. Authority in literature.   7. Monarchy in
literature.   8. Queens in literature.   I. Title.   II. Series.
PR461.H68   1999
820.9'351—dc21   99-21545
CIP

Women crowd closely upon the great high-road of the past. The unobtrusive domestic creature which is held up to us as the great model and type of the sex, could never be guessed at as its representative, did we form our ideas according to experience and evidence, instead of under the happy guidance of the conventional and imaginary. Every other kind and fashion of woman, except that correct and abstract being, is to be found in history; women who are princes, heroines, martyrs, givers of good and of evil counsel, leaders of parties, makers of wars. Their robes mingle with the succincter garments of statesmen and soldiers round them, with an equality of position and interest such as no theory knows.

Margaret Oliphant, *Historical Sketches of the Reign of George Second*

Contents

Illustrations

Preface

Women in history, strangely enough, seem always to impart to the chronicle a certain heat of personal feeling to which their companions are not subject. Whether it is that the historian is impatient to find himself arrested by the troublesome personality of a woman, and that a certain resentment of her intrusion colours all his appreciation of her; or that her appearance naturally possesses an individuality which breaks the line, it is difficult to tell; but the calmest chronicler becomes a partisan when he treats of [Queens] Mary and Elizabeth.

Margaret Oliphant, *Historical Sketches of the Reign of Queen Anne*

HAVING SPENT THE past six years researching Queen Victoria, it is difficult not to be partisan about her cultural effects, her thoroughgoing vivacity and longevity as a historical figure, and her capacity to produce a "certain heat" in her biographers and aficionados, as well as in the scholarly community. In this study I approach this formidable "woman in history" as a historical figure, a figure of speech, a cultural figure underlying Victorian writers' signifying practices, and as a writing agent herself. Because of Victoria's many disparate fictional and historical meanings and manifestations, it has been difficult to focus on one aspect of her reign or cultural capital. But this is a condition to be celebrated. As one Victorian scholar has generously suggested to me, because of her very diversity and complexity, there is room for many to study this fascinating monarch. Recognition of the various effects and aspects of the woman whose name defines the age also induces us to recognize the divergences and complexities in what once seemed to be a historically seamless era.

Indeed, as Margaret Oliphant posits, historians lose their purported objectivity when women become the subject of study. As this popular, prolific nineteenth-century writer recognizes, Victorian representation—whether in history or fiction—explicitly troubles and is troubled by legal, historical, and fictional constructions of women. Oliphant localizes that trouble in historical queens, whose very existence undermines generic representations of woman's nonsubjectivity and lack of sovereignty. By making such a move, the novelist suggests that representation might escape the bind that binary constructions of gender produce by focusing less on sex characteristics and more on individual characteristics. This tactical maneuver broadens understandings of the self and suggests that women who make trouble about gender positively change and enrich the previously limited course of history.

By focusing on the gender of authority and the feminization of aesthetic and political representation in the Victorian age, this study has helped me to be more sensitive to the indeterminacy and incommensurability of the personalities, historical forces, and literature we examine as cultural critics, and to acknowledge the richness and density of the web we refer to as the Victorian period. "Arrested" by Queen Victoria's unruly meanings, I have also been fascinated by the ways in which professional Victorian writers, viewed as geniuses by their own age and ours, are demystified when they encounter Queen Victoria's "troublesome personality" in their writing. It is also fascinating to examine the ways in which Victoria self-consciously demystifies and reinforces herself as a cultural icon, particularly through her insistence upon wearing the mantel of writer. Intuitively sensing the authority to be added to her already monumental cultural power, Victoria co-opted the author's professional perquisites even as writers sought to augment their trade by trading places, as it were, with the queen.

Acknowledgments

THIS PROJECT COULD not have been completed without the help of many people. They include the ever gracious Lady Sheila de Bellaigue, registrar of the Royal Archives at Windsor Castle, the staff at the National Library of Scotland, the National Art Library at the Victoria and Albert Museum, and the Harry Ransom Humanities Research Center at the University of Texas at Austin, which provided access to the Gernsheim Collection and the Robert Wolff Collection. Scott Duvall, curator of the Victorian Collection at the Brigham Young University Special Collections, was also a tremendous help. The staff in Special Collections at the Southern Illinois University Library are also to be thanked. Princeton University Library graciously supplied materials from the Meirs Collection of Cruikshank, Graphic Arts Collections, Visual Materials Division, Department of Rare Books and Special Collections. Also, by gracious permission of the Royal Archives © Her Majesty Queen Elizabeth II, other important materials were provided. I am grateful as well for generous grants from the English Department, College of Humanities, and the Women's Research Institute at Brigham Young University. A research grant from the University of New Mexico made it possible to complete the project. I thank *Philological Quarterly* for giving me the space to study Dickens and Barrett Browning in earlier versions of chapters 3 and 4. Revised portions of my chapter in *Remaking Queen Victoria,* edited by Margaret Homans and Adrienne Munich and published by Cambridge University Press, who kindly gave permission for their use here, appear in chapter 1 of this study.

In addition, I want to express thanks to Elizabeth Young, Luis Leme, Jalene Wangsgaard, Susan Cannata, SueAnn Schatz, and Chandra Parker for their rigorous, unstinting service. I want to thank Cathie Brettschneider and Julie Falconer for their patient and astute handling of the manuscript. For their generosity and integrity, Adrienne Munich, Margaret Homans, Minrose Gwin, and Alexander Welsh also command my respect and esteem. I must also thank my exemplary colleagues Claudia Harris, Brandie Siegfried, Susan Howe, Kent Harrison, Kristine Hansen, Suzanne Lundquist, Fred Gedicks, Grant Boswell, Tom Plummer, Steve Goates, Steve Walker, Rick Duerden, Scott Abbott, Sam Rushforth, and Bill Evenson. My brothers Kent and Mark Turley also must be thanked for their generosity. Finally, my gratitude, as always, to Michael, Melissa, and Kate.

ROYALTIES

Introduction: "Home Lessons" for the Woman Who Would Be Queen

There is something in the position of sovereign which seems to develop and call forth the qualities of a woman beyond that of any other occupation.

Margaret Oliphant, *Historical Sketches of the Reign of George Second*

DEEPLY CONFLICTED ABOUT, antagonistic toward, yet on the whole profoundly loyal to the concept of a queen regnant, Victorians viewed their female monarch as an acceptable, if sometimes disturbing, historical aberration. As both a sovereign and a woman, Victoria was the unsettling focal point for a number of anomalies: She was a reigning queen in an age whose dominant ideology situated women as queens in the private sphere and warned them against participation in the public sphere. While the age concocted the platitude "he to rule, she to obey," Victorians also prided themselves on being the subjects of a long-reigning, efficient, and often masterful female sovereign. Virtually always associated with her gender and its effect on her reign, her subjects, and the nation-state, Victoria—as many of her subjects asserted—"womanized" or "feminized" the age. At the same time, her reign helped to launch discussions about what "queenly womanhood" was. Indeed, upon Victoria's accession, anxieties about and emotional attachments to "queenly womanhood" significantly informed public discussions about political sovereignty, individual subjectivity, and representation.

Recognition of Victoria's importance to studies of Victorian culture has occurred only recently. As Adrienne Munich notes in *Queen Victoria's*

Secrets, "Victorianists do not regard Victoria as central to her era, though no one denies her function as a cultural icon."[1] But to fail to see Victoria as pivotal is to miss how crucial gender issues were to the Victorians. Recent feminist scholarship on Victoria has expanded our understanding of the queen and, consequently, of the age over which she ruled, pointing out that constraints upon and controversies about sex roles inflected all of Victorian life in diverse, discordant, complicated ways. As a result, Victoria herself is now coming to be seen as a crucial representation of those incongruities, as at once the imperial monarch and the domestic angel, the exemplar of supreme power and the model of wifely submission, the commanding force in British politics and the reclusive widow who shunned the political limelight.

Dorothy Thompson was the first to develop a full-scale feminist scholarly approach to Victoria, focusing on the way a queen's gender troubles sovereignty. Elizabeth Langland, in *Nobody's Angels*, has illustrated the frictions that resulted from the fact that under Victoria "women" and "power" became correlative terms rather than entities relegated to separate spheres. Too, *The Woman Question* (by Helsinger, Sheets, and Veeder) includes a chapter that examines the complexity of this queen. Asserting that Victoria's reign accentuated Victorian debates about "differences between men and women," Adrienne Munich focuses on the "cultural work" Victoria "performed" and the ways she used ideologies about the roles of women to her own advantage. Margaret Homans also examines Victoria's political savvy, suggesting that the British monarch brilliantly and consciously performed her conflicted roles, simultaneously displaying her magnificent civic power and her private, middle-class domesticity.[2]

Remaking Queen Victoria, a new collection of essays edited by Munich and Homans, is another invaluable illustration of Victoria's complexity. While Susan Casteras argues that "Victoria Regina . . . was the monarch, a cultural artifact, and a symbol of political power, patriotism, and public consensus," Munich and Homans suggest that there are "many Victorias." In their view, Victoria is a "diffus[e]" figure whose long reign allows us to have "entry" into many diverse "cultural formation[s]" with "disparate legacies." As *Remaking Queen Victoria* further suggests, the queen "meant different things to different groups" and "does not have a fixed identity to which others accede or object: instead, her image is created even as it is read, and destabilized even when it is treated as monolithic." Thus one of the underlying assumptions of *Remaking Queen Victoria* is that, as an individual and as a cultural sign, Victoria was situated in a web of larger cultural forces that were conflictual, simultaneous, and always in process.[3]

I, too, analyze the complexities inherent in the roles Victoria filled as a woman and sovereign. In particular, this study adds another component to the investigation by examining the relationship between Victoria and Victorian writers, a subject that has received little attention in scholarly studies of the queen. While I focus on the dynamics between Victoria and specific Victorian writers, I recognize that my analysis of those dynamics cannot be conclusive about Victoria's meanings. Certainly, much of the complicated cultural web within which I situate my discussion is beyond the scope of this book. But by centering my study on the intertextuality of Victoria and Victorian writers, I hope to display the complexity of Victorian gender ideologies, in particular the gendering of the professional writer, as well as the dynamics of the feminization of the age.

The descriptive term "feminization" is itself troubled, especially when it is associated with Victoria: It alludes to the increasing political empowerment of women in the nineteenth century; yet it also refers to the loss of power that occurs when an entity becomes associated with the feminine. The ideological ambiguity of the term "feminization," then, underlines my discussion of Victoria and Victorian writers. Obviously Victoria was not the only force implicated in the feminization of the age, and neither was she always an active agent informing the age's dominant ideologies. She was probably more acted upon by that ideology than she was its prime mover. As Homans suggests, "If monarchs do have individual agency at all, it takes, by the time of Victoria, the form of influencing ideological shifts, and for Victoria this power lay in manipulating the spectacle of royalty, as well as in being manipulated by it."[4]

Nevertheless, if the age was feminized, certainly the monarch's gender accentuated that feminization, putting the sovereign and the subject in a troubled feminine position. While we may assume, in addition, that both Victorian writers and their queen were actuated by the complicated culture within which they lived, we must also recognize that both were explicitly involved in representing that increasingly feminized culture. Vitally implicated in the representation of gender, in the gender of authority vis-à-vis authorship, and in the feminization of the age, the queen and many Victorian writers often represented themselves as having each other's representative powers. On the most elementary level of analysis, we can say that the queen took great pleasure in her success as a popular writer. At the same time, some Victorian authors exhibited a thinly disguised envy of the authority that royalty automatically conferred on Victoria, an authority that they themselves had to work hard to achieve. Whether or not they were explicitly aware of a desire to trade places professionally, Victorian writers and the queen competed with each other for the right to represent the culture.

In chapter 1, assuming the connection between political and literary representations, I examine the anomalous ways the queen regnant was represented in legal texts and compare these with Victoria's own hybrid construction of her legally constituted identity. Chapter 2 lays the groundwork for studying the historical construction of British writers and their monarch as antagonists competing over the right to represent the nation. To a great extent, the Victorian writer's gender became a marker of the right to wear the laurel crown. With this in mind, I look at how contemporary writers represented Queen Victoria and examine some of the ways in which her reign both undermined and supported the British gendering of professional authority. Chapters 3 through 5 focus on the exchanges between Victoria and three specific writers, Charles Dickens, Elizabeth Barrett Browning, and Margaret Oliphant. Dickens, Barrett Browning, and Oliphant all picture—and attempt to consolidate—their trade by both explicitly and subliminally comparing their profession with the monarch's. Likewise, in her exchanges with these authors, Victoria either minimizes the value of the writer's trade, or, with a mixture of shrewdness and naiveté, directs the professional author's attention to her own published writings.

I do not want to give the impression that I see Queen Victoria as a necessary or monolithic entity possessing the essence of power, of which Victorian writers desired to dispossess her. Neither do I view authentic power or authority as necessarily inherent in the profession of writer. My study is based on the premise that powerful political systems are riddled with self-contradictory loopholes that undermine the law's authority. Thus, as I maintain throughout this work, the dialectic of power is unpredictable, synergistic, and contradictory. As Dickens illustrated so well, inertia, indifference, and ineffectuality are as much a part of the fabulous, seemingly monolithic Ideological State Apparatus of the Circumlocution Office as is the will to supervisory power. To be sure, systems intended explicitly to dominate often end up showing "how *not* to do it" (my emphasis). As a corollary to this assumption, I believe that individuals are not simply subjected to culturally mandated gender roles. As Regenia Gagnier suggests, subjects can and do mediate and transform discursive institutional efforts to discipline the self. Or, as one Victorian feminist put it, if woman's role is submission, "even when the submission is forced, there are a thousand ways in which resistance can and will take place."[5]

Thus I view the relationships between writers and Victoria as a complicated mix of personal desires and inadequacies, always related to gender and always underwritten by the need to maintain personal and professional sovereignty. As I see it, the legal, political, and professional instability of the queen's and the writer's sovereignty made it even more desirable to attempt to dominate the culture through representation. Concomitantly, I view the individual writer and monarch as entities constructed through and by the unstable culture they hoped to represent. Hence my study participates in a demystification of canonized Victorian authors, a modus operandi that nevertheless, in my case at least, does not seek to banish them from the canon. Indeed, such demystification humanizes these writers whom our age has tended to lionize, and, as a result, helps to democratize the relationship between reader and writer, allowing reciprocal empathy to be part of the trade.

My study assumes, then, that the author is not dead, and neither is the queen. In other words, in contrast to postmodern deconstructions of selfhood, my analysis of the queen's and writers' mutual envy takes them as real individuals who experienced a real interior life that was simultaneously intertwined with their immersion in their culture. This is not to say that we can fully identify their reality. Nor can we erase the multiple, varied, intertextual, and conflicted fictional emanations and personas with which Victorian authors and their queen were and are associated. I would, in fact, expand Adrienne Munich's apt description of Victoria's "excess of representation"[6] to include the rich, complicated, intense personas and representations of and by Oliphant, Barrett Browning, and Dickens. The awareness that these were real people who experienced the ineffable vagaries of life while also acknowledging their abundant fictionality, allows us, I think, to show more justice toward and understanding of the complexity of human experience. It also helps us to tackle the seemingly intractable problems that result from essentialist views of gender and power.

My intent is to complicate the way we look at both canonical and non-canonical Victorian writers vis-à-vis the queen, and to examine the ways in which this monarch troubles and triggers representation, gender construction, and authority while she is also already subject to them. Trading places in their quest for cultural capital, Queen Victoria and Victorian authors consciously and subliminally competed for domination over a realm that could not be figured on a geographical map. Competing over representation, these "representative" Victorians prefigured modern concerns about who creates, controls, and distributes a culture's knowledge systems and oversees inter- and intracultural exchanges within those systems. The professionalization of two seemingly superfluous modern careers—that of the author and that of the monarch—in nineteenth-century capitalist Britain suggests what the stakes might have entailed in the competition for representative power. I will also examine how both demands for and fears of the feminization of the age always influenced contemporary evaluations of the queen's representative power.

For many, Victoria was doubly a queen because she was the epitome of the queenly woman as well as the actual monarch. In his nostalgic *The Queen's Resolve: And Her "Doubly Royal" Reign*, for example, Charles Bullock refers in his subtitle to Victoria's fulfillment of the role of queen in both the private and public spheres, yet clearly he is only writing about Victoria because she is the political queen, not because she is the exemplar of the unknown wives of England. Conflating and thus camouflaging the disparities in the two queenly roles, Bullock approvingly quotes the *Spectator*'s assessment of Queen Victoria's accomplishments. "When you go deep enough," says the *Spectator*, "a Royal family is only a family." And in "any well-ordered family," it is the mother who "is essentially the focus of all sympathy." While other people "may understand," the queen/mother "feels." According to the *Spectator*, the queen is appropriately referred to as "the mother of her people" because "she could not have been [queen] had she not been a mother indeed."[7]

Bullock also believes that the maternal queen's authority rests on her acknowledgment of the male subject as the rightful bulwark of the state. Arguing that the "home" lesson is the most important feature of his book,

Bullock teaches that in Victoria's reign, "Every man's home should be his 'palace.'" To illustrate his point, Bullock quotes a commoner's sympathetic lament that Princess Victoria is destined to rule a kingdom rather than a simple hearth. Writing just a year before her accession, the anonymous poet notes that "The voice of millions will thy rule proclaim." But this fate brings the working-class writer no joy, for in the next stanza he exclaims,

> *Oh! I could feel for thee—sincerely feel!*
> *And wish thou wert not fated to such care,*
> *But had some calm home where thou might'st reveal*
> *The heart's affections to the quiet there!*
> *Then—then indeed I might thee gratulate,*
> *And say thou wert the very loved of fate!*[8]

Thus both Bullock and the anonymous poet condescendingly examine the queen's womanly role, and, though loyal to her, implicitly suggest that her gender mitigates their presumption of familiarity. After all, as a woman, her first priority should be the "home lesson."

Like Bullock, the anonymous author of the Jubilee pamphlet "The Queen of Queens" imagines the natural connection between Queen Victoria and all Englishwomen. In a written type of the *tableau vivant*, the author dramatizes three fictional representatives of the women of England who come to pay tribute to their exemplar, the queen. First a middle-class mother steps forward and proclaims, "Great Queen but Greater Woman, we love you much because you have reigned over us so wisely, and we love you more because you have opened your kindly woman's heart to us in our troubles and in our joys." She continues, "Every office which a woman can fill you have filled with dignity and honour. You have ennobled for us the homely rank of matron, of wife, of mother; you have sanctified anew the sweet relationships of domestic life." Asserting that Victoria is a "bright example" to all women, the spokeswoman concludes that the queen has "been what every English woman ought to be, in the household which she is called upon to control."[9]

Likewise, when the maidens of England designate a virgin to speak their piece to the sovereign, she values the queen's femininity above her wisdom as a ruler. As this spokeswoman remarks, "we love you more because you have reigned ever in the hearts of simple English maidens, teaching them to keep Innocency, and shielding them by the strength of your Virtues from sorrow and from harm." Asserting that Victoria's "blameless life" serves as a pattern for all virgins, the nominal leader of the maidens praises Her Majesty for having "taught us all, from the highest to the lowest, how a lady ought to think and speak, and what a lady ought to do." Moreover, "the girls of every rank among us, in every mansion and in every village home, thank you for helping them to keep what is best worth keeping, and love you for the sweet lessons of your glorious reign."[10] With scarcely a reference to the queen's political sovereignty, the "sweet lessons" have to do with the "home" lessons directly applicable to all girls: being a queenly woman means manifesting the qualities of virtue, submission, and above all chastity.

When it comes to the spokesperson for the young girls, traditional Victorian notions of femininity are infiltrated with the New Woman's aspirations. The queenly girl starts out with the obligatory appositive, "Great Queen but greater Mother . . . you have made us just as happy as you have made the boys and we love you every bit as much as they do." But what does this maiden mean by suddenly bringing boys into the picture? Surprisingly, the young woman includes boys in her address because Victoria has allegedly brought about what Mary Wollstonecraft could not, the equality of the sexes. As the young lady explains,

> *Things might have been so very different with us, if you hadn't been so nice. Grandmamma says that sixty years ago women were looked upon as inferior animals, and little girls of course as more inferior still; and sisters were snubbed by their younger brothers, and made to fetch and carry. Our brothers never attempt to snub us now; we shouldn't stand it for a moment; and if they tried it on we should shut them up and laugh at them. There are lots of things that I can do just as well as any of my brothers can, and rather better. But sixty years ago, Grandmamma says, I shouldn't have been allowed to try, and I don't think that is quite fair. You have made it all right for me and my happy playmates, dear gracious Queen of Queens.*[11]

This anonymous writer, who begins with quite conventional praise for the queen's home lessons, not only asserts Victoria's efficient feminine rule of England but also implies that a woman's reign is always accompanied by gender troubles. In this case, her feminine difference domesticates political relations while it also politicizes the domestic.

If chastity was the distinct Victorian marker of the queenly woman's separation from the public woman, it is not too surprising to find another Jubilee celebrant simultaneously praising and interrogating the queen's sexual probity. Asking "Who can find a virtuous woman?," the writer ambiguously answers his own query, remarking, "Who can say that this description does not appertain to our beloved Queen." But in posing his question rhetorically, the writer actually leads the reader to question Her Majesty's purity rather than to assume it. In this way the ostensibly loyal subject shows that he can catechize and thus subject the queen to his own authority. Similarly, the queen's gender is the troublesome focal point of another occasional piece written by lyricist F. W. Orde Ward for the 1897 Jubilee. Avowing that "It was the / Almighty made her strong," though "her woman's acts were weak," Ward celebrates the queen's astounding accomplishment of simply surviving as a female monarch.[12] Indeed, her gender blinds Ward to any other categorical evaluations of her tenure and textually always makes her troublesome and vulnerable.

In still another occasional piece, an anonymous writer describes the power relations between the queen and her male troops, ostensibly in order to praise the monarch. Entitled "Queen's Address to the Volunteer Army," the poem begins with Victoria addressing the army:

> *Men of a thousand hills!—*
> *O Children of my Clan!*
> *I know your love is far above*
> *What woman beareth man!*

The categorical definition of woman as the inferior gender is extended when, in a later stanza, the writer has Victoria proudly declare her feelings for the troops: "I only know I feel as though / Victoria were a king!"[13] Figured as a mere mimic of the true masculine essence of sovereign power, in this verse Victoria becomes the caretaker woman monarch who would—but never can—be king. Thus the writer subliminally shows that his masculinity puts him in closer proximity to true sovereignty than any woman could ever achieve.

Such confused identity formation based on gender occurs also in "The King Comes!" In this occasional piece celebrating Edward VII's reign, H. Somerset Bullock attempts to praise and bury Edward's predecessor, Queen Victoria. But Victoria's importunate femininity as well as her extremely effective rule overshadow the festivities for the new king.

> *THE KING comes!*—ah, but the Queen is dead.
> *KINGLINESS claims the realm!*
> *MANLINESS holds the helm!*
> Ah, but the Mother is sped.

The overdetermined engendering of sovereignty reaches a climax in the last two stanzas, which include the lines:

> *THE KING comes! SON of our Mother-Queen,*
> *SON of the MOTHER who yearned*
> *With a love that ever burned*
> And ah, what that love has been!

Though he capitalizes the masculine form of monarchy for good measure and minimizes the feminine form with italics, the writer still cannot evade the formidable presence of Victoria brooding over her son's accession in the final lines of the poem. Although "THE KING comes! Seeing GOD'S THRONE above," the final line nevertheless reiterates, *"Reigns still Victoria's love."* [14] Having figured gender as exclusionary, the poet can only imagine the queen's sex as haunting and ultimately canceling out a King's rule.

In these representations of gender, female sovereignty always acts as a threat to masculinity even when it is constructed as maternal or virginal. Nevertheless, in British history the politically constituted male subject relies on the potential political subjectivity of a particular female citizen—the queen—to ensure the continuation of generic monarchical government at particular historical moments. Those moments take place, of course, when there is no male legally placed to inherit the royal robes. This contingency requires that a disruption of cultural gender constructs be always potentially available yet usually suppressed. Hence, as all of these authors were well aware, British law required men to pay obeisance to a queen regnant while it figured women in general as subordinate to male subjects. How British legal constructions of sovereignty engendered representational confusion is the subject of the following chapter.

I

"In the Reign of Queen Dick": Legal Fictions and the Constitution of Female Sovereignty

She was queen, then, at length. She was the central figure of a fiction as splendid as the Kenilworth of Sir Walter Scott, and all the world looked with interest upon its gorgeous illusions. . . . she seemed to the imaginations of men the most brilliant and most enviable of human beings. . . . She could not, at first, quite reconcile her mind to be a fiction.

James Parton,
*Eminent
Women of the
Age*

*Disguise our bondage as we will,
'Tis woman, woman, rules us still.*

Thomas
Moore,
"Sovereign
Woman"

VICTORIAN SUBJECTIVITY WAS both cause and effect of the Industrial Revolution. As small-scale home industries were displaced by modern factories to accommodate the requirements of the evolving commercial marketplace, social and domestic relations were likewise disrupted. The needs of the market demanded a new division of labor and a new type of laborer—*homo economicus.* Men who had worked as independent laborers, often in cottage industries shoulder to shoulder with their wives, now worked outside the home for wages; women, in turn, were gradually transformed from economic producers into "house-keepers" and, eventually, "home-makers." Thus emerged the new expectations of the sexes and the new gender identities that we associate with the Victorian era, including the formulation of "opposite" sexes, in Thomas Laqueur's specialized use of the term,[1] and the concept of "separate spheres" of influence and action for men and women.

At the same time, scientists like Malthus and Darwin formulated new narratives about human history that drastically affected conceptions of human identity. Faced with acute population increases, a feisty lower class, and radical alterations in the production, use, and distribution of capital, Victorians grappled with the need to reorganize the criteria for who was and who was not a political subject. Literary texts during this period constructed and displayed competing and conflicting projections of selfhood that contained, comprised, and compromised the onslaught of changes that Victorians were experiencing in virtually every sphere of life.

Given the fragmentation of Victorian subjectivity, Britain's longest-reigning monarch, Queen Victoria, seemed the never-ending subject as well as the representative of national identity. Known as "the Great White Mother," "the Grandmother of Europe," and "the Mother of Peoples," Victoria was figured as a primal, permanent essence. She was the personage who kept "the balance steady," for though "the greatest statesmen" were always contingent because subject to election, "the Queen," as novelist Margaret Oliphant noted, "is never out of office."[2] Representing Parliament as a house of cards that folded easily under the sway of Victoria, a *Punch* cartoon entitled "The Queen dissolving Parliament" graphically illustrated the queen's royal self-sufficiency and longevity (fig. 1). Indeed, as another editorial cartoon, "Light Sovereigns, or the Balance of Power," vividly asserted, among the world's sovereigns Victoria was ne plus ultra (fig. 2).[3] After her death, memorials emphasized how difficult it was to remember another monarch or to imagine British identity apart from Victoria. The *Illustrated London News* coverage of her death is typical. Suggesting that Victoria's loss has disrupted the use of language itself, the memorialist notes the corresponding rupture in the British subject: "The passing of that name [Queen Victoria] from the symbols of our allegiance, from the forms of worship, from the current speech, is a shock to the imagination of which we have no parallel. . . . Popular as the Prince of Wales most justly is, 'Our King' is a phrase so strange upon our lips that it almost makes a stranger of him. Within the last few days I have heard men murmuring 'the King,' as if they were groping in their memo-

Fig. 1. "The Queen dissolving Parliament," featured in *Punch* on 7 August 1847.

ries for some ancient and unfamiliar charm." In the same issue, another writer observes that the queen's subjects have "lost in Victoria not only a personage, but almost an institution." As another unnamed eulogist asserts, after three score years on the throne, the queen had become so associated with power and perpetuity that at her passing the "century seemed to belong to her."[4] Here the "gorgeous illusion" is that the breathtaking institutionalization of female sovereignty established during Victoria's long reign gave her the right of possession not only of herself but of all her subjects and of the age itself.

These florid tributes illustrate Mary Poovey's argument that during the nineteenth century England came to imagine itself as a unified, sovereign nation-state.[5] But also inherent in these memorials is the stunning realization that during Victoria's reign the concepts of masculine sovereignty and subjecthood were temporarily alienated. This is extraordinary, for when John Locke asserted the legal principle that "every man has a property in his own person," every man knew that this description of individual sovereignty did not include women. In Britain, political subjectivity had always been legally gendered as masculine. Endorsing what

Fig. 2. "Light Sovereigns, or the Balance of Power" (1842). Illustrates Victoria's monumental political weight in comparison with other nineteenth-century monarchs. Gernsheim Collection, Harry Ransom Humanities Research Center, The University of Texas at Austin.

Philip Corrigan and Derek Sayer call the "pervasive masculinity of 'the State,'"[6] British political institutions relied upon a binary model of gender to define identity. The one legal exception was that a queen regnant had "the same powers, prerogatives, rights, dignities, and duties, as if she had been a king." However, the norm of masculine authority was reiterated in the addendum to the constitutional description of the queen regnant's role: Not until the "failure of male issue" was sovereignty conferred on the female.[7] The constitutional implication seemed to be that a queen's reign represented a kind of interregnum until the norm could be reestablished in the reign of a king. Likewise, as I explain in more detail in chapter 3, in eighteenth-century English slang, the phrase "that happened during the reign of Queen Dick," used to refer to an event that could never happen. The impossible situation referred to, of course, was that a queen could not be male. Coupled with the constitutional conception that a reigning queen was essentially an interim sovereign in the case of a "failure of male issue," the colloquialism implies the absurdity—though it is a necessary one—of queenship itself.

Under Victoria, however, these assumptions were tested, for the queen's reign imprinted a feminized embodiment of the nation upon the minds of British subjects. For a very long time indeed, Victoria undermined the "pervasive masculinity of 'the State.'" No longer could the British people live according to the "gorgeous illusion" that "A kingdom in all its parts is like a man. . . . The king is the head; the people form the other parts."[8] During Victoria's reign, ironically, the ideological rationale that the rejection of Salic law was a means of preventing political disruptions in the transfer of sovereignty resulted in the interrogation of the concepts of sovereignty and subjecthood as they related to gender. Furthermore, Victoria's reign brought into sharp relief the specious legal argument that women were not legal subjects except in the case of the queen. Thus we must adapt Mary Louise Pratt's otherwise accurate assertion that the nineteenth-century nation-state imagined women "as dependent rather than sovereign" and as not possessing "intrinsically the rights of citizens." I would argue that when we add Victoria to the discussion of female subjectivity in England—and how can we fail to include her?—we must say that nineteenth-century Britain conceived of women as both dependent *and* sovereign. Recognizing the anomaly of women's nonsubjectivity adds support to Pratt's argument that because women were viewed as nonsubjects, nations "exist[ed] in permanent instability."[9] As I see it, part of that instability was due to the fact that a woman, who was always legally contingent, could also become the incarnation of the law and the signifier of meaning. With that possibility, what was to stop the idea that any woman—not just the queen—had the potential to be a political subject? Indeed, the law's self-contradiction was the only thing preventing the collapse of the seemingly natural separate spheres. If genders can be viewed as "master 'narratives' that shape the way people see their lives," [10] we must acknowledge that there was more than one Victorian narrative on separate spheres and the subject's position within them. In fact, multiple narratives produced a cultural view of gender that, while seemingly unified, also reflected contrapuntal, dynamic processes at work.

In the following chapters of this study, I investigate the conjunction of state authority and the literary writer's authority and examine some of the ways in which Victoria and Victorian writers traded places, as it were, in their attempts to reign over the domain of representation itself. Victorian contemporary Hans Vaihinger well understood that Victorian representations held more power than the reality they depicted. In his theory of fictions, *The Philosophy of "As If,"* Vaihinger writes that the concept of "As If," by which he means a "consciously false idea," was the foundation of all nation-states. Arguing that no field of human endeavor is exempt from the use of "gorgeous illusions," Vaihinger focuses on the fictions he sees as underlying the hard sciences, ethics, aesthetics, and law during the Victorian era. [11] Ironically, it becomes clear that Vaihinger uncritically accepts the view that Western culture's master narratives were the rightful domain of an elite male group: The philosopher who is so insightful about the power of fiction to shape a world view is oblivious to the dominance achieved by the always self-interested male groups who legislated and controlled the "as if" that was representation.

The conflicted fictions located in English law are particularly revealing in the matter of Queen Victoria's powers of representation vis-à-vis the writer's fictional powers, because the aesthetic criteria for genre and style were founded upon natural law, which was also the ostensible basis for constitutional law. Since this study analyzes the gendered dynamics of cultural representation as revealed through the relationship between writer and queen, it is important to examine the ways in which the law and its makers and commentators represented Victoria. This inquiry will demonstrate that although the rejection of Salic law served the interests of the male state by ensuring its continuity, the exception to that law allowed the concepts of "woman" and "queen" to disrupt the authority of legal texts. Extracts from jurists Sir William Blackstone and Frederic Maitland and parliamentarians Charles Bradlaugh and Benjamin Disraeli, as well as other commentators on the legal concept of the queen regnant, show that the British Constitution was always subjective—that it had a particular gendered subject in mind—despite its high-minded claims of impartiality.

For all of its stunning erudition, for example, Blackstone's remarkable compilation of British law cannot help but reveal the often irrational means by which its patriarchal makers sustained their authority. Describing the law's jurisdiction over the private sphere in the *Commentaries,* Blackstone begins his discussion of domestic relations with the idea that the "three great relations in private life" are those of *"master and servant," "husband and wife,"* and *"parent and child."* [12] In this narrative, the wife is to the husband as the child is to the parent and the servant is to the master; and the relations of power seem indisputable. But these analogies immediately break down because the traits associated with their particular terms, and therefore the power relations between terms, are unstable markers: The disempowered male child can look forward to an empowered status when he becomes a husband and father; meanwhile, the female parent is simultaneously figured as a child and servant. In this section of the law, then, gender is a crucial signifier that can do the work it is intended to do only by being inconstant in its consequences. Indeed, according to these rules of proper womanhood, Victoria herself would have had to be at once childlike underling and sovereign queen of her family and nation.

This instability is also inscribed in the law's view of the marital relationship. Regarding the legal subjectivity of husband and wife, Blackstone iterates the infamous notion of coverture: "By marriage, the husband and wife are one person in law: that is, the very being or legal existence of the woman is suspended during the marriage, or at least is incorporated and consolidated into that of the husband; under whose wing, protection, and *cover,* she performs everything; . . . and her condition during her marriage is called her *coverture.*" Erasing the woman's legal identity, Blackstone accepts the insecure position this constitutional vision of wifehood establishes, for, as he concludes, "the disabilities which the wife lies under are for the most part intended for her protection and benefit: so great a favorite is the female sex of the laws of England." [13] Simultaneously figuring woman as the darling of the law and a legal nonentity, coverture relies upon the problematic legal notion of the "corporation sole," which merges at least two real identities into a legally established fictional body. Thus, if one of the meanings of subjectivity is that the subject "is a body that is separate . . . from other human bodies," [14] then a woman's sexually different body was unincorporated in the concept of the corporation sole. Victoria's special case as *femme sole* complicates the legal design of coverture by introducing a potentially subversive exception to the rule.

It did not take a legal expert to expose the discrepancies in Blackstone's dependence on natural law as a means of authorizing the British Constitution's distribution of political power among its male and female subjects. If, as Blackstone asserts, valid human laws "derive all their force, and all their authority, mediately or immediately" [15] from the law of nature, then the notion of the absolute relation between sovereignty and masculinity does not hold true in nature, as any schoolchild knows. Indeed, Mrs. Trimmer's *Fabulous Histories,* one of young Princess Victoria's schoolbooks, includes a tale that illustrates the discrepancy between British law and the law of nature. Following the lives and lessons of the Benson family, Trimmer describes a scene in which Mrs. Benson teaches her son the "home" lesson that bees' loyalty to their sovereign is a pattern for Englishmen. "I wish our good king, could see all his subjects so closely united in his interest!," exclaims Mrs. Benson, and admonishes her son to "love your King, for he is to be considered as the father of his country." The son, Frederick, rather gleefully responds, "But mamma, . . . it is the Queen that the Bees love, and we have a queen too." Caught by the inadequacy of the male-identified constitution (in nature there are always exceptions to biological grounds for gendered hierarchies), Mrs. Benson explains, "I believe her majesty is as much honoured by her subjects as a queen bee in her hive, though she has not so full a command over them, for it is a king that governs England as your papa governs his family, and the queen is to be considered as the mother of the country." [16]

Mrs. Benson's simplistic transmittal of the natural law on which the British Constitution is based unravels, because divine sanction of masculine authority, in both the animal and the human kingdoms, is difficult to maintain during the reign of a queen. The queen's very body—be it insect or human—upsets the allegedly immutable character of body politics manifested in English law. George Cruikshank's editorial cartoon

"The British Bee Hive" graphically portrays this disjunction. In this popular artist's representation of national life, everyone in British society is categorized according to his duty, which is directly associated with the queen, for she resides at the top of the metaphorical beehive. Meanwhile, the English Constitution—which considers the sovereign both above and below the law, and which inscribes a queen as unnatural but acceptable when a male sovereign is wanting—is depicted as on a level just below Her Majesty.[17] Unable to depict the queen visually as being both above and below the law, the cartoon uses a metaphor from the natural world. Graphically illustrating the constitution's instability, the cartoon also depicts the unreliability of English law and the discrepant position it attaches to gender (fig. 3).

The instability apparent in "The British Bee Hive" is almost exactly reproduced in Blackstone's *Commentaries*. In addition to equating monarchy with the male, English law also designated man as the universal subject and the king as the chief overseer of law. But in a convenient lapse that reveals the law's distribution of special privileges, Blackstone explains that there is no "legal authority" that can "either delay or resist" the king. In other words, the king cannot legally be held accountable for the conduct of public affairs. This vexed reasoning rests on the assertion that the "king can do no wrong" and that the sovereign is not "answerable [to] his people" if his behavior is "exceptionable."[18] Paradoxically, Blackstone portrays the king as both above the law (he cannot break the law) and below it (he cannot abrogate the law). Thus, according to the *Commentaries,* the male sovereign incarnates a divinely based law that excludes its chief representative—and by association, his male subjects—from consistent adherence.

But if both masculinity and femininity are problematic in the *Commentaries,* this legal disquisition also suggests the anomaly of the concept of "subjectivity" itself. Other eighteenth-century philosophers asserted the absolute fragmentation of subjectivity, as well. Commencing with the proposition that reality can only be known in the present moment, John Locke, David Hume, and Jeremy Bentham proceeded to alarming conclusions. For example, if reality was knowable only in the present moment, then concepts of the self and of law—which by definition require extension through time and representation—were arbitrary, fictional constructions. As John Bender interprets Locke, if the "self is a

Fig. 3. George Cruikshank's etching of "The British Bee Hive," 1867. Princeton University Library. Meirs Collection of Cruikshank. Graphic Arts Collections. Visual Materials Division. Department of Rare Books and Special Collections.

continuing legal and rhetorical fiction bounded by its own perceptions, which are retained individually in memory and collectively in laws," then the "very act of conscious being becomes fictive, and the self a legal entity." Queen Victoria was not far removed from such abstract conceptions of subjectivity, for Prince Albert, who had studied and been influenced by German Romantic philosophers, made the following almost postmodern statement about selfhood:

> *The identity of the Individual is, so to speak, interrupted and a kind of Dualism, springs up, by reason of this, that the 'I which has been,' with all its impressions, remembrances, experiences, feelings, which were also those of youth, is attached to a particular spot, with its local and personal associations, and appears to what may be called 'the new I' like a vestment of the soul which has been lost, from which nevertheless 'the new I' cannot disconnect itself because its identity is in fact continuous! Hence the painful struggle, I might almost say, spasm of the soul.*[19]

Juxtaposed with the work of other eighteenth-century philosophers, Blackstone's definition of real and fictional selves undermines his central conviction that English law represents the pinnacle of human thought and the "pitch of perfection." Blackstone's description of the rootlessness of selfhood may be seen most starkly when he divides "persons" into natural and artificial types: "Natural persons are such as the God of nature formed us; artificial are such as are created and devised by human laws for the purposes of society and government, which are called corporations or bodies politic."[20] Though obviously Blackstone is referring to the artificial construction of groups as nations or corporations, the definition of artificial persons also suggests the fictionality of selfhood. One might argue, then, that this written account of the unwritten constitution, an account that asserts its divine, unchanging foundation, also admits that the gendered self, rather than a member of a fixed generic category, is in fact constructed by the temporal narratives of the self-interested, male-dominated institutions that impose those categories.

In light of Blackstone's juridical wranglings with fictional and real selves, it is interesting to look at the nineteenth-century English jurist Frederic Maitland, who gives the legal concept of the "fictional self" a sound and cynical drubbing in his own commentaries on English law.

Questioning the method of "illustrat[ing] one fiction by another," Maitland stringently notes that "we may say that the artificial person is a fictitious substance conceived as supporting legal attributes." Maitland especially dislikes the corporation sole, a legal concept "which seems to approach self-contradiction." Asserting that the term is problematic because its meaning is vague, Maitland shows how it sometimes refers to a kind of abstract, archetypal person, while at other times it refers to a single individual and in still other cases can designate "corporations aggregate." The British "corporations sole," Maitland frets, is "a queer creature that is always turning out to be a mere mortal man just when we have need of an immortal person."[21] Insisting, then, that at least in legal terms the self must be conceived of as having integrity, Maitland strongly rejects the notion of the corporation sole.

Maitland's dislike of the concept of the corporation sole also informs his critique of another fictional concept used to uphold the integrity of the nation, the concept that the British sovereign's subjectivity resides in two bodies. In the following passage, Maitland acerbically censures the notion of the king's two bodies:

> *What we see in England, at least what we see if we look only at the surface, is, not that the State is personified or that the State's personality is openly acknowledged, but (I must borrow from one of Mr. Gilbert's operas) that the king is "parsonified." Since that feat was performed, we have been, more or less explicitly, trying to persuade ourselves that our law does not recognize the personality or corporate character of the State or Nation or Commonwealth, and has no need to do anything of the sort if only it will admit that the king, or, yet worse, the Crown, is not unlike a parson.*[22]

Here Maitland takes issue with Britain's tradition of depicting the king in the same way it has figured the parson. The king in this way is legally fictionalized as having an individual body but also as representing the body politic. To Maitland the problem is that the British have come to view those two entities as "indivisible." Under this doctrine, Maitland explains, "the body natural by the conjunction of the body politic to it (which body politic contains the office, government and majesty royal) is magnified and by the said consolidation hath in it the body politic." To make matters worse, the law fictionalizes things even further, teaching citizens that though the king "has 'two bodies' and 'two capacities' he

'hath but one person.'" Assessing the source of such legal thinking, Maitland argues that jurists expected that without the "legal fiction" of the
indivisibility of the king's two bodies, citizens would believe that they
owed "allegiance" to the "corporation sole" (the individual entity of
kingship) rather than to "the mortal man."[23] As Maitland asserts, avowals
of the indivisibility of the king's two bodies plunge British legal experts
"into talk about kings who do not die, who are never under age, who are
ubiquitous, who do no wrong and (says Blackstone) think no wrong."
Maitland suggests with arch understatement that "such talk has not been
innocuous." Arguing that "Many things may be doubtful if we try to
make two persons of one man, or to provide one person with two bodies," he explains, "So long as the State is not seen to be a person, we must
either make an unwarrantably free use of the King's name, or else we
must for ever be laboriously stopping holes through which a criminal
might glide."[24]

Perhaps Victoria's reign made Maitland's fin-de-siècle critique of
English constitutional law possible, for her position as a high-profile
anomaly brought constitutional notions of sovereignty into question.
Maitland's interrogation of the corporation sole demands analysis of the
constitution's implicit constructions of gender and class, both of which
came under heavy fire in the nineteenth century. Maitland's critique of
the fiction of the king's two bodies also opens a window through which
to examine how that concept changes when the gender of the monarch
changes. Where the concept of the king's two bodies was problematic,
the idea of a queen's two bodies seemed downright unworkable, for her
corpus was already considered a failure as well as a fictional replacement
of the king's body. That is, the English queen was allowed to act as a
fictional man and to wield a man's power only when it was implicitly
understood and acknowledged that she could never *really* be anything
more than a counterfeit. Hence, by asserting absolutes while at the same
time permitting the inevitable, occasional exception to the absolute rule,
the quasi-legal fabrication of queenhood as the failure of male issue both
overdetermined and undermined the sovereignty and gender of the few
queens regnant in British history.

Blackstone made still another attempt to pass off to English subjects
two bodies in the guise of an indivisible one. Piously asserting that the
law is "a rule of action which is prescribed by some superior being," that
is, God, Blackstone expected his readers to infer that God's body is the

identity that gives authority to British law. But as Blackstone's introduction to the *Commentaries* makes clear, the superior being he is most concerned with is not God, but the "gentlemen of independent estates and fortune," who were "the most useful as well as considerable body of men in the nation." Seeing God's authority as invested in this body of men, Blackstone assumes that they are rightly "the guardians of the English Constitution; the makers, repealers and interpreters of the English law; delegated to watch, to check, and to avert every dangerous innovation, . . . bound by every tie of nature, of honor and religion, to transmit that constitution and those laws to their posterity, amended if possible, at least without any derogation." Having come to the conclusion that God is a gentleman, Blackstone imagines a thoroughly hierarchical masculine universe with the pinnacle, God, being implicitly associated with the interests and values of the English male aristocracy. Hence, if the legal fiction of the *Commentaries* is that the law is a bond between men and a property passed on from man to man, "man" must be understood as "gentleman."[25]

As I shall show presently, many Victorian male writers made this same assumption about the masculine essence inherent in the primal connection between the divine and the human. This ideology also complicated their views of the queen, of course. Certainly member of Parliament and future Prime Minister Benjamin Disraeli wrote *Sybil* as a testament to the truth of Blackstone's legal connection between the gentleman and God. Disraeli's rhetorical flourishes of homage to the young queen are in fact window dressing for his celebration of the kingly qualities of the male aristocrats who support her. Full of chivalrous condescension to the new female monarch, Disraeli's anticipation of the queen's reign includes the fear that her royal femininity will affect masculine claims to power:

> *In a palace in a garden—not in a haughty keep, proud with the fame but dark with the violence of ages; not in a regal pile, bright with the splendour, but soiled with the intrigues, of courts and factions—in a palace in a garden, meet scene for youth, and innocence, and beauty— came a voice that told the maiden that she must ascend her throne!*
>
> *The council of England is summoned for the first time within her bowers. There are assembled the prelates and captains and chief men of her realm; the priests of the religion that consoles, the heroes of the*

sword that has conquered, the votaries of the craft that has decided the fate of empires; men grey with thought, and fame, and age; who are the stewards of divine mysteries, who have toiled in secret cabinets, who have encountered in battle the hosts of Europe, who have struggled in the less merciful strife of aspiring senates; men too, some of them, lords of a thousand vassals and chief proprietors of provinces, yet not one of them whose heart does not at this moment tremble as he awaits the first presence of the maiden who must now ascend her throne.

A hum of half-suppressed conversation which would attempt to conceal the excitement, which some of the greatest of them have since acknowledged, fills that brilliant assemblage; the sea of plumes, and glittering stars, and gorgeous dresses. Hush! the portals open; she comes; the silence is as deep as that of a noontide forest. Attended for a moment by her royal mother and the ladies of her Court, who bow and then retire, VICTORIA ascends her throne; a girl, alone, and for the first time, amid an assemblage of men.

In a sweet and thrilling voice, and with a composed mien which indicates rather the absorbing sense of august duty than an absence of emotion, THE QUEEN announces her accession to the throne of her ancestors, and her humble hope that divine Providence will guard over the fulfillment of her lofty trust.

The prelates and captains and chief men of her realm then advance to the throne, and, kneeling before her, pledge their troth, and take the sacred oaths of allegiance and supremacy.

Allegiance to one who rules over the land that the great Macedonian could not conquer; and over a continent of which even Columbus never dreamed: to the Queen of every sea, and of nations in every zone.

It is not of these that I would speak; but of a nation nearer her footstool, and which at this moment looks to her with anxiety, with affection, perhaps with hope. Fair and serene, she has the blood and beauty of the Saxon. Will it be her proud destiny at length to bear relief to suffering millions, and, with that soft hand which might inspire troubadours and guerdon knights, break the last links in the chain of Saxon thraldom?[26]

In this extensive passage, Disraeli replaces political power with sexual difference as the focus of attention. The gritty, masculine world of politics stands in contrast to the innocent, virginal queen, who seems in Disraeli's "gorgeous illusion" never to have been in the company of men, and who is expected to enter that vast masculine company alone. Leaving her protected private sphere to enter the public sphere of men, Victoria occupies a fragile domain not naturally inhabited by women. One gathers that if she were entering this sphere on any other terms than as queen, the response would be less excessively courtly. In fact, her difference is ominously sexual, for the maiden must endure a mysterious rite of passage while the men "tremble" expectantly. To gain her throne, the princess displays her body and her beauty to their ranks and accepts the allegiance—and oppressive protection—of the wise male attendants.

Endorsing the constitution's ostensible integrity, this passage worships the woman sovereign while asserting that her reign is in fact a mere interregnum. Like Blackstone, Disraeli represents rightful reign as masculine in general, a credo underscored by the reference to the highest sovereign, a male god. If Victoria is an appropriate female figurehead commanding obedience, she is also cause for male anxiety. Their natural right to rule having been subverted by the inconsistencies of their own patriarchal law, the male aristocrats are forced to sublimate their resulting gender anxiety. This sublimation takes the predictable form of the elevation of the maiden queen to a pedestal where she becomes a passive, angelic figurehead whom the men can rule in the guise of serving her.

For member of Parliament Charles Bradlaugh, the mystical connection between English gentlemen and God was intolerably partial. But in his efforts to stand for a more republican England, Bradlaugh was unable or unwilling to imagine a female monarch's two bodies—the sovereign and the woman—as legitimately inhabiting one person. In *The Impeachment of the House of Brunswick,* Bradlaugh figures Victoria's political superiority as illegitimate not only because her position took sovereignty away from its rightful possessors—the masses of British male commoners— but also because she was a woman. Portraying the queen as a fallen woman who prostitutes the resources of the nation, Bradlaugh wonders why she expects the nation-state to provide a silver spoon, as it were, for her nine royal do-nothings. Bradlaugh depicts the queen's consort as her personal stud and caustically asserts that the "memory of the Prince is dear to the people; he has left us nine children to keep out of the taxpayers' pockets, his own large private accumulations of wealth being

inapplicable to their maintenance." "Her Majesty," he sarcastically proclaims, "is now enormously rich, and—as she is like her Royal grandmother—grows richer daily. She is also generous, Parliament annually
voting her moneys to enable her to be so without touching her own
purse." Relating Victoria's own bodily gratification to the economic condition of the body politic at large, the would-be queen-unmaker berates
the monarch for draining the economic energies of her people by grati-
fying her own excessive sexual energies.[27]

The queen was not amused by Bradlaugh's attempts to replace England's "gorgeous illusion" of monarchy with a republican worldview. It
is not surprising, then, that Victoria was disturbed by this man's powerful
political imagination. In her journal of 1880, Victoria refers to the "hor-
rid Bradlaugh" and wonders why something cannot be done to expel
him from Parliament when "so many oppose his sitting."[28] In fact, on no
less than forty occasions the queen expressed her animosity toward him
in official correspondence with her prime minister, and in 1874, Victoria
or her councilors—it is unclear who initiated the proceedings—considered whether it was legally possible to crush the man whose critical representations of the monarch reached an ever wider audience. In a letter
to Victoria of 28 January 1874, her secretary Ponsonby wrote of Bradlaugh's fiery American speaking tour, "Mr. Bradlaugh occasionally at-
tacks Your Majesty but in very cautious and measured terms never saying
anything which could be considered personally offensive. But in assailing
the Prince of Wales he accuses him of passing a worse than useless life and
says he is utterly unfitted to reign. But it is doubtful whether he has said
anything which would render him liable to prosecution. He is a clever,
cautious and therefore more dangerous man than the wild orators who
heedlessly declaim on whatever comes uppermost."[29] Thus both the con-
servative aristocrat Disraeli and the radical populist Bradlaugh agree on
one point, the disturbing position of a female sovereign in relation to
their own definitions of natural law and political rule.

Walter Bagehot's overdetermined "gorgeous illusions" about the
queen's legal potency never reached Bradlaugh's or Disraeli's intensity;
nor did the queen feel her own sovereignty threatened by Bagehot as she
evidently did by Bradlaugh. Nevertheless, Bagehot's summary of the
queen's constitutional powers combines praise with anxieties concerning
the culture's master narratives about gender. "She could," he noted,

"make every citizen in the United Kingdom, male or female, a peer" and "every parish in the United Kingdom a 'university.'" She could also, he added, not only "dismiss most of the civil servants; she could pardon all offenders." The repetition of "she could" culminates in an ominous conclusion: "In a word, the Queen could . . . upset all the action of civil government . . . , could disgrace the nation by a bad war or peace, and could, by disbanding our forces, . . . leave us defenceless against foreign nations."[30] Arguing that the essence of national and individual sovereignty is the "upset[ting]" of the very rules that institute that sovereignty, Bagehot invokes a legally defined male citizen who simultaneously identifies himself with the queen's failure of masculinity and associates himself with her powerful feminine excesses. In either case, his rhetoric produces the impression that something is not quite right in the state of England when the nation is represented in the body of a queen.

Victorian political activist William Fox also covered over anxieties about male impotence in his abridged synopsis of the queen's legal power. In the context of the patriarchal times, even Fox's linking of "she" with "sovereignty" becomes an almost baleful refrain that views the queen as always on the verge of violating natural and constitutional law:

> *She selects the persons who are to fill the great offices of State. . . . The tremendous question of peace or war is in her breast. She is the empire to foreign powers; for it seems that courts know nothing of nations but their princes. She administers the laws, by her deputies the judges; and in the making of the laws she has a negative upon the results of the collective legislatorial wisdom of the nation. . . . Her obstinacy may indefinitely postpone, her treachery may cruelly disappoint, the hopes of millions suffering under accumulated wrongs. She has the disposal of immense revenues, and is the fountain of honour. She is the head of the army, which is sworn to her service; and the head of the Church, selecting the men, who . . . may lead souls to heaven or mislead them to perdition. All this and more, not only may, but, when the contingency occurs of a woman's being next in succession, must be consigned to her charge, or the constitution is destroyed.*[31]

In this lengthy oration, patriarchal law inflates the meaning of sexual difference to an extreme degree. The passage also implies that when sexual difference determines legal definitions of subjectivity, the individual self cannot help but be figured in terms of failure and excess. As Fox inadvertently implies, female sovereignty equates the anomalous subject with the queen, who is simultaneously all-powerful and "contingent." Thus, as with Bagehot, the "gorgeous illusions" Fox entertains about his queen seem always to teeter on the verge of chaos and nightmare.

To seemingly more enlightened times, it is shocking to confront the condescending attitudes Victorian male commoners took toward Queen Victoria merely because she was a woman. They embody the perspective that only a man can tell a queen how to rule properly, how, that is, to fulfil her anomalous constitutional role. As a review of English law shows, that role was defined constitutionally as resulting from the failure of male issue, or in other words from an absence of masculinity. Thus many men who wrote about her legal position assume that Victoria was in need of a little fatherly advice about how to fulfil the father's law. An example of one of these "home lessons" comes from a writer signing himself "Old England," who seeks to instruct the queen by comparing an ungoverned house to a governed one: In a governed house the husband and father rule and the wife is "next in authority." In this master narrative about England's political crisis, gender roles are crucial. As "Old England" explains, the results of the "nongovernment" of a household are that the "father is an improvident man, the husband is an unkind man, the master is a tyrant." Furthermore, in a household that is nongoverned—and unnatural—the wife "disputes" with the husband "for pre-eminence." The next step, of course, is to analogize the government of a household with the government of a nation, the predictable conclusion being that a female-ruled nation is unnatural and ungovernable. Patriarchal "Old England" associates new (ungovernable) England with female rule when he asserts that "To govern a country is not to flatter a young queen" or "to surround the person of the queen with female politicians of low political attachments."[32]

It would be hard to imagine a subject taking such a condescending position on the reign of a new king. But, at least in writing, Victorian male Tories and Radicals felt little compunction about demeaning their queen in this way. In perhaps the most blatant of such cautions to Victoria at the beginning of her reign, one of her male subjects, the anonymous radical writer of the pamphlet "Letter to the Queen on the State of the Monarchy," asserts that Victoria's accession has brought the monarchy to a crisis: "Madam, the monarchical principle is exposed to a new and a rude trial of its strength in your person."[33] This statement relies on nothing less than naked masculine intimidation of the female position, and the writer goes further still in arguing that things will only get worse for her if she does not come around to his republican wisdom.

Clearly, according to this writer, it is Victoria's femininity and youth that endanger England's current political position. "It is your fate to have the experiment tried in your person, how far a monarchy can stand secure in the nineteenth century, when all the powers of the executive government are intrusted to a woman, and that woman a child." Claiming to be "an experienced man, well stricken in years," and professing that "I bend myself respectfully before *you,*" he in fact has no scruples about patronizing the young queen and continues, "a girl of eighteen . . . in my own or any other family in Europe, would be treated as a child, ordered to do as was most agreeable or convenient to others,—whose inclinations would never be consulted,—whose opinion would never be thought of,—whose consent would never be asked upon any one thing appertaining to any other human being but yourself, beyond the choice of a gown or a cap, to gain your approval of my opinions."[34] The message is clear: As a mere female child, Victoria has no right to be the monarch and she should simply accept her status as an interim ruler and allow herself to be guided by her male betters. Furthermore, she should be schooled in the legislative desires of male betters such as himself, who are demanding the vote as a sign of their true masculine sovereign selfhood.

This letter apparently created a stir during Victoria's early royal career, for at least two male respondents took issue with the anonymous writer's insubordinate tone. As one of the queen's anonymous champions pointed out, the language of the "Letter on the State of the Monarchy" was "insolent" on two counts. First of all, "from a man to a young and unoffending female" it was "brutal." But "from a subject to a sovereign" it indicated "a disloyal and traitorous heart, combined with a total ignorance of the relative standing and duty of him who writes, and of the royal personage who is addressed." Note, however, that on both counts, the queen's defender resorts to patriarchal religious and ostensible natural laws regarding the sexes. The assumption is that men should act chivalrously toward women because women are the weaker sex. Furthermore, a true old-fashioned Tory, this writer invokes the divine right of kings as the rationale for obeying the queen, asserting that the British "will obey this 'Girl of Eighteen,' because the holy oil is upon her, because she reigns by the grace of God; because she is God upon earth to us, for all matters of temporal rule, good order, and civil blessings. We bow down before Him who is Invisible in His visible representative." [35] Here again the queen is only a stand-in for the real power behind the throne, the male God whose invisible omnipotence is temporarily immanent in the body of a woman. Victoria has no need, apparently, to bow to the writer of this letter, but she must bow to the masculine source of authority itself.

Victoria continued to receive this kind of mail even as a seasoned matron. In "Letter to the Queen, On her Retirement from Public Life," another anonymous critic condescendingly teaches Victoria her "home lessons." Signing himself simply "One of Her Majesty's Most Loyal Subjects," this writer bewails the fact that unlike George IV and William IV, Victoria seemed "much less acquainted than" English kings had been with the extent of the monarch's "royal prerogatives." "You were, therefore not so well prepared as they had been to maintain them." Blaming Victoria's political naiveté on the fact that she is a woman and therefore naturally focused on home lessons, the self-styled loyal subject remarks that "the allurements of the home circle engrossed so much of your attention as to render you indifferent, if not insensible, to the loss of political power." "Your early and happy marriage turning your thoughts to those domestic delights in which you have ever taken so much pleasure, prevented you from detecting, or, if you did detect it, from lamenting the anomalous nature of the position in which you were placed; and thus it has come to pass that the very events which have the most contributed to your own comfort, have also contributed in a great measure to the transfer from the hands of the Sovereign to those of the people of the last vestige of political power possessed by the former." [36]

The writer does acknowledge that "The harmony of your domestic relations contributed to preserve and still further to popularise the idea that the family should be the unit of society, an idea which more than any other has helped to develop and mould our national character; and which I believe to be at the bottom of our national greatness." [37] But at this point the queen's correspondent abandons all pretense to objectivity and records a litany of troubles that he attributes to the queen's preference for home lessons over worldlier affairs. He worries, among other things, that because she has withdrawn so much from public view she has failed to set an example for the upper classes, who correspondingly no longer feel the duties of noblesse oblige, whether to help the poor or to help run their country. As a result, the poor and lower classes have become filled with contempt for their betters, angry at their lack of political power, and easy prey to radical agitators. Without the queen's moral influence, the old Tory fears, the rich will become even more decadent and the poor will see them as such. The polemic then makes explicit the connection between the queen's gender and the nation's downfall. Young women, he notes, are becoming "fast" and finding it fashionable to indulge in vice. Assuming that men are doomed when women refuse to act as moral exemplars, which is of course one of the tenets of the Victorian notion of separate spheres, the writer explicitly notes that the queen has "stood aloof while the process of class demoralisation has been going on." At the end of his letter he stoops to goad Victoria with a mean-spirited vision of her beloved lost husband: "How deeply would not that estimable Prince, could he revisit, the scene of his philanthropic labours, deplore the deterioration of society, which could not but force itself upon his notice." Undercutting his own assumption that men must rely on women's moral superiority, the author implies here that Albert was more virtuous than the queen and that if he were still alive would act as the nation's moral center, a position the queen has failed to fill.[38] Hopelessly entangled in the inconsistencies of Victorian gender ideology, this writer can only blame the supposed author of the age's feminization for its moral disintegration.

Thus far I have looked at male representations of Victoria's sovereignty, largely because, as with the Woman Question itself, men were more likely than women to publish their opinions on such matters. Indeed, it could be dangerous for women to express their views of topics that so thoroughly affected their own relatively powerless lives. We shall now turn to some of the "gorgeous illusions" Victorian women held about the lawful status of their queen in an era when, as Victorian W. Anderson Smith asserted, "all England, the very government of England is womanised."[39] Tutored in the dominant gender ideology that made all domestic "queens" of the household submissive to male rule, Victorian women were faced, in their queen, with a deviant model of femininity that complicated the concepts of womanhood and sovereignty. Viewed as explicitly informing the subjectivity of every Victorian female, Victoria's womanhood was both endangered and endangering because she was queen. And, as with the male critiques of this sovereign, it is womanhood that is the focus of essays written by women. Not legal subjects themselves, these women tended to focus on the natural laws governing Victorian womanhood.

Sensing the endangered status of queenliness, Sarah Stickney Ellis attempted to rescue "womanhood" by incorporating in her definition of female sovereignty the characteristics prominently associated with femininity. In *The Women of England,* this immensely popular writer remarked the moral and political kinship between queenly womanhood and the female sovereign, warning that "The British throne being now graced by a female sovereign, . . . it is surely not a time for the female part of the community to fall away from the high standard of moral excellence, to which they have been accustomed to look, in the formation of their domestic habits."[40] Ellis's political position is more complex than it first appears, as she simultaneously undermines and substantiates her own queenly womanhood. For one thing, by publicly inscribing the meaning of the queenly woman's essentially private femininity, Ellis called into question her own pursuit of a profession. Yet Ellis's rhetoric is masterful, partly because her twofold purpose is to reiterate woman's failure of masculinity and to establish herself as an exception to the rule. As such an exception, she directly associates herself with Victoria, the ruler who was by definition the paramount exception to the rule. In fact, Ellis assumes the sovereignty of her own queenly womanhood, aligns that sovereignty with her authority as a writer, and thereby establishes her moral authority. Indeed, Ellis implies that Victoria's acquiescence to her, Ellis's, authoritative voice on the subject of female sovereignty indicates the popular antifeminist's supremacy over the queen herself.

Though Marie Corelli's extensive memorial to the queen focuses primarily on Victoria's femininity, Corelli adeptly transforms her acclamation of Victoria's femininity into a wily argument for the superiority of a woman's rule. Viewing the queen as the exemplar of femininity par excellence, Corelli constructs a hagiography of woman at the different stages of life in order to eulogize the age's supreme woman. "An incarnation of womanhood," the princess as a girl was "simple and modest, unaffected and graceful." As a wife and mother, "she was devoted to her duties, and adored her husband and children." "As a widow," she fulfilled her feminine task of being the "faithful worshipper of a beloved memory." To Corelli, then, Victoria seemed merely an extension and magnification of the Victorian myth of the angel in the house. Applauding "England's Good Angel," Corelli asserts that Victoria chose to be a wife and mother first and queen second: "Occupying the proudest position on earth, her days were passed in the quietest pleasures,—and she stood before us, a daily unmatched example of the inestimable value of Home and home-life, with all its peaceful surroundings and sacred influences."[41] Like Ellis, Corelli explicitly connects the queen's womanhood with the femininity of her female subjects. Her reason, she says, for writing this tribute to the queen's "imperishable glory" is to present "this noblest Woman's life" as a "special lesson" to all women. "Every great nation needs" "true, good" mothers, and since Victoria is the "supreme example" of motherhood, it is through her femininity that she has best served her country, particularly since England was "fast losing" the "invaluable influence of pure and modest womanhood." Asserting an essence inherent in womanhood and specifically in English womanhood, Corelli perceives in Victoria a knowledge of the secret of woman's power: that Englishwomen were the "Queen-roses of the world, and did so influence men to love their homes and to work for the glory of their country that they were able to leave it greater than they found it."[42]

According to Corelli, women who departed from Victoria's example of queenly womanhood destroyed the essence of femininity and thus lessened its powerful influence on the nation's identity. Calling for a new kind of woman—a return to the essence of womanhood exemplified by Queen Victoria—Corelli offers a critique of the self-interestedness that has led to the downfall of English womanhood. The queen's death, she hopes, will result in a rebirth of the feminine virtues she exemplified: "We shall demand of women that the matrons deserve our homage and the maidens our respect,—that the aged command our reverence, and the young our tenderness. We shall perhaps learn by-and-bye that paint and dyed hair are not beautifiers of any woman's face, and we shall give the wearers of such the kindly com-passionate cold shoulder. We may even ask—who knows!—that certain of our 'ladies' shall give up smoking and the use of stable slang."[43]

But at this point it is perhaps well to consider Corelli's belief that woman's femininity made her the perfect sovereign. For in fact Corelli's *Passing of the Great Queen* lauds Victoria's power as monarch, a power equal to that of any man. To Corelli, men are often too masculine, as it were, for the royal profession. Men in governmental positions frequently display little foresight; when difficulties arise, they lose "their heads in emergency," throwing "aside their responsibilities in desperate dismay." In contrast, Queen Victoria's "heart was true," and "her trust in God never faltered." Thus Corelli views Queen Victoria as the prototype of sovereignty itself, not just of female sovereignty, for "she taught all her fellow sovereigns the dignity of sovereignty." Corelli adds that the supremacy of masculine physical strength has nothing to do with the ability to rule a nation. In Queen Victoria's case, "woman's hand, so small and delicate, held all things in the clasp of a fearless love and faith such as we are told can remove mountains." "If the woman herself be pure and true" to her essential feminine nature, then, in Corelli's view, she has as natural a legal claim to sovereignty as does a man.[44]

While Ellis championed self-authorizing illusions about the queen's feminine sovereignty and Corelli authorized femininity as complementary to sovereignty, Victorian suffragists used Victoria's reign as a logical support for their feminist political agenda. In spite of Victoria's view of the women's movement as "alarming," "unnatural," "dangerous & unchristian," the queen's reign highlighted the anomalous nature of British laws regarding women. One of the feminists' most potent arguments exploited the contradiction between the constitutional assertion of a woman's right to rule and the legal code's restriction of the vote to male property holders. A newspaper article entitled "The Franchise for Women" pointed out that though "the highest political prerogative and dignity in this land is held by a woman," and though "no law can be enacted without her concurrence, no writ issued but in her name," women are "'not parts of the body politic at all.'" "A woman appoints and dismisses the great officers of state," notes the female writer of this brief, yet "'women do not belong to the body politic, but remain a non-political element side by side with the male population.'" "If such is the theory of our Constitution," she concludes, "then, at any rate, the Constitution is not consistent with itself."[45]

Another feminist journalist contends that "where a Queen reigns, and where queens have reigned, . . . it is slightly inconsequent to say that women are and always have been regarded as incapable of exercising political power, because they are entirely unfit for it." Feminist activist Barbara Bodichon decries the "picture of unreason, and scarcely disguised injustice" apparent in "the argument of [female] incapacity" to vote. Pointing out that such logic "loses much of its force at present, 'when a woman sits at the helm of government in England,'" Bodichon trumps opposing arguments by invoking "the most glorious ruler" ever to sit on the throne, Queen Elizabeth I.[46] Like Frederic Maitland, these feminists exploited the inconsistencies of British law and showed how the notion of the monarch's two bodies became sexualized when the sovereign was a queen.

Given that Victoria was central to representations of female empowerment, it is hardly coincidental that her reign coincided with Frances Swiney's feminist manifesto. Creating her own sometimes bizarre natural law—a commingling of Darwinian biology and the legal precedent of the king's two bodies—Swiney argued that the human race would eventually evolve into the sole, true, original sex, the female. In *The Cosmic Procession or the Feminine Principle in Evolution,* Swiney unabashedly asserted that the female sex was superior to the male and that woman was the origin from which all evolution began and the end to which all evolution would lead. Because woman was the great creator, she was the "standard in Nature," while maleness was "an intermediate phase of development." Swiney exulted in all the signs of the evolving "feminisation" of the age,[47] and it is tempting to suggest that she had the queen explicitly in mind when she attempted to replace a masculinist representation of power with her own feminist master narrative.

Victoria's participation in the feminization of the age highlighted contradictions in the legal classification of the gendered subject. Revealing the personal effects of such inconsistent legal illusions as coverture, the king's two bodies, and the corporation sole, Victoria and Albert themselves expressed a great deal of anxiety about legal, social, and natural laws governing their multiple public and private identities. It is important to note how the royal couple interpreted and responded to these laws and how they rationalized their anomalous legal performances of sovereignty, gender, and marriage. How, for example, did the couple handle the legal notion of coverture, and how was the concept of the king's two bodies replicated, if at all, when it came to a female sovereign? How did they represent these anomalies to themselves and to their subjects in an age in which representation, as Mary Poovey argues, became the ruling essence of culture?[48]

Albert's and Victoria's abundant written accounts of their experience of gender vis-à-vis their roles as consort and queen indicate the baffling nature of their task. While they occasionally expressed anxiety about how they undermined societal gender norms, the royal couple also attempted to perform their sex roles as if there were no fundamental contradictions in the Victorian ideology of gender. Though legally she escaped the effects of coverture because she was the queen regnant, Victoria was still beholden to the culture's disjunctive formulation of natural and juridical laws. Almost without exception, writers who represented the queen—including the queen herself—judged her according to notions about women's natural duties and abilities. Likewise, as consort, Prince Albert inhabited the private sphere—and it is amusing that Victoria referred to him as her "Angel" in the house—yet as Victoria's husband and royal advisor, he was both the antithesis and the ideal of Victorian masculinity. Representing their relationship as a stable enactment of bourgeois normality, the royal couple was able, to a remarkable extent, to cover over the gender anxieties that they themselves graphically embodied. Thus, even if the royal pair had never pondered their own deviancy from convention, their performance of gender automatically upset Victorian sex roles. While it is true, in Margaret Homans's words, that the "history of Victoria and Albert's relationship is an ambiguous text of sexual and political powers held and given up on both sides,"[49] the couple nevertheless finessed their digression from the law with considerable expertise.

Peter Gay refers to the Victorian male's pervading fear that his masculinity was in peril, a disposition I see as directly related to the queen's visible disruption of Victorian gender norms. If there was a sense of manhood in danger, we might expect Prince Albert to be the most prominently visible embodiment of this fear. The royal couple's aberrant performance of gender was implied in every artistic depiction of Albert, particularly when in death he became the absent center of Victoria's reign. For example, when George Gilbert Scott, one of the architects of the Albert Memorial, documented the process of creating the shrine to Victoria's grief, he unintentionally pinpointed the prince's anomalous legal position. Scott stated that the most difficult artistic decision was whether to sculpt the prince consort in a standing or sitting position. As another artist involved in the project wrote, the question about Albert's placement presented "difficulties to the sculptor of the gravest nature": "If represented standing, the figure would in position repeat the four figures placed on a level with it against the columns, and also the principal figure in each of the four groups immediately below. This might justly be termed bad composition: moreover, the figure thus would fail to have the appearance of being enthroned and presiding over all that surrounds it."[50] Ultimately, the decision was made to sculpt the prince in a sitting position so that the statue of Albert would be in aesthetic harmony with the other sculpted figures. But the architects' overdetermined discussions about the memorial suggest ideological as well as aesthetic anxieties. Represented as both a presiding and an overshadowed figure, Albert necessarily created a "bad composition" because of his peculiar legal position.

Albert's Uncle Leopold expressed his nephew's gender confusion: "the Queen being Queen Regnant, 'Prince Albert's position was to all intents and purposes that of a Queen Consort,'" and therefore "'the same privileges and charges ought to be attached to it which were attached to Queen Adelaide's position.'"[51] Leopold's designation of Albert as queen consort underlines the royal uncle's own conflicted motivations: He is torn between the masculine pride that identifies virility with sovereignty and a sense of justice that insists that the male consort's prerogatives should be equal to those of previous female consorts. Victoria herself wrote in a memorandum to the prime minister as late as 1856 that "It is a strange omission in our Constitution that while the wife of a King has the highest rank and dignity in the realm after her husband assigned to her by law, the husband of a Queen regnant is entirely ignored by the law." She is particularly attentive to the incongruity of this legal omission in a culture that views "a Titular King" as "a complete novelty." Expressing astonishment at this "strange anomaly," she notes that whereas a "husband has in this country such particular rights and such great power over his wife, and as the Queen is married just as any other woman is, and swears to obey her lord and master, as such," according to the law, nevertheless her own husband "has no rank or defined position." [52]

The problem obviously distressed the queen, who recorded in her journal her worries about the prince's "awkward and painful position." Reasoning that the "Queen Consort" is legally provided with "rights" and "provisions" by English law, why was it that "the reigning Queen's Husband, should not have the same"? "The position of a Prince Consort, must be painful and humiliating to any man," wrote Victoria, so much so "that at times I almost felt it would have been fairer to him for me not to have married him." Elsewhere she wrote of her own "anomalous position" as the "Queen Regnant," and worried that though "dear Papa, God knows, does everything—it is a reversal of the right order of things which distresses me much and which no one, but such a perfection, such an angel as he is—could bear and carry through." [53] These textual signs of Victoria's perplexity indicate that she intuitively recognized the law's confusion: Whereas she was queen by virtue of her failure of masculinity, a condition that elevated her to the position of privileged subject, Albert, as male consort, was also figured as a failure of masculinity, though in his case this made him a cipher.

The peculiarity of the prince consort's position was something of a public joke as well as a private one between Victoria and Lord Melbourne. In 1901 *The Gentlewoman* addressed the problem of precedence. Lacking a formal legal rank, Albert had to rely during the numerous ritual ceremonies at court on the "grace and favour" of "the Sovereigns [Victoria] visited" and of the monarchs who visited her. *The Gentlewoman* gave excruciating examples: In 1856, though "the Emperor of the French treated the Prince as a Royal personage, his own uncle declined to come to Paris, because he would not give precedence to the Prince." On another occasion "the King of Prussia would not give place to the Queen's husband which common civility required, because of the presence of the Archduke, the third son of an uncle of the reigning Emperor of Austria, who would not give the *pas,* and whom the King would not offend." To the royal couple's great embarrassment, "The only legal position, according to international law, which the husband of the Queen enjoyed was that of a younger brother of the Duke of Saxe-Coburg." Explicitly remarking on the inconsistency of the law, *The Gentlewoman* concluded that

Albert had to endure such humiliations because "the English law did not know him." [54]

Albert and Victoria were also the subject of less elevated debates about their legal problems. A street song celebrating Victoria's marriage called attention to the way that a queen regnant's accession and marriage magnify the instability of so-called natural law. The jocular ditty suggested that when performing her part in the ceremony, the queen must vow to "love" and "honour," but never promise to "'obey.'" [55] Other popular accounts of the marriage worried about who should be the head of the household. In a famous apocryphal depiction of the queen's frequent spats with her consort, for instance, it was said that one day an angry Albert locked himself in his room. When an equally enraged Victoria knocked on his door and he asked, "Who is there?" she replied, "The Queen of England." Albert refused to respond to her continued rapping until she knocked more gently and finally answered his question, "Who is there?" with "Your wife, Albert." [56] In another account of the queen's marriage, Victoria reportedly avowed that "it was her wish to be married in all respects like any other woman, according to the revered usage of the Church of England, and that, though not as a *queen,* as a *woman,* she was ready to promise all things contained in that portion of the Liturgy." [57]

Similarly, in a poem that appeared in *Fraser's Magazine* on the occasion of the consort's twenty-first birthday, Albert was depicted as a comic figure because the English Constitution did not recognize him. Denigrating Albert's masquerade of masculinity as a British military leader, the poetaster pointed out the shameful reality that Albert's power was located in a woman. "What tool of fight / Hath he e'er held? Of none what e'er I know." The poem continues, "No angry blood / Was shed to raise him to his station bright—/ Sword, pike, lance, musket, handspike, fierce of blow, / He never handled." Instead, Albert found "a way far different to fame, / And power, and glory," one that allowed him to be "safe within his regal nest." The poem snidely concludes that the prince "Spend[s his] days and nights in jollity and game." [58] This doggerel clearly manifests anxiety about the prince's royalty depending on his marriage to a queen rather than coming naturally from the inheritance of his father's crown or through battle. For this writer, then, Albert's dependence on "safe[ly]" inhabiting the Queen's "regal nest" represented a dangerous threat to masculine authority.

The concluding lines of the poem resort to Bradlaugh's tactics, sexualizing the queen's sovereignty and thus bastardizing Albert and any of his progeny:

> *The only thing that I can see to blame*
> *   Is that the people, whom we all detest,*
> *   Are not by him, and her he loves the best*
> *(Or ought to do), kicked out like cripples lame.*
> *Answers the prince: "Tis easy, sir, to say,*
> *   But not at all so easy to be done.*
> *   Why, as to letter-back close sticks the queen*
> *In effigy, for which your pence you pay,*
> *   Sticks to the real queen old Melbourne on."*[59]

In these final tortured lines, the poet compares the relationship between the queen's effigy on a stamp affixed to an envelope with the real queen's relationship to her prime minister. According to this view, to put a man and woman on equal footing in the public sphere inevitably results in the man's emasculation and the woman's sexualization. To this writer, sexual difference will necessarily lead to sexual infidelity if a husband inhabits the private sphere while his wife enters the public.

Eighty years later, Lytton Strachey reiterated this hypersensitivity to sexual difference vis-à-vis the royal couple's marriage. In his "gorgeous illusion" of the monarch's reign, *Queen Victoria,* the Bloomsbury figure spends far more time lauding the consort than he does the ruling sovereign. In the purplest of prose, Strachey implicitly bemoans the subversion of patriarchal law accompanying the accession of a female sovereign:

> *There was something that he wanted and that he could never get. What*
> *was it? Some absolute, some ineffable sympathy? Some extraordinary,*
> *some sublime success? Possibly, it was a mixture of both. To dominate*
> *and to be understood! To conquer, by the same triumphant influence,*
> *the submission and the appreciation of men—that would be worth*
> *while indeed! . . . Doubtless he had made some slight impression: it*
> *was true that he had gained the respect of his fellow workers, that his*
> *probity, his industry, his exactitude, had been recognised, that he was a*

highly influential, an extremely important man. But how far, how very far, was all this from the goal of his ambitions! . . . England lumbered on, impervious and self-satisfied, in her old intolerable course. He threw himself across the path of the monster with rigid purpose and set teeth, but he was brushed aside.[60]

Clearly the gender of sovereignty is at issue in this overdetermined passage. That England is represented as female and monster surely suggests, for all of Strachey's tongue-in-cheek coyness, that it was the queen herself who stood in the way of the natural order of things in both the private and public spheres.

Strachey's narrative also reveals anxiety about the Prince's virility. In his portrait of Albert as an overworked secretary to the queen, the biographer explicitly represents the middle-aged prince as increasingly afflicted with physical ailments. Thus Strachey is appalled at the inverted model of sexual difference displayed by the royal couple: "Beside Victoria, [Albert] presented a painful contrast. She, too, was stout, but it was with the plumpness of a vigorous matron; and an eager vitality was everywhere visible—in her energetic bearing, her protruding, enquiring glances, her small, fat, capable and commanding hands. If only, by some sympathetic magic, she could have conveyed into that portly, flabby figure, that desiccated and discouraged brain, a measure of the stamina and the self-assurance which were so pre-eminently hers!"[61] Essentializing sexual difference, Strachey imagines that Victoria's failure of masculinity incorporates Albert as impotent female. But Strachey's desire for a virile prince also necessitates a transposition of Victorian gender roles: He wishes that both sexually and metaphorically the queen could infuse the masculine nonentity Albert—and, by inference, all Victorian men—with her own identity and potency.

Preempting contemporary and future public interrogations of Albert's masculinity, *The Early Years of His Royal Highness the Prince Consort,* compiled after his death *"Under the Direction of Her Majesty the Queen,"* attempts to do away with the stereotype of the emasculated Albert by constructing him as the thoroughly ideal new man who governs without presiding and leads without dictating. As *The Early Years* carefully explains, Albert "was, indeed, the type of a new era—an era of power; but not of that kind of power represented by the armor of his noble ancestors, the power of mere physical strength, courage, or endurance, displayed at the head of armies or of fleets, but the moral power of character, the power of intellectual culture, of extensive knowledge, of earnest thought; the power of the sagacious statesman, of the *single-minded good man.*" [62] *Power* is the key term here, as the text forces on the reader the argument that Albert is still masculine even though the English law does not recognize him. By defining Albert's power as an influence for moral good, however, this description positions him squarely within the terrain of the female angel in the house, whose prerogative was moral influence rather than political power. Thus, in a way, Victoria's pet name for her consort, "Angel," came back to haunt the "gorgeous illusions" constructed to memorialize him after his demise.

Certainly Albert's letters about his royal role are haunted by the need to be at once covered, as in coverture, by his wife but also to act as the head of her household. *The Early Years,* of which Victoria may have written extensive sections herself, makes much of his claim that his only desire was "to sink his own individual existence in that of his wife—to aim at no power by himself or for himself—to shun all ostentation—to assume no separate responsibility before the public." However, though Albert claims in a letter to Prince Lowenstein to be "very happy and contented" with this shadowy position, he also writes that the "difficulty in filling my place with the proper dignity is, that I am only the husband, not the master in the house." In another letter, in response to the question of his identity as Victoria's marriage partner, the foreign prince refuses to appear as "puling," "effeminate," or "delica[te]" and desires a more "virile" identity to balance the potent powers of the queen.[63] *The Early Years,* then, highlights Albert's natural masculine leadership in order to compensate for his legal status as a nullity. Albert "continually and anxiously . . . watch[es] every part of the public business, in order to be able to advise and assist [Victoria] at any moment in any of the multifarious and difficult questions brought before her." With the claim that he is "the natural head of her family, superintendent of her household, manager of her private affairs," *The Early Years* naturalizes the prince consort's capacity as the queen's "sole confidential adviser in politics, and only assistant in her communications with the officers of the government." [64] As with Blackstone's *Commentaries,* however, the representation of the consort in *The Early Years* relies on contradictory attitudes toward gender roles. Glorifying the prince consort's earnest refusal to usurp his wife's legal authority, the memorial at the same time asserts that masculinity is the "natural" and original source of sovereign power.

Victoria's own gender anxieties are apparent throughout her relationship with Albert, and *The Early Years* goes to great lengths to rationalize her sovereignty in light of her role as wife. In the following passage, an anonymous narrator, possibly the queen herself, is careful to assert that while in the first giddy months of marriage the queen may have subordinated her lord and master, "fortunately, however, for the country, and still more fortunately for the happiness of the royal couple themselves, things did not long remain in this condition."

> *Thanks to the firmness, but, at the same time, gentleness with which the Prince insisted on filling his proper position as head of the family—thanks also to the clear judgment and right feeling of the Queen, as well as to her singularly honest and straightforward nature—but thanks, more than all, to the mutual love and perfect confidence which bound the Queen and Prince to each other, it was impossible to keep up any separation or difference of interests or duties between them. To those who would urge upon the Queen that, as sovereign, she must be the head of the house and the family, as well as of the state, and that her husband was, after all, but one of her subjects, her Majesty would reply that she had solemnly engaged at the altar to "obey" as well as to "love and honor," and this sacred obligation she could consent neither to limit nor refine away.*[65]

As this excerpt indicates subliminally, if the couple was viewed as the prototypical fulfillment of dominant Victorian gender ideology, their behavior was neither normative nor natural according to that same ideology, for, obviously, the "condition" to which the text obliquely refers is the exceptional one of a woman ruling because of the failure of male issue. Albert ostensibly resolved this "condition" when he insisted, gently or otherwise, on training Victoria in the home lesson that she must submit to his natural masculine authority. As this passage reveals, Victoria insisted in the beginning on ruling the country without Albert's advice. *The Early Years* implies that during this early period the royal couple's gender-bending threatened the stability of their home and the nation.

The text insists that the royal marriage did in fact become more conventional, but this only confuses matters further. The ambiguous narrator of the passage (we don't know if it is Queen Victoria, Grey, or a "compilation"), assumes the contradictory status of the doctrine of separate spheres as s/he also erases any "differences" between the couple's gendered bodies by inscribing their merging of public duties and their private love into a kind of corporation sole.

Excessively rewriting but never resolving the royal pair's legal quandary, *The Early Years* cannot erase the fact that at the moment Albert became Victoria's center he also became a nonentity. Nor does this text unravel Prince Albert's need to prove his masculinity while serving a woman sovereign, or, for that matter, Queen Victoria's obligation to prove her femininity while yet ruling a male subject. Once again, Albert's masculinity is made to appear overshadowed but still powerful. At the same time, the queen must appear submissive in her role as woman and stymied by her role as sovereign—yet she must never absolve herself of sovereign power while she represents herself as self-lessly feminine. Of course Victoria cannot reflexively proclaim the essence of femininity as the natural right to rule; instead she is careful to acknowledge the masculine right to rule. The queen "entirely," "unreservedly and confidingly" recognizes the need to "throw herself upon her husband's support, relying in all questions of difficulty on his judgement, and acting in all things by his advice."[66] Yet it should be noted that all of this was articulated publicly only *after* the prince's death, when there was no longer any question of her submission to his rule.

Given her need to respect the accepted conventions of gender, it would seem that the only legal position Victoria could take on female suffrage was a negative one. And in fact her letter to Gladstone regarding the suffragist's demands does indeed appear to condemn the movement.

> *The Queen is a woman herself—& knows what an anomaly her own position is:—but that can be reconciled with reason & propriety tho' it is a terribly difficult & trying one. But to tear away all the barriers wh surround a woman, & to propose that they shld study with men—things wh cld not be named before them—certainly not in a mixed audience—wld be to introduce a total disregard of what must be considered as belonging to the rules & principles of morality.*

The Queen feels so strongly upon this dangerous & unchristian &
unnatural cry and movement of 'woman's rights,'—in wh she knows
Mr. Gladstone agrees . . . that she is most anxious that Mr. Glad-
stone & others shld take some steps to check this alarming danger & to
make whatever use they can of her name. . . .
Let woman be what God intended; a helpmate for a man—but
with totally different duties & vocations.[67]

Despite Victoria's attempt to appear to conform to Victorian gender roles and her evident acceptance of the submission of woman, her argument falls apart on close examination. She says that she has reconciled herself to her anomalous position but leaves the "terrible" and "trying" details of that process of reconciliation a mystery, thus concealing her true power. Likewise, designating her own position as unique and anomalous, she authorizes herself as an identifier, if not the actual identity, of cultural norms and asserts that she is above the law she embodies. Hence, while Victoria argues that the naturalized generic category of "woman" is "totally different" from and subordinate to the category of "man," she speaks as a powerful sovereign, vigorously and condescendingly teaching the male prime minister his role in the whole debate. By urging her male subordinate Gladstone to use her name—which she knew was the sign of law—to denounce the suffrage movement and urge women to abide by the Victorian "rules of morality," Victoria contests the ostensible natural law regarding the sexes. Nevertheless, it is by appearing to have learned her "home" lesson—that she is a failure of male issue—that Victoria ensures her right to rule.

For all of the queen's obeisance to Victorian gender norms, then, evidently she was conflicted about her own sovereignty vis-à-vis her femininity. Indeed, there is a strong case for arguing that she enjoyed being sovereign. In June 1837, she wrote in her journal, "I really have immensely to do; I receive so many communications from my Ministers but I like it very much." In July of the same year she exclaimed, "I *delight* in this work." In 1838, after a year of reigning, she triumphantly admitted that "of all other lives, the one I had . . . a life of hard work was what I preferred."[68] But as a subject formed both within and yet above the doctrine of separate spheres, Victoria saw herself as limited to two extreme options—she could either continue to resist her mother's obsessive machinations to be her guardian, or she could resort to what she referred to as the "shocking alternative" of marriage. Having explained to Prime Minister Melbourne the aversion she felt toward the wedded state, Victoria recorded the conversation in her journal: "I said, Why need I marry at all for 3 or 4 years? did he see the necessity? I did not think so, still this & certainly the present state is dreadful; always, as he says on the verge of a quarrell; I said I dreaded the thought of marrying; that I was so accustomed to have my own way, that I thought it was 10 to 1 that I shouldn't agree with anybody." When Victoria changed her mind and decided to marry Albert immediately, Lord Melbourne supported her decision with the comment, "a woman cannot stand alone for long, in whatever situation she is." [69] Once she married, Victoria regretted having taken so long to do so, and after Albert's death she rejected any suggestion that she had ever really enjoyed her unmarried state.[70] In 1845, for example, she celebrated eight years of reigning, but thanked God "a million times more for the preservation of my blessed domestic happiness!" [71] Thus, as Margaret Homans argues, Victoria created her own form of "female authority only by means of the ideology of female submission." [72]

Nevertheless, this monarch also expressed an inability to give up the power she obtained through the appearance of submission. Victoria was unwilling, for instance, to refute Melbourne's belief that in normal circumstances a woman's property becomes her husband's but Victoria was a special case, a *"femme sole."* [73] Moreover, since Victoria never abdicated, one must question her pronouncement that "I am every day more convinced that *we women, if* we *are* to be *good* women, *feminine* and *amiable* and *domestic,* are *not fitted to reign;* at least it is *contre gré* that they drive themselves to the *work* which it entails." In fact, Victoria went on in the next breath to undermine the essentialist view of femininity with the equivocation that "this cannot now be helped, and it is the duty of every one to fulfil all that they are called upon to do, in whatever situation they may be!" [74] Accepting, then, the generic association of masculinity with the erection of public sovereignty, Victoria also sought to defy the standard that relegated women to the private sphere. For one thing, she refused to give up the power allegedly so "unnatural" to women and implied that her subjects would have to accept her contravention of the norm. The term "duty"—implying loyalty to law, however inconsistent—works ambiguously to imply the constraints of generic institutions as well as the means by which to exceed their confining boundaries. Reasoning that her unique status as female sovereign necessitated her rejection of essentialist definitions of gender, Victoria destabilized the disciplinary powers of sexual difference and opened a loophole within which Victorians could rationalize their own "duty" to gender norms.

Victoria's uncompromising fidelity to her professional career is further institutionalized in Edwin Landseer's famous portrait "Sorrow," which explicitly displays the widowed queen's needy devotion to Albert (fig. 4). Executed soon after the Prince's death, the painting features the queen, dressed in her somber mourning clothes, sitting astride a black horse. At first glance, the figure of the queen appears to epitomize the suffering widow. But at the same time that the portrait displays her personal sorrow, it also represents her professionalism, for the array of papers she peruses are not letters of sympathy or Albert's memorabilia but dispatches from her prime minister. Thus even in this spectacularly excessive representation of mourning, Victoria signifies her duty to rule despite the loss of her own ostensible ruler. In fact her journal entries after Albert's

Fig. 4. "Queen Victoria at Osborne" (1865), commonly known as "Sorrow," by Sir Edwin Landseer, is one of the many portrayals of Victoria's widowhood. The Royal Collection © Her Majesty Queen Elizabeth II.

death indicate that even while she mourned his loss she was receiving, reading, and responding to voluminous memoranda regarding matters of state.

Shrewdly, too, the queen did not authorize publication of those parts of her journal that show enthusiasm for her public duties, nor did she authorize the inclusion of descriptions of her public duties in *Leaves*. As Arthur Helps writes in the preface to *Leaves*, "references to political questions, or to the affairs of Government, have, for obvious reasons, been studiously omitted."[75] However, as Victoria's private secretary, Sir Arthur Ponsonby, asserts, the political queen was very much in evidence at the Scottish retreats described in *Leaves:* "It would not require much research," he says, "to pick out a date recording some colourless, unimportant incident and to find in her correspondence on the same day some letter to the Prime Minister or the Private Secretary expressing in the most vehement language her desire to interfere in high matters of national importance."[76]

In addition, though all of Victoria's published books were memorials to Albert, her position as queen regnant could not help but have the effect of replicating her sovereign authority as well as Albert's dependence on her. In spite of her obsessive attempts to ensure Albert's personal and national identity in the form of architectural and literary monuments, Victoria's memorials, as Margaret Oliphant notes, had the unintended effect of making herself, rather than her husband, "known."[77] For that matter, any artwork memorializing another in the name of the queen would always manifest her authority, for the subject of commemoration would not have been honored in the first place had Victoria not authorized the testimonial.

Having examined the contingency of the gendered subject that is incorporated in the British Constitution, I turn in the next chapter to the Victorian literary writer's legal interventions. Building on the British legal construction of gender, chapter two focuses on how Victorian writers implicitly and explicitly attempted to establish their Shelleyan positions as "legislators" who professed superior aesthetic and ethical representations of the law. I am particularly interested in how these writer-legislators inscribed their access to a higher law in the context of their relationship to the epitome of state law, Queen Victoria, who herself was

a popular author. These already complex tensions were further complicated by the queen's and the writer's genders. Heightening the Victorian
queen's representative powers by adding to the already numerous "gorgeous illusions" about the female monarch, the Victorian literati also insisted upon using those representations to increase their own prestige and
to assure the distribution of their literary representations.

II

The Royal Crown and the Laurel Crown: Gendering Sovereign Subjects and Professions

The Queen was . . . in herself the representative of England.

Marie Corelli, The Passing of the Great Queen

[E]ven while they [poets] deny and abjure, they are yet compelled to serve, the Power which is seated upon the throne of their own soul. . . . Poets are the unacknowledged legislators of the world.

Percy Bysshe Shelley, "A Defence of Poetry"

THE PREVIOUS CHAPTER illustrates some of the powerful legal fictions underwriting the Victorian construction of sovereign subjectivity as well as some of the apprehensions aroused when a woman signified the law of the land. These apprehensions had everything to do with who was the proper representative of authority and who was the appropriate subject of representation. This chapter focuses on the powers and praxis of representation, particularly on the ways in which Victorian writers constructed their representative powers vis-à-vis the queen's. In their "gorgeous illusions" of the queen, many Victorian writers subliminally grappled with tensions about their own discursive prowess, their possession of cultural capital, and their display of imperishable authority. The enigma of gender was central to the author's display of writerly authority. Indeed, the contingency of masculine authority and the latent potency of all women implicit in the reign of a queen produced many fictional allusions to female sovereignty in general and to Queen Victoria in particular. Male writers often implicitly raised questions about constitutional authority in their writings on the queen. For example, who is innately privileged to define or represent subjects, and who rightfully embodies the ostensible sovereignty of the self? The male writers I examine, though loyal to their monarch, also reiterated patriarchal views of sovereignty and representation. The female writers I discuss, though they often evoked and even co-opted the queen's "femininity" and ascendancy, were equally ambivalent about Victoria, though all seemed to find in her an explicit image of female potency that informed constructions of their own authority.

Fortifying their professional authority against escalating pressures that simultaneously fictionalized, multiplied, and eradicated the identity of the sovereign self, Victorian writers—like other Victorian professionals—documented, organized, and directed British subjectivity in an increasingly complicated episteme. But if Victorian writers elaborated subjectivity ever more meticulously and legislated through their body of work what the British Constitution lacked or confused in its legal descriptions of subjectivity, they could not deny that it was Victoria whose female body represented Victorians. Certainly the Victorian belief in the queen's sexual difference influenced the writer's inscriptions of sovereignty, subjectivity, and representation itself. Sexual difference, that is, governed the Victorian author's awareness of his or her self as a writer, and, as I will show, that awareness was often linked with the writer's consciousness of the sovereign's sexual difference.

Noting the correlation between state authority and the writer's authority, Patrick Parrinder suggests that there is a connection between literature and national pride.[1] Aesthetic representations of British subjects, in other words, coincide with political notions of representation. Representation as cultural practice was complicated by nineteenth-century discourses about political representation. These discourses included declarations about and justifications of who should actively participate in the nation-state's governing bodies, who should express the will and values of the people, and who should be allowed to influence decisions about the state's finances and its domestic and foreign policies. In the Victorian period, contests over this kind of representation were frequent, continuous, and sometimes fierce, as women in general and groups of middle- and lower-class men demanded political representation.

Symbolic representation of the nation–state was as important as the mechanisms through which political representation was actually distributed. The terms of symbolic representation involved deciding who or what should mediate Britain's identity to the rest of the globe and to Britons themselves. Of course in England the monarch had traditionally filled this role. Over the course of the nineteenth century, however, the powers of the British monarch were increasingly aligned with the cultural rather than political meaning of representation. The British monarch had long since lost explicit powers to make political decisions for the country as power was taken over by the prime minister and ruling party. Under Victoria, however, the monarchy learned to create more professional "gorgeous illusions" of its power and influence. As David Cannadine notes, though political statecraft became invested elsewhere, the monarch's symbolic meaning expanded in the nineteenth century as Victoria's public appearances became the "centre of grand ceremonial."[2]

In the previous chapter, I used the anonymous "Letter to the Queen, on her Retirement from Public Life" to illustrate how at least some Victorians were concerned that the queen's gender might interfere with her constitutional duties as sovereign. The writer of that letter was alarmed that, following Albert's death, Victorian writers traded places with the queen. Linking Victoria's "Retirement from Public Life" with the country's political downfall, "One of Her Majesty's Most Loyal Subjects" articulated the queen's crucial role of being the "personal representative" of "the nation at large": "How awkward it is for the inhabitants of one country to express shortly and with perspicuity their sentiments with respect to the inhabitants of another country unless they have recourse to imagery is testified by the habit into which painters and writers have fallen of symbolising the nation they describe or depict under some ideal form, either that of a conventional figure, as Britannia, or John Bull, or the British lion, or of some living notability, as the ruler of the particular State which they wish to personify."[3]

Acknowledging the ways in which the artist's and monarch's representational powers are similar, this writer feared that if the queen gave up her symbolic potency, these other professional purveyors of the sovereign image would assume her higher, more consequential representative powers. In other words, if "the Sovereign is the apex of our social system" and "the acknowledged head of society," she should, then, "brook no rival."[4] But, as the loyal subject acknowledged, in a socioeconomically competitive society there will be rivals, and in Victorian England professionals commonly vied with each other in their efforts to rise to the top of their field.

This same writer nevertheless went on to explain that "Away from the Court, or in its absence, individual leaders of fashion may assemble their respective coteries, and endeavour to outdo each other in the splendour of their appointments or the extent of their influence." The bottom line, however, was that "where the Sovereign outshines all, and compels all, friends and foes alike, to yield a respectful homage to her, these lesser luminaries, though they may emit a more or less intense light in their own circles, are deprived of all power to burn." As the loyal correspondent insisted, the queen is the signified through which all signifiers receive their meaning. Flatly asserting that "Controversy and emulation" should "cease when the competitors approach the throne," the essayist explained that the monarch is the "one to whom all must pay equal deference," and therefore, "In the presence of Royalty the supereminence of the Queen stills the strife of the Many."[5]

It was unnatural for Victorian writers to co-opt Victoria's representative powers. The letter referred in particular to the powerful sway of the sensation novel, "in which vice is described in glowing and attractive terms, and the practice of it extenuated, if not extolled, while virtue is decried or damned with faint praise." When the sensational novel first came out, he noted, it attracted great attention, just as the queen did when she acceded to the throne. But when Victoria abdicated her responsibilities, "Society, wanting its natural head and guide," had to resort to "the productions of so-called poets," for, since Victoria had rejected her own moral leadership, "There was no one sufficiently influential who was inclined or who had the power to mould public opinion." Victorian writers were more than willing to fill that gap.

> *Can we doubt that if the influence of the Court had been put in motion to check the reception of those baleful works,—if, to use the words of the late Prince Consort, "the Court—that is, the Queen—had set the example" of condemning them, the views of the Court would have prevailed in the highest ranks of society, and the authors and authoresses of them, unable to obtain that toleration for their earliest efforts which*

*was all they needed to give them a foothold, would have slunk back into
the obscurity whence they ought never to have emerged?*[6]

If, as this anonymous writer complained, Victorian writers were co-opting the queen's symbolic powers, few if any of them could compete with the queen's representative powers in sheer material terms. For one thing, they did not yet own their own "royalties" in the way that she possessed her royal perquisites. Authorized to acquire vast estates, gifts, and royal accoutrements to display to the world her country's majestic sovereignty, the queen represented material excess. Lytton Strachey captured her brilliantly: "Victoria was a woman not only of vast property but of innumerable possessions. She had inherited an immense quantity of furniture, of ornaments, of china, of plate, of valuable objects of every kind; her purchases, throughout a long life, made a formidable addition to these stores; and there flowed in upon her, besides, from every quarter of the globe, a constant stream of gifts." Preserving every article in her possession, Victoria had them replaced with exact copies when they wore out. Fascinated by Victoria's material excess, Strachey points out the queen's obsessive protection of the material signs of her own sovereignty: "Over this enormous mass she exercised an unceasing and minute supervision, and the arrangement and the contemplation of it, in all its details, filled her with an intimate satisfaction."[7]

Not only did Victoria hoard the royal valuables, she multiplied their representational power by having each article photographed and each image kept in her vast collection of photographic facsimiles. Strachey notes that not one but a variety of photographs from different viewpoints were taken of each item. Next to each photograph in her elaborate collection of albums "an entry was made, indicating the number of the article, the number of the room in which it was kept, its exact position in the room and all its principal characteristics."[8] One of Victoria's own retainers confirms Strachey's account: "Every photo, when affixed to the page, is surrounded by various *data,* which include the number and name of the room in which the article is kept, the number of the article itself, its size, any marks or signs that may be on it, and a full description of it from every point of view," including whether or not the item was the queen's own personal property. The compilation of these photographic catalogues was "one of the most expensive of the Queen's fads" for it was never ending. "Very fond of her catalogues," the queen sent for one every few days and pored over it.[9] Whether by personal preference or out of a sense of tradition, according to the present curators of the Royal Archives at Windsor Castle, every English sovereign since Victoria has continued her mind-boggling practice of having royal possessions photographed and catalogued.

Victoria was also "very fond of being painted" and was the subject of "many hundreds" of statues, busts, and pictures, each of which she "eagerly anticipate[d] and carefully criticise[d]," "as though to see the reproduction of her face was quite a novel experience." According to her attendant, it was also Victoria's "weakness" to "be photographed in every possible condition of her daily life."[10] Exact copies of herself were also distributed commercially among her subjects when one of the first paparazzi, John Edwin Mayall, sold eager Victorian consumers thousands of *cartes de visites* featuring the royal family. Victoria herself got caught up in the craze: As one of her ladies-in-waiting wrote home, "I have been writing to all the fine ladies in London for their and their husbands photographs for the queen," who, she claimed, "could be bought and sold, for a photograph" (fig. 5). The queen also sent photographs of herself as a gift to at least one author, Charles Dickens. The long-lived sovereign collected thirty-six volumes of these *cartes de visites* in addition to at least eighty-four family photograph albums, which included 100,000 photos.[11]

In *The Commodity Culture of Victorian England,* Thomas Richards asserts that the Jubilees were as much about selling the queen's image in material terms as they were about spectacularizing and selling her in political terms, for Victoria's image gave uniform identity to the chaotic array of advertisements displayed during the Jubilee celebrations. The list of Jubilee products sold with her image on them is astonishing. Of course the queen's likeness was to be found on specialty items such as jewelry, coins, and stamps. But in addition there were "mugs, jugs, plates, plaques, busts, and statuettes; glasses, pipes, paper clips, cups and saucers, candy boxes (both wooden and metal), thimbles, watches, tea caddies, napkin rings, spoons, mirrors, magazines; flags, aprons, handkerchiefs, dishcloths; and a host of magazines, invitations, menus, photographs, and prints."[12]

Being queen meant more than just exhibiting the country's economic wealth on and in her person, more, too, than reproducing that

Fig. 5. "Queen Victoria and Prince Albert, May 15th 1860." J. J. E. Mayall. The Royal Collection © Her Majesty Queen Elizabeth II.

wealth in symbols of her person such as those described above. Since she inherited royal commodities from previous sovereigns, Victoria also added to the stockpile of material representations of the state when she herself received gifts from foreign leaders. But as the above list suggests, commodified representations of Victoria served as imitations of the original, authoritative source of identity and economically legislated the meaning of Victorian self-possession. The linkage of commercial representation with royalty linked the project of the Industrial Revolution to Victoria's reign. With her face stamped on each coin of the realm, as well, (one of those coins designated a "crown"), Victoria was legally, politically, and economically associated with the distribution of money. Thus the female sovereign represented British identity as circulating, imitative, fragmentary, exchangeable, and utterly commercial.

Richards explicitly points out the close connection made in the mid-nineteenth century between Victoria—the sign of the law of the land—and the commodity—"the living letter of the law of supply and demand." The enthronement of the commodity as king accompanied the monarchy's declining political powers of representation and its increasingly potent symbolic representation. As Richards and, more recently, Anne McClintock have shown, the nineteenth-century advertising industry's "gorgeous illusions" of the queen depended on the image of the maternal, domesticating monarch to distribute its ideology and its material goods to the empire. Organizing all culture "around economic representations," commodity culture linked the female monarch with the massive increase of consumers, commercial products, and commercial representations designed to create desire for those products. Indeed, as Richards argues, her identity was equated with her subjects' identities as consumers, for "in department stores the consumer" was constructed as a "queen" while the queen was constructed as a consumer, and both were treated as "equals in the eyes of the market." [13]

In her unpublished fictional commemoration of the first Jubilee ("The Good Hermione"), Victorian writer Mary Braddon denounces the mercantile character of the event. Braddon's narrator fumes that before "this Jubilee Memorial was settled all the busybodies . . . came forward with their particular fads, & everyone wanted his or her little adventure to profit by the queen's Jubilee. . . . everyone of all shades & denominations, clamoured for institutions, or halls, or museums, or almshouses, or schools, or creches, or recreation rooms, or libraries, to be built out of Jubilee money & endowed with Jubilee money." [14] This part of Braddon's "gorgeous illusion" about Victoria stands out because it appears on the last pages of her unfinished manuscript, which suggests that these were Braddon's final thoughts about royalty in the age of the author's contested fiscal royalties. One wonders, indeed, whether Braddon's foreboding description of the commercial takeover of the Jubilee had anything to do with her own inability to complete her representation of the queen.

In fact, Braddon's description of the capitalist trajectory of the royal celebration eclipses Victoria's powers by showing the market's dominance over any political sovereign, over sovereignty itself. Previously cheerful, the narrator becomes positively glum when confronting the mercantile tone of the affair. "Everyone," she grumbles, "declared that the aggrandisement of his or her particular fad wd be the most appropriate tribute for our admiring nation to [make] to its Queen. . . . All the genteel beggars went about with little velvet bags crying 'Please to remember the Jubilee' just as you may see dirty little boys at the beginning of the oyster season running about with oyster shells, & pestering passers by with 'please to remember the grotto.'" [15] This rampant commercialism pollutes and disfigures the event, which no longer simply commemorates Victoria's long, distinguished reign but inaugurates the long reign of commercial consumption to come. Braddon recognizes in this lament her inability, and that of any other literary representation, to overcome the massive commercial forces that benefitted from both authorized and unauthorized representations of the queen.

But if the queen's image was strongly associated with British commerce, wealth, and consumerism, Victoria adeptly covered over the materialist implications of the commercial appropriation of her person by publishing a representation of her private life, the domestic values of which depended on but at the same time concealed her own expansive consumerism. Becoming a published author must have been important to Victoria, for her family and advisors strongly urged her not to publicize during her lifetime two extracts from her journals (*Leaves from the Journal of Our Life in the Highlands* and *More Leaves from a Journal of Our Life in the Highlands*), reasoning that to do so would be to vulgarize her royal authority. Victoria did not heed the advice, and her journals became bestsellers. Strachey explains the significance of Victoria's authorship when he says that it "was through her writings that [Victoria] touched the heart of the public." Deftly pinpointing the way *Leaves* represented the bourgeois domestic idyll with which Victoria's subjects strongly identified and to which their identities were subjected, Strachey writes: "The middle-classes . . . were pleased. They liked a love-match; they liked a household which combined the advantages of royalty and virtue, and in which they seemed to see, reflected as in some resplendent looking-glass, the ideal image of the very lives they led themselves. Their own existences, less exalted, but oh! so soothingly similar, acquired an added excellence. . . . [Victoria was] . . . the embodiment, the living apex of a new era in the generations of mankind." [16]

Because she wrote voluminously, and because she saw herself as the people's representative, it should have been no surprise that Victoria sought to accrue to herself the fanfare of having successfully published her own representation of British life and sovereign selfhood. Giles St. Aubyn points out that between her personal and official correspondence, Victoria spent a great deal of time reading and writing. Penning an average of 2,500 words daily, by the end of her reign Victoria had written an astonishing total of sixty million words. The queen wrote twelve hundred letters to Palmerston alone. But it was not the memoirs of her professional life that she chose to publish. Instead, she publicized the purportedly truer private life. The female monarch read her audience's desires well, for *Leaves* outsold many books that came out in 1868, including Wilkie Collins's *The Moonstone,* Robert Browning's *Ring and the Book,* and Louisa May Alcott's *Little Women.* The queen was not shy about her success either. Writing to her daughter Vicky, who was embarrassed by what she saw as her mother's tawdry entrance into the writer's domain, which had everything to do with economic royalties, Victoria gleefully exclaimed that "Eighteen thousand copies were sold in a week." [17]

It is fascinating to discover that Victoria's books vied successfully with the works of such popular novelists as Wilkie Collins and Robert Browning. One realizes, too, that as a best-selling writer, Victoria brilliantly negotiated the author's competitive profession. The competition was about achieving mastery over representation and its material and cultural affects and effects. Having entered that professional playing field, Victoria was subject to its criticism, and apparently a number of Victorians took potshots at her writing skills. If, as we have seen, one of her "loyal subjects" feared that writers had appropriated her representative powers, another loyal servant defended her writing prowess: "It was at one time rather the fashion to decry the Queen's powers as an authoress—or rather as an expressive writer. . . . The writings of the Queen's which the public have been permitted to see have essentially the elements of great work, perfect simplicity of expression, and admirable self-restraint. The Queen never gushes or over-writes, and of what other feminine writer can such words be truly said?" Here again, the queen's gender is viewed as the overriding basis for evaluation. Still, the writer continues, "If the Queen had been destined by Fate to write in lieu of ruling, she must have left a great mark on the literature of the century." [18] An avid reader of novels, Victoria sensed what this writer assumed: that the professional author was coming increasingly to be viewed as the most qualified person to represent Victorians to themselves.

Given Victoria's venture into publishing, in a strict sense it might be said that she competed with literary writers in their own arena. From her work in the Royal Archives, Lynne Vallone has shown that as a young girl Victoria seems to have had ambitions to take a writer's work and rewrite it literally in her own image. For example, as princess, Victoria took Maria Edgeworth's *Harry and Lucy,* in which the boy is the central protagonist, and rewrote it so that her own barely disguised female alter ego became the central character. In this case, writing and sovereign authority colluded and competed for the power to represent culture. Likewise, Victoria seems to have been in the habit of presenting *Leaves* as a gift to professional authors—she gave it to George Eliot, Charles Dickens, and Margaret Oliphant. It is fascinating to conjecture what exactly was in the queen's mind when she made this gesture, whether it was humbug or humble pie toward the authors she admired. In either case, the queen had to have viewed *Leaves* as representative of her reign, her personal life, and her ability to represent.

It seems, then, that Victoria believed that her profession as queen gave her the prerogatives of the professional writer. But she was not alone in making this connection. Percy Shelley explicitly linked the two representational trajectories when he famously remarked that the "throne" of the literary writers' "own soul" authorized them to be the "unacknowledged legislators of the World." A political activist as well as a poet, Shelley imaged poetry as a political means of "awakening" in the people of a nation "a beneficial change in opinion or institution." [19] In keeping with Shelley's vision, the Victorian novel's increasing attention to the individual's emotional and psychological states accompanied the nation-state's move toward expanding the ranks of the legally enfranchised political subject. Shelley, in fact, approved of poetic "monarchy" but not of political, and he held the representative powers of royalty far below those of literature.

At the end of the nineteenth century, Rudyard Kipling implied much the same thing in his poem "Recessional," written as a check on the 1897 Jubilee celebrations. Describing the presumed high point of the queen's incumbency, Kipling incisively debunked her representative powers in his prophetic representation of the declining authority of Victoria's England. But this portrait of the queen's last years has poignant overtones for the writer also, for just as the monarchy had lost political power and gained immense symbolic powers of representation, literary authority was also both diminished and lionized in the nineteenth century. During this period writers struggled to establish themselves as professionals, a position that would give them "self-determined valuation rather than subordination to the market." Hoping to achieve the recognition that literature was "a specialized and special service offered by the possessor of poetic knowledge for the edification of others," professional writers also sought the economic rewards that went along with such recognition, sought, at least "a measure of social independence and economic security." [20] But it was difficult to wear the laurel crown when royalties and copyright were fiercely contested. As J. A. Sutherland points out, "Who actually 'owned' literary property was never actually stated on contracts after the Copyright Amendment Act of 1842." "Before this a publisher might well talk of a novel as 'my exclusive property.'" [21]

If Victorian writers inherited the eighteenth-century view of authors as "hacks who sold ideas by the word," their evolving profession also trailed clouds of glory from the tradition of "leisured men of letters" of the past.[22] Viewed at once as a Shelleyan poet-prophet expressing the culture's greatest truths, the Victorian writer was also seen as a commercial being deeply embroiled in concerns about profit. As Catherine Gallagher suggests, the historical conjunction of the "activities of authoring, of procuring illegitimate income, and of alienating one's self through prostitution" became closely associated in the nineteenth century.[23] Most important for the purposes of this study is that these contradictory images of the author are invested with disturbing representations of gender. For example, the identification of poet with prophet echoes Blackstone's constitutional attempts to associate English gentlemen with God. The prophet imagery also links the poetic act of representation with the fructifying powers of a fathering sage.

In contrast, the image of the poet as prostitute genders the disfigurement of the writing subject as feminine. Such images also neatly divide the commercial aspects of writing from the transcendent, respectively gendering the former as feminine and the latter as masculine. How could the female writer inscribe herself within these gendered models of representation? If women writers were associated with the mercantile underside of the writing profession, they were also viewed as prostituting their natures and their limited talents by being prolific and bad or, at best, mediocre copiers of male texts. Given that the production and consumption of texts was governed predominantly by male publishers and advertisers, a woman writer could never be defined without bringing in overtones of the call girl.

For Victorian male writers, the problem has everything to do with the "feminization" of the age to which so many scholars have referred.[24] Adrienne Munich's discussion of the "erotomania" that compelled seven men to try to assassinate the queen reinforces my argument that gender constructs and the feminization of the age underwrite the male writer's loyalty to the female monarch. Margaret Homans has argued in the same vein that the feminization of the English monarchy was necessary to the feminization of the subject in a capitalist economy. As she suggests, Victoria "had to be available for idealization and, by the same token, to be manifestly willing to relinquish active agency in political affairs, so that others [men] could perform remarkable deeds in her name."[25]

The process of feminization has everything to do with Nancy Armstrong's notion that as a being subjected to the market, the modern capitalist subject is feminine. Building on Armstrong's argument, Tamar Heller has elaborated on the way the writer's profession became feminized during the Victorian age, as the marketplace became "the site not of male self-definition, but of the erasure of masculine identity through an economic neediness that makes men like women. Women are associated with lack of economic independence either through their feminine reliance on men within the Victorian family or, alternatively, through their unfeminine dependence on the marketplace when they are writing for money." Explaining that to the Victorian mind "women's influence is linked to oppression and secrecy," Heller points out that Victorian women writers were also necessarily engaged in subversion and secrecy because they were writing professionally in a culture in which the "proper" woman did not work. "Both femininity and fiction (what is smoothed and polished for the popular taste)" came to seem to the Victorians antithetical to the "'plain and true record' of facts" associated with masculine writers.[26]

If woman in the Victorian era becomes associated in many ways with the "fictional," Queen Victoria is a focal point for those associations. Her very image relying on contradictions within and subversions of Victorian definitions of femininity and sovereignty, Victoria was the ultimate fiction—a powerful representation that was at once unreliable and duplicitous and tremendously influential. A master at manipulating representations of her role as queen and as domestic angel in the house,[27] Victoria, like the Victorian woman writer, could always be suspected of the will to secretly subvert men's power through feminine influence. Victoria's own authorized fictions—*Leaves* and *More Leaves*—reinforced her political authority by concealing it under elaborate representations of her own domestic bliss. Thus she subversively accrued to herself the professional authority of queen and writer while secretly subverting the ostensible source of all authority—the masculine.

Victoria's authorization of portraits and photographs of herself to be distributed among her subjects effected the same kind of manipulative representation. As Susan Casteras points out, the invention of photography "was one of the most crucial factors in disseminating Victoria's image so widely in her own country and abroad." As a result, Victoria "gained a constant presence in the presses and a tangible likeness in the minds and eyes of subjects."[28] The wide distribution of her photos had an effect not unlike that experienced by an author whose serial novels were widely circulated. The photographic images as well as the portrait of herself on the postal stamp made Victoria a formidable competitor to anyone avowing his or her representative authority.

The "feminization" of the Victorian age, then, cannot be separated from the empowered and destabilized femininity of the most famous woman of the age, Queen Victoria herself. Indeed, the sheer massiveness of her representation, her own fictionality, and her authorship also implicate her in Victorian male writers' fears that the age had lost its virility. The queen's own invasion of the male writer's terrain added to his fear that women were taking over his profession. And since she came to power only through the failure of male issue, she was an anomalous representative under whom it would be difficult for the male artist to portray himself as the rightful transmitter of cultural values[29] that looked increasingly feminized. If the "Power that was seated" on the "throne" of his "own soul" was associated with a political throne inhabited by a queen, it would be a perplexing project to represent the linkage between his own male authority, the pervasive masculinity of the state, and the pervasive masculinity of canonical literary writing.

Closely aligned with the subversion of male identity, particularly the male writer's identity, is Victoria's implicit connection with the crown's historical antagonism toward the writer's profession. Susan Stewart's chronology of the copyright establishes the historical link between laws about writing and the friction between government (the monarch) and writers. As Stewart shows, the establishment of printing resulted in "The Star Chamber, England's special prerogative court," which dealt with acts of treason in printed form. Thus, from the start, copyright law suggested the antithetical positions of the crown and writing citizens. Illustrating the argument that "'in England censorship was always centralized and derived from the royal prerogative,'" Stewart shows how written dissent from or criticism of the monarch was viewed as having powerful negative representational effects.[30] Stewart's historical account, then, provides a context within which to read the negative comments about Victoria made by Victorian writers, among them Barrett Browning, Dickens, and Oliphant. In some ways, their critique of the queen carried with it historical traces of the original reason for copyright law: the writer's dissent from or even treason against the monarch's representative authority, and his own aspiration to representative authority.

For a writer to lament the feminization of the age, then, was to be at once seditious and loyal to the constitutionally mandated queen who was so much a part of that feminization. Rueful disquisitions on the age's loss of virility were generally expressed subversively.[31] Louis Montrose's study of the way male writers portrayed Queen Elizabeth is useful for studying similar fears of emasculation during Queen Victoria's reign. Montrose finds that Shakespearean plays manifest an unease with the reign of a powerful woman ruler. Although Elizabeth's male subjects were loyal to Elizabeth because they were loyal to man-made law, Montrose argues that in literary representations they also sublimated the masculinist belief in their right to rule. For instance, *A Midsummer Night's Dream* represents the male fantasy of overthrowing the interregnum of a female monarch, carried out through the male subject's sexualization and domestication of the queen's political body. Similarly, Adrienne Munich typifies the dynamics of royal containment in the Victorian period in her discussion of Gilbert and Sullivan's Savoy operas, which, she argues, are based on the subliminal desire to overthrow a large, powerful, mad older woman in order to restore orderly patriarchy.[32]

Containing Victoria's body by sexualizing and often prostituting it became common practice for many male writers. Indeed, many Victorian male authors took for granted their right to enter the queen's bedroom. In his doggerel verse, for example, the pseudonymous Patricius Terentius Thadaeus O'Toole could not resist making broad innuendoes about the wedding night and what Albert would "give" his bride. In the climactic scene, Albert essentially presides over the erection of male sovereignty:

> *Prince Albert did not linger, but took her wedding finger*
> *And on it put a ring, or I'm under a mistake;*
> *"For better or for worser—when sick," says he, "I'll nurse her;*
> *I'll give her my goods and purse, sir" (*that same *his heart*
> *won't break;)*
> *And something else he added, which from my mind has faded."*[33]

Other memorials of the royal marriage go further and link the distribution of the queen's wealth with the dispersal of her sexuality. One contemporary editorial cartoon, for example, features the couple's betrothal metaphorically, with Albert fishing for the queen's favor. In this cartoon, a passive, domestic young Victoria, showing no sign of her public power, waits in the background for her suitor to catch his limit. Illustrating the interpenetration of the erotic and the economic, the cartoon puts the Prince and his monetary expectations in the foreground (fig. 6).[34]

Fig. 6. "Fishing Scene in Windsor Park" (1839) by Foz.

Likewise, a contemporary street song celebrates the prince's romantic/economic "interest" in Victoria and their future progeny:

> O slumber my darling
> While I sing thee a sermon
> Thy mother's a Guelph
> And thy father's a German.
> The hills and the dales
> And John Bull's money,
> All shall belong
> My dear darling to thee.[35]

Later in her reign, of course, the queen had to endure the gossip surrounding her highland steward John Brown. But what I find as interesting is the fantasy of one of her lowlier subjects who would be king. Englishman and late nineteenth-century prophet of the Mormon church, Wilford Woodruff noted in his journal of 14 June 1880 that he had "dreamed this morning that Queen Victoria had received the gospel and Been Baptized." "Appear[ing] vary [*sic*] humble," in the dream she is married to Woodruff, and she "thanks" him for the favor.[36] Of course, Woodruff, the leader of a polygamous church, was fantasizing about Victoria as just another of his many wives. But in this self-serving reverie, Woodruff subliminally fortifies his role as prophet by associating himself with the queen's imprimatur, a subconscious instance, perhaps, of subordinating the powerful female sovereign in order to compensate for his own lack of power as the leader of a fledgling church with little authority in the eyes of the world.

Lytton Strachey also sexualizes the queen in order to delegitimate her sovereignty, here describing the young princess: "One seems to hold in one's hand a small smooth crystal pebble, without a flaw and without a scintillation, and so transparent that one can see through it at a glance." But "perhaps, after all, to the discerning eye, the purity would not be absolute. The careful searcher might detect, in the virgin soil, the first faint traces of an unexpected vein." Strachey goes on somewhat excessively (in a four-and-a-half-page-long-paragraph, no less) to recount Victoria's many flirtations with her boy cousins, covertly and inexplicably depicting the future queen, who "was just seventeen" and a "budding organism," as a potential prostitute.[37] Strachey's representation of the queen's adolescent dalliances as revealing a flawed "vein" in her personality implies her sexual vanity as well. Calling up the old double standard, he holds the queen to an ideal of sexual purity that does not apply to kings as well; a king need only worry that his consort remain sexually pure.

Victoria's queenly femininity vis-à-vis her sexuality also appears as a subliminal element in a sex manual for women that came out during the queen's reign. In *Queenly Womanhood* (the counterpart to *Princely Manhood*), cleric and self-styled marriage counselor Smith H. Platt cashes in on the royal couple's preeminence. Platt also metaphorically takes the queen into the bedroom in his attempt to reassert masculine prerogatives in the guise of chivalric but meaningless obeisance to the power of queenly womanhood. Using the image of female sovereignty to point out that a woman's true "Victory" is to be found in submission to the masculine sex, Platt endeavors to restore the proper gender hierarchy, which has everything to do with male sexuality. His purpose being to teach the reader—the woman who would be queen—"HOW TO LIVE A VICTOR ALWAYS" over sexual desire, Platt encourages women to enjoy physical desires, but "Not in such a way as to CULTIVATE THEM."

Rather, the queenly woman should constrain herself in order that the "full, self-collected" sexual energies might "be held in reserve, fortifying the consciousness with a sense of superiority over self, that will itself go far toward preserving self-control." [38] The implication is that if a woman indulges her erotic, economic, or political desires, she forfeits the right to be called a queen. Victoria was the true "VICTOR" and queenly woman, then, not because she filled the political role of sovereign but because she submitted to her natural ruler, Albert.

Constituting woman's sexuality as the counterpart of man's supposedly uncontrollable erotic "nature" and, thus, his confused sense of self, Platt exalts woman's self-contained omnipotence, especially when contrasted to man's sexual instability:

> *A man should go into training for a conflict with his appetites just as keenly as he does for the university Eight, the only difference being that the training will be more beneficial and more protracted. Besides diet and exercise, let him be constantly employed; in fact, let him have so many metaphorical irons in the fire that he will find it difficult to snatch ten minutes for private meditation; let his sleep be very limited, and the temperature he moves in as nearly cold as he can bear; let neither his eye nor his ear be voluntarily open to anything that could possibly excite the passions; if he see or hear accidentally what might have this tendency, let him at once resort to his dumb-bells, or any other muscular precaution till he is quite fatigued; whenever any sensual image occurs involuntarily to his mind, let him fly to the same resource, or else to the intellectual company of friends, till he feels secure of no return on the enemy's part.* [39]

Defining the sexes as inhabiting absolutely polarized separate spheres, Platt automatically ensures the self-contradiction of both. Unable to deny the obvious instability of the man, who should be the acknowledged superior in the marital relationship, Platt concludes that the more self-controlled woman must submit to the man in order that the natural order be maintained. Her superior self-control should only be enacted in an interregnum of sorts, which acts as a guarantee that the man will retain the kingly position he so rightly deserves.

Woman, then, must give up her queenly sovereignty if the marital relationship and the social order are to be maintained. Suggesting that "marriage is desirable in most of both sexes," Platt asserts that the "female particularly should ponder well the obligations involved" because men "tend to savagery when their passions are concerned" and "his passional wants" will most likely exceed hers. The logic is that since his is the stronger urge, and hers the weaker, as in all battles the weaker must submit: "The wife should therefore consider that although her part may be a painful one at the time, it is a martyrdom of the flesh which she may be called to make, and which has its reward in this world and in the world to come." Therefore, even where pregnancy might lead to death, Platt advises the woman to succumb to her husband's desires. Would it be worse for a wife to "suffer physically" or for a husband to fall to extra-marital temptation? The obvious answer is that "if it comes to this, no true wife will hesitate, even though the sacrifices may *seem* to be a species of immolation, abhorrent to the sensibilities of her nature." [40] Thus Platt trains the female reader that in order to be a queen she must be willing to pay homage—both physically and emotionally—to her kingly master, a subject so wrenched by his sexual desires that every moment is a battle to maintain his stability.

Thomas Carlyle, Alfred Lord Tennyson, and John Ruskin do not explicitly refer to the queen's sexuality in their representations of her, but all three felt it necessary to instruct her—and the queenly woman—in the proper duties of womanhood. This instruction is related, I believe, to anxieties about their own sovereign powers as writers and as men. In Carlyle's case, fear of the feminized age seems directly related to his economic need to be successful in his profession. Figuring writers as the chosen few, whose masculinity is the primal source of their authority, Carlyle exhorts aspiring authors to "Be *men*" before they attempt "to be *writers!*" [41] Mystifying male virility, Carlyle lauds the "perpetual priest-hood" [42] of male genius, dramatically suggesting that no political entity—which would include the queen—can rival the writer's authority. Carlyle asserts that of "all Priesthoods, Aristocracies, Governing Classes at present extant in the world, there is no class comparable for importance to that Priesthood of the Writers of Books." [43] Here Carlyle anticipates Edward Said's definition of the author as the ultimate macho "father" who "enforce[s]," "influence[s]," "possess[es]," "originates," "begin[s]," "founds," "increase[s]," "controls," "produces," "invents," "initiate[s]," "institute[s]," and "establish[es]." [44]

In another study, [45] I discuss Carlyle's discursive representation of his tormenting, lifelong mysterious stomach ailment, which rendered him inert, passive, and sickly—qualities associated with femininity. In a diatribe directed against the passions and appetites produced by the temptress woman, the future author warns a friend that the "letcher's fate" is that anyone who finds him "shall *geld* him." [46] Combined with his comments about the gender of authorship, this comment is just another example of how *the* most authoritative writer of the Victorian era associates his profession with the success or failure of his masculinity. A writer concerned with the virility of representational powers, Carlyle continually refers to Queen Victoria in the diminutive form. In accounts of his meetings with or sightings of the queen from 1838 to 1878, Carlyle refers to Victoria as the "poor little Queen," "Poor little Victory!" "Unhappy little child," and the "hapless little fool." [47] By infantilizing the queen— who did not remain a child, in spite of Carlyle—one of the most authoritative writers of the age subliminally "establishes" and "enforces" his own supremacy at the expense of her own.

In a less combative style than Carlyle's, Tennyson implies that acknowledging the true male possessor of the royal crown is central to the project of *Idylls of the King*. Like Mrs. Trimmer's tales for children, in the prefatory matter of the *Idylls* the male poet denies the reality of female sovereignty by representing Albert as the active, ruling presence in England and Victoria as an almost incidental, passive consort. Elliot Gilbert notes that Tennyson's depiction was not, of course, accurate, for "Victoria is the true holder and wielder of power, the repository of enormous inherited authority, while Albert possesses what influence and significance he does almost solely through his marriage." Thus Gilbert argues, as I do, that the reversal of gender roles expresses not only the predominance but also the increasingly destabilized position of the doctrine of separate spheres in Victorian culture. Tennyson certainly honors the queen, but it is for her domestic rather than political features. In fact, in his eulogy of the queen, the poet laureate firmly positions Victoria as first and foremost a mother and wife:

> *Her court was pure; her life serene;*
> *God gave her peace; her land reposed;*
> *A thousand claims to reverence closed*
> *In her as Mother, Wife, and Queen.*[48]

In *The Princess*, which portrays a powerful female sovereign who threatens to rule and even to live without men, Tennyson explicitly represents the male writer's subliminal response to being ruled by a female monarch. By no means a feminist manifesto, *The Princess* endorses the doctrine of separate spheres, the notion that sexual difference creates erotic attraction, and the belief that masculinity is defined against its opposite—the feminine. Deflecting the plot of this potentially radical political narrative, Tennyson ends up spinning a traditional romance in which love teaches the wayward princess her home lessons, and she submits happily to the rule of her prince. Christopher Ricks suggests that *The Princess* exactly mirrors Queen Victoria's situation before she was married: like Princess Ida, after initially rejecting marriage because she so much enjoyed the excitement of being independent and having a professional career, Victoria accepted and glorified the duties of marriage and motherhood.[49]

But perhaps more important than the actual narrative about Princess Ida is the story that frames it. At an upper-class fete where young men and women are bantering about women's rights, Lilia, the most beautiful and talented woman present, makes the most compelling arguments in favor. The men decide to use this playful battle of the sexes as an excuse to spend the day telling the tale of a princess, modeled after Lilia, who believes in "ladies' rights." But it is assumed by the characters (and their creator) that the young men will perform the task of representation, while the young women will provide intermittent, incidental songs to break up the narrative—an assignment similar to Victoria's constitutional position as female monarch fulfilling a kind of interregnum. The chief male storyteller decides that the men "will say whatever comes" to them "And let the ladies sing us, if they will, / From time to time, some ballad or a song / To give us breathing-space."[50]

Aesthetic and political power, obviously, reside in the males of this story, yet the narrator is uneasy about including women in the making of the Princess Ida narrative, and a battle of the sexes occurs over what genre to use. Should it be a ballad, as the women want, or a burlesque, as the men desire? Describing himself as "Betwixt" the "mockers and the realists," the narrator ends up not pleasing anyone. Instead he supervises the creation of a text that "mov[es]" in a "strange diagonal." And even though the band of storytellers troops back to their host's mansion supposedly "joyful" after their afternoon sport, overhead "bats wheel'd, and owls whoop'd" and, still more ominously, "the walls / Blacken'd about" them.[51] The narrator attempts to remain good-natured about the addition of women to the increasingly contested field of literary representation. But the implication is that dangerous and unforseen consequences can come from toying with established sexual boundaries and the categories of sexual difference. In the end, nightmares hover over this tale of men's ostensible good will toward women.

John Ruskin's chivalry is engendered with similar anxieties. Certainly in "Of Queen's Gardens," he deplores the notion that woman's mission is separate from man's, but he cannot quit the belief that masculinity is the originary source of power. And his didactic disquisition on "queenly powers" makes it clear that a woman's wisdom, power, and position have their origins in the primal site of masculine omnipotence. By Ruskin's logic, then, the queenly woman fulfils her role at the king's pleasure, and only when the king is absent can she fully enact her lesser, queenly role. In contrast, the source of all law, "kingly power," is immovable, "without tremor, without quiver of balance, established and enthroned upon a foundation of eternal law which nothing can alter nor overthrow." Assuming the self-consistency of patriarchal law, like Blackstone and Carlyle, Ruskin argues that "all literature and all education are only useful so far as they tend to confirm this calm, beneficent, and *therefore* kingly, power." [52]

Assuming a natural hierarchy of gender within which women receive power from kings, the male commoner sanctions his authorial representations by inscribing his own precedence over the female monarch, that precedence deriving from the simple fact that he is male. Ruskin then considers what "portion or kind of this royal authority, arising out of noble education, may rightly be possessed by women; and how far they also are called to a true queenly power." In Ruskin's view, "queenly" power has little or nothing to do with ruling a nation-state, or with artistic representations of the British subject. In the companion piece to "Of Queen's Gardens," "Of King's Treasures," Ruskin explicitly links masculinity with the seminal literary texts that form the man of letters. "Of King's Treasures" genders books themselves as masculine and sees in them the recorded wisdom and nobility of the ages. He concludes that if men would be kings, as they naturally should be, then they must associate with kingly predecessors, found in male-authored, male-identified books. Like Carlyle, Ruskin uses such imagery to establish himself as a majestic sage whose literary and political representations overrule the representative powers of a mere queen regnant. Men of letters are "the true kings of the nation," who are "learned in the *peerage* of words," and know "the words of true descent and ancient blood."[53] Like Blackstone, Ruskin also figures masculinity as a God-given royal heritage passed down from man to man through the ages.

More sensuous than these Victorian predecessors, in an unpublished dramatic parody, Swinburne literalizes Victoria's identity as excess of representation, instability of representation, and circulation of representation. Swinburne's fictional queen has a twin sister, whose existence automatically puts the female monarch's authority into question. In order to remove this rival candidate for the throne, Sir Robert Peel has her kidnapped, and the queen's Other eventually grows up to become a prostitute. After her twin is informed of her royal heritage, an outraged Victoria attempts to expel her sexually promiscuous counterpart. In a similar plot, entitled *La Soeur de la reine,* Swinburne features an illegitimate daughter of the Duchess of Kent named "Miss Kitty," who challenges the tyrannical queen. When Lord John Russell, one of Victoria's former lovers (who include Sir Robert Peel and William Wordsworth, among others), threatens to reveal the monarch's scandalous life, the queen vows to have him executed. In yet another Swinburnean play, Prince Albert pretends to have joined forces with the Chartists in order to gain the throne for himself.[54]

By satirizing the ostensible chief representative of conventional Victorian sexuality, Swinburne brilliantly questions the ideological underpinnings of what was viewed as sexual normality. He also comically undermines aristocratic pretensions. But I would also suggest that the writer's humorous fuss about the sovereign's sexuality—and his implicit belief that her sexuality informs her professional capability—also has something to do with Swinburne's anxieties about his own poetic potency. A writer who explicitly associates his sexuality with aesthetic creativity and the power to represent the culture, Swinburne robs Victoria of her authority by making her into a tyrannical adulteress, an object of satire, indeed, a comic figure of ridicule. A woman, even a queen, could hardly defend herself against such representations, for—just because he was male and a writer—Swinburne benefitted from the double standard that allowed him to write irreverently about the female monarch without fear of repercussions.

H. Rider Haggard's adoration of the historical Queen Victoria turns sexual, too, as the protagonist of *She*—a book Victoria owned[55]—topples the long-lived queen or She-goddess in both the bedroom and the throne room. Indeed, Haggard's *She* is a perfect illustration of Louis Montrose's suggestion that male writers consciously treat a queen with chivalric intent while subliminally deposing her. A representation of an omnipotent queen who has outlived her usefulness, this male bonding adventure is replete with explicit loyalty to Queen Victoria. The protagonist, Holly, explains to the puzzled She-goddess that Queen Victoria "was venerated and beloved by all right-thinking people in her vast realms."[56] Haggard implicates his own masculinist intentions, as She—who must be obeyed and who is thus in conflict with patriarchal law—cannot understand how a subjugated people could feel loyalty for their subjugator queen.

The narrator plays the same coy game when he asserts that "this history of a woman on whom, clothed in the majesty of her almost endless years, the shadow of Eternity itself lay like the dark wing of Night, was some gigantic allegory of which I could not catch the meaning." Despite this apologia, the allegory is almost blatant. Ayesha, with her unrestrained powers, emotionalism, and scornful assertion that "I am above the law,"[57] is like the queen William Fox and Bagehot describe, one who teeters on the edge of misrule. Like Victoria, too, in her obsessive, prolonged love for a dead man, Ayesha, in her own form of memorial, preserves her deceased lover through mummification rather than memorialization. Like the British queen, Ayesha knows her proper place as an interregnum monarch. She exclaims that as soon as she recaptures her lover, Kallicrates—in the reincarnated form of Leo Vincey—the two will return to his native England, where he, not she, will reign.

Holly "absolutely shudder[s]" when he contemplates Ayesha's desire to come to England, for he has little doubt that she will "assume absolute rule over the British dominions, and probably over the whole earth, and, though I was sure that she would speedily make ours the most glorious and prosperous empire that the world had ever seen, it would be at the cost of a terrible sacrifice of life." The "terrible sacrifice" that Holly fears is revealed in his worries that Ayesha is being "used by Providence as a means to change the order of the world." When Ayesha finally, inevitably dies, Holly is relieved. Having "opposed herself against the Eternal law," she would have "revolutionised society, and even perchance have changed the destiny of Mankind."[58] Clearly Holly, like Fox and Bagehot, worries that a queen's reign changes the "natural" order of rule by men, and the implication is that Haggard sees Victoria as "revolutionizing" gender relations. Haggard's overdetermined view of sexual difference also interprets the "destiny of Mankind" in its gendered form, disguising his masculinist project under rhetorical appeals to the universal good.

More important for my argument, however, is that Haggard's fears about the upset of the gendered status quo are linked to his anxieties about the aesthetics of representation. This becomes clear in the scene in which Ayesha takes Leo and Holly to "the very Fountain and Heart of Life" in the "bosom of the great world." Here in the primal site of reproduction, it is Ayesha who cannot stand the flames. When she steps into the eternal fire, she grows old and disintegrates before the men's eyes. Meanwhile, just before She's dramatic death, Holly experiences an aesthetic epiphany when he stands near the same flame:

> *I know that I felt as though all the varied genius of which the human intellect is capable had descended upon me. I could have spoken in blank verse of Shakespearean beauty, all sorts of great ideas flashed through my mind; it was as though the bonds of my flesh had been loosened, and left the spirit free to soar to the empyrean of its native power. . . . I seemed to live more keenly, to reach to a higher joy, and sip the goblet of a subtler thought than ever it had been my lot to do before. I was another and most glorified self, and all the avenues of the Possible were for a space laid open to the footsteps of the Real.*[59]

It seems to me no accident that Haggard, writing in the twilight of Victoria's reign, juxtaposes the moment when Holly verges on his most sublime aesthetic powers of representation, with Ayesha's annihilation as the figure who represents her people. Indeed, after this climax, the Englishmen restore the "natural" order, the long interregnum, occupied by a bereft queen obsessed with her departed lover, finally at an end.

So far we have looked at how the Victorian naturalization of male authority resulted in barely concealed anxieties that took the rhetorical form of teaching the queen and women their "home lessons." The obsessive—and burdensome—need for such rhetorical strategies suggests the inconsistency inherent in male-authored, ostensibly self-consistent law and illustrates how Victoria's reign subverted and interrogated the supposedly natural, constitutional laws concerning gender roles. Let us turn now to the anxieties and ambivalence women writers experienced during the reign of the queen. In an age in which women writers were trying to achieve equal economic and literary status with their male counterparts, one might assume that they would have welcomed the reign of a queen. This is true in many cases, for quite a few Victorian women writers, as we have seen already, found in the female monarch a means of imagining a way to overcome the deprivations resulting from rigid, bifurcated gender roles. Others, such as Marie Corelli and Christina Rossetti, honor the idea of "queen" and magnify it beyond the individual Queen Victoria to represent a generic "feminine" potency best represented in their own work. These writers seem generously able to share the powers of queenliness with their actual monarch. A few female writers, however, including Elizabeth Barrett Browning and George Eliot, were embarrassed that the intellectually puny Queen Victoria represented both womanhood and the nation-state.

Marie Corelli, in *The Passing of the Great Queen,* explicitly compares the representative powers of the professional writer and the monarch. Taking a seemingly insignificant detour in her elegy for the sovereign, Corelli muses, "whenever I have heard people discussing the Prince, now the King, [I have] taken care to exercise those particular privileges belonging to the profession of Literature, which are, to hear, to observe, and to chronicle such things as may be useful to remember in the history of the time." The author recognizes that she is "deemed altogether unimportant by that particular section of Society which judges Literature merely as a sort of bill-posting or press-reporting." This portion of society "can never be brought to realize that all day and every day, millions of pens are constantly at work, writing down such impressions of the hour as will out-last thrones, and be read by future generations." Those privileged writers include "even [myself], one of the least of these wielders of pens."[60] Beginning with the idea that her writing is only a subordinate praxis meant to provide citizens with an illustration of the supreme representative of England, Corelli goes on to associate the monarch's powers with the writer's prowess. Having established that reciprocity, she quietly asserts that the writer always outlives the political sovereign because the writer's representations of the monarch will last through the ages. The monarch, in contrast, has representational power only during her actual reign.

Christina Rossetti is also concerned with queenly omnipotence in her description of Victoria. Defying the Victorian norm of genteel womanhood, Rossetti expresses intense emotions about womanly duties and queenly professions in her poem about Victoria's personal sorrow. In "Our widowed Queen," Rossetti eulogizes Prince Albert while also insisting that Victoria's political and symbolic powers were not diminished by her consort's death. The doctrine of separate spheres is central, for the poem begins with an image of Albert as the head of the household who continues to protect and guide his fragile spouse even after his death.

> *The Husband of the widow care for her [Victoria],*
> *The Father of the fatherless:*
> *The faithful Friend, the abiding Comforter,*
> *Watch over her to bless.*[61]

But though "Husband" Albert looms as a ponderous, guiding presence, he also takes on features associated with Victorian femininity. Figuring Albert in much the same way Victoria did, as an "Angel," Rossetti feminizes the prince's role, emphasizing his power to do good and to provide emotional comfort. Associating Albert with a feminized Christ, the poem continues by beseeching Christ, the British kingdom, and the queen's children to sustain the grieving sovereign.

Although the poem appears to be more about the dead prince and his resurrection than about Victoria, it also addresses the queen's sovereign vitality and suggests that it will outlast Victoria's grief. Indeed, Rossetti shows that even in the most reduced personal circumstances, the person of the queen cannot be separated from political power. For one thing, the poet never refers to Victoria as "Wife" in the way she designates Albert as "Husband." Victoria is "Queen upon her throne," "desolate Woman in her home," and "Mother," to both her literal offspring and her subjects. But Albert is only "Husband"; he cannot be imagined as a parent to the "Sons and Daughters of the realm" as Victoria is. Because Victoria "holds the helm," Albert's death has no effect on the stability of the realm, whereas Victoria's death would completely "desolate" the kingdom and require a substantive shift in power.[62] It is significant, too, that having shifted the source of sovereignty from the male to the female, Rossetti also implicitly exhibits her own poetic potency.

Though the authors of *Queens of Literature of the Victorian Period* refer to George Eliot as one of these queens,[63] Eliot did not seem to share Rossetti's compassion for Victoria. In *Felix Holt, the Radical,* Eliot's narrator condescendingly says of the English monarch that "Our little humbug of a queen is more endurable than the rest of her race because she calls forth a chivalrous feeling."[64] Perhaps Eliot was responding to the queen's authorial ambitions, for the queen had sent her a copy of *Leaves.* But in her thank-you letter to Arthur Helps, the queen's clerk of the Privy Council, Eliot exhibits her remarkable stylistic suavity and political tact, at once implying her own superiority to the queen while representing herself as the queen's loyal subject. Thanking Helps for "the handsome gift" of *Leaves,* Eliot remarks that she "read the Queen's Journal with more sympathy because I am a woman of about the same age." Curiously, given Eliot's unorthodox living arrangements, she adds that she and the queen are also alike in that Eliot had her "personal happiness bound up in a dear husband whose loss would render my life simply a series of social duties and private memories." She continues, "I like that page in which the Queen prays for the very house which has sheltered her happily. On closing the book I felt that I had been following a thoroughly upright affectionate nature, and I thank you for giving me that healthy pleasure."[65] In this epistle, Eliot, a master writer whose fiction will indeed outlast the ages, fictionalizes her own nonconformity to gender roles, equating her "gorgeous illusions" of queenly womanhood with the queen's. Thus Eliot subliminally shows that what she shares with the queen is more than gender, age, and wifely devotion. What she shares is the necessity to paint a picture of herself as totally dedicated to the doctrine of separate spheres while still leading a vigorously independent professional life. Implying that the queen can incorporate at least two roles (woman and sovereign) in one feminine body, Eliot creates a bond with the monarch by merging her own and the queen's professional and personal lives. Yet Eliot also skillfully asserts her own superiority with her allusion to the queen's limited imaginative capacities. In a subtle form of showmanship masked as sincere regard, Eliot maintains her own sovereignty in the realm of authorship.

Often remarking that she was born " 'in the year of Queen Victoria's accession,' "[66] sensation novelist Mary Braddon knew that this was only a gorgeous illusion, for in fact she was born in 1835. But associating herself with the queen was apparently important to her. On 23 June 1897,

Braddon recorded that she watched the events of the second Jubilee "from roof of Lyceum."[67] In her novel *During Her Majesty's Pleasure,* a certain Lady Chilworth kills her husband because, fearing scandal, he refuses to let her go to their gravely ill daughter, who was conceived out of wedlock. The courts put Lady Chilworth in an insane asylum for her crime, whence, after sixteen years of incarceration, she escapes and goes to her daughter. Lady Chilworth tells the sad story to her daughter: "I was to be there all my life—a prisoner—at Her Majesty's pleasure! *His* Majesty's pleasure! They told me the old Queen was dead!" Associated with the law's distribution of justice, "her majesty's pleasure" in Braddon's inscription becomes a subversive reaction to the oppression of women, a subversion Braddon seems to link implicitly with Victoria. Only men, she suggests, take pleasure in the confinement of women.[68]

Braddon took pleasure in Victoria's majesty and in 1886 she commemorated the first Jubilee with a fictionalized children's version of Queen Victoria's reign, entitled "The Good Hermione." An acerbic persona, the female narrator of this unpublished manuscript astutely recounts the queen's intelligent performance of her public role. But she is nevertheless conflicted about how to portray female sovereignty and envisions Hermione, Victoria's fictional alter ego, as at once a feminine monarch guided by male mentors and a cosmic queen who is the primal source of sovereignty. Similarly, while she gently portrays the innocent queen's gorgeous illusions about sovereignty, the sophisticated, worldly-wise narrator benefits from describing her own illusions about the incomparable site of female sovereignty.

Braddon describes Victoria as an Amazon-like figure whose influence straddles the centuries. We see the queen's almost omnipotent essence in Braddon's initial description of the setting. Displacing the mythic origins of British male monarchy, the narrator mystifies queenhood in her historicization of the concept. "Before even the tree that made the great King's Table had begun to grow there lived and reigned over the Kingdom of Lyonesse a Queen who was happier and greater than that good King Arthur." This queen "lived for a hundred years and reigned for more than three quarters of a century over a prosperous people." Seeing Victoria's alter ego as triumphantly reigning "when King Arthur's Table was only an acorn," Braddon imagines female sovereignty as the original source of majestic power. Indeed, according to this version of

British history, "Never did the state of [England] flourish so well or make such progress as under the kindly rule of this Queen." [69]

In displacing King Arthur's primacy, Braddon also implies that woman is not only the original site of power—she is also the fountainhead of purity, which must be aligned with successful rule. Braddon makes much of the signs of the princess's innocence when she learns that she is queen. "Burst[ing] into tears," Hermione exclaims, "God help me . . . I am only a poor weak girl." At first the "burden seemed too great for her," for she thinks of "the dreadful responsibility of ruling and reigning over so many millions of human beings—she thought of all the poor, and the sick, and the unhappy, and the wicked, prisoners, and murderers condemned to death, all the bad & the good & the glad & the sorry for whose welfare & salvation she wd henceforward have [responsibility]." [70]

But Braddon goes beyond the obligatory sentimentalizing of the queen's tears and anxieties, and almost immediately the "girl like tears gave place to smiles. She clapped her hands suddenly, inched up her long white dressing gown and ran out of the room" to tell her mother the news. In addition to the stereotypical feminine feelings of duty and humility, Braddon intimates, a woman faced with the prospect of becoming the world's most powerful ruler feels joyful and ambitious. Moreover, at the thought of all the kings who had preceded her, Hermione, though a "poor weak girl," recognizes that gender has nothing to do with the capacity to rule. Braddon's narrator wryly notes that the young queen recalls "what a mess my uncles made of the Kingdom tho' they were men of the world, & what a muddle my poor well-meaning grandfather" made when he lost "one of the biggest jewels out of the crown," a reference to George III's loss of the American colonies. Later in the story it becomes clear that in spite of the supposed pitfall of Hermione's gender, she, unlike her male forebears, reigns over a "vast rich land," and her kingdom "grew stronger year by year, & year by year her territories widened." [71]

Hermione's response to this power is exultant rather than fearful, and she seems able to merge her private life with her queenly duties without much difficulty. There "now began for Hermione the most delightful & the most wonderful life that ever a young girl led. She was but just out of the nursery, & she was Queen of the great Kingdom of Lyonesse, with all its colonies & dependencies in distant seas." Having "just laid aside her doll," the queen's "play things were treaties & acts of parliament, her playfellows were Cabinet Ministers." Alluding to Hermione's triumph over Sunland (India), Braddon writes, "Think what a wonderful thing it was for this girl queen, this young mother with her thoughts in her nursery & her babies, to be ruler over that distant land, the oldest, grandest, richest country in the world, the land of highest mountains, & mightiest rivers, & cities of palaces."[72]

Assuming that the youthful female monarch needs masculine guidance, the narrator concedes that "In the council chamber she was serious, earnest, eager for information & advice, submissive to superior age & knowledge." But Braddon also insists that Hermione is "never forgetful of her own dignity" or superior position when she prudently seeks the advice of seasoned counselors. In fact, Braddon's narrator urges all girls to follow in the footsteps of Hermione/Victoria. In an aside concerning Alexandra's leaving home to marry Prince Edward, she warns against small-mindedness: "I hope you children—you girls, I mean—will all feel very sorry when you leave the home circle, & that yr vapid little minds will not be chockfull of yr trousseaux, & yr wedding gowns." Using Hermione as a model for womanhood, Braddon remarks that the queen "was not one of those feather-headed girls who think of nothing but their frocks. There was a vein of seriousness in Queen Hermione, that went side by side with a gay & happy temper, & an enjoyment of all the right & pleasant things in this life. She had brought up her children to think seriously about serious things—& the girls especially had taken the colour of the mother's mind into their own young thoughts."[73]

Despite the relatively liberated rhetoric, Braddon is always careful to remember the queen's sex and the behavior considered appropriate to it. Indeed, Braddon never lets Hermione forget that she is a female, even if she will not allow her to be thought of as just a mere girl. Insisting that Victoria does not lose her femininity just because she happens to be the most powerful woman in the world, the narrator argues that her femininity only enhances the performance of her public duties. The fairy-tale memorial describes the queen as made of "that tenderer clay [which] Nature has made on purpose for wives and mothers." There was nothing strong minded or masculine in her character, except her courage "which was virile." Victoria was, the narrator concludes, "in all things distinctly womanlike & distinctly human." "Above all & before all,"

Victoria "was a woman, & she was never more queenly than when she was most womanlike." [74]

For Braddon's sagacious female narrator, Hermione's womanliness resides in the fact that she "loved her home & its surroundings, & she interested herself in the wellbeing of all who served her: from the preacher whose awakening sermons she heard with humble reverent spirit, to the . . . cowboy on the home farm. She loved to look in at the simple pleasures of her dependents . . . after all the gaieties & splendour natural when our sphere had ceased to delight her. Their dances & rustic feasts, their bridals & baptisms were full of interest for her. She knew their histories & respected the graces of those simple honest lives." [75]

Here the narrator implies that Hermione is in fact much more powerful than any king, because she includes her womanhood—and her domestic womanly duties—in the performance of her public role. Because she incorporates feminine expertise on familial and social relations into her public duties, that is, Hermione/Victoria becomes an even more powerful monarch. Thus Braddon's "gorgeous illusion" of a female monarch is relatively multidimensional. While this queen's womanhood precedes and produces the most brilliant English example of royal power, she always retains the sensitivity and humility associated with femininity. That femininity, however, only further empowers the monarch, allowing her to merge and perform the majestic and maternal in a variety of situations. Hermione/Victoria is not just a "poor weak girl." Without losing her purity of heart, she naturally displaces the supremacy of male monarchy. It is apparent, too, that Braddon uses this fairy tale, in part, to teach Victorian girls the home lesson that they too can have great power without giving up their "womanly" attributes. Braddon uses her children's tale to instruct her readers that "manhood" is not necessarily inherent—and may even be detrimental to—the performance of monarchical duties. At the same time, Braddon creates an authorial female persona whose majestic, witty discourse surpasses Victoria's queenliness while still demonstrating the consummate essence of female sovereignty.

Of course Victoria's influence was not only confined to the British isles. Nineteenth-century American author Sarah Orne Jewett includes in *The Country of the Pointed Firs* a narrative about an eccentric old woman who refers to herself as "the Queen's Twin." Like the real Mary Braddon, the fictional queen's Twin, Abby Martin, "come[s] to feel a real interest in the Queen" because "They were born the very same day, and you would be astonished to see what a number o' other things have corresponded." Not only has Mrs. Martin married a man named Albert and had a child named Albert, she also keeps a room, "sacred as a meetin'-house," with a vast array of pictures of the queen. Abby's mental landscape itself becomes a memorial to the queen, for "If you want to hear about Queen Victoria, why Mis' Abby Martin'll tell you everything." [76] Abby's need to identify with the queen is so intense that, despite her excruciatingly limited circumstances, she saves up enough money to travel to London. There she sees the queen in a procession and then leaves the city immediately, for she knows that nothing else could possibly equal the experience of seeing her royal double in the flesh. "I saw her plain," the elated Abby explains, "and she looked right at me so pleasant and happy, just as if she knew there was something different between us from other folks." Jewitt uses the fictional Abby Martin to suggest the kind of influence the queen's *Leaves* might have had on the common woman. "It's been a treasure to my heart," says Abby, "just as if 'twas written right to me. I always read it Sundays now, for my Sunday treat. Before that I used to have to imagine a good deal, but when I come to read her book, I knew what I expected was all true. We do think alike about so many things." [77]

Abby Martin's identification with the queen carries ominous overtones that don't appear in Eliot, Rossetti, or Corelli. She has "always been in very poor, strugglin' circumstances. . . . She's been patient an' hard-workin' all her life, and always high above makin' mean complaints of other folks. I expect all this business about the Queen has buoyed her over many a shoal place in life. Yes, you might say that Abby'd been a slave, but there ain't any slave but has some freedom." In this astute description, the narrator recognizes that one class of female is weighed down with the culture's brute expectations of woman as household drudge so that a higher class of woman can be the angel in that house. Mrs. Martin dimly recognizes this market relationship when she acknowledges that "I've always lived right here. I ain't like the Queen's Majesty, for this is the only palace I've got." Ironically, the queen's twin must equivocate about the stark economic differences between herself and the queen in order to maintain some sense of her own sovereignty. "I don't require what the Queen does, but sometimes I've thought 'twas left to me to do the plain things she don't have time for. I expect she's a beautiful housekeeper, nobody couldn't have done better in her high place, and she's been as good a mother as she's been a queen."[78]

Abby constructs a "gorgeous illusion" that intimates her own majestic identity: "'You see there is something between us, being born just at the same time; 'tis what they call a birthright. She's had great tasks put upon her, being the Queen, an' mine has been the humble lot; but she's done the best she could, nobody can say to the contrary, and there's something between us; she's been the great lesson I've had to live by. She's been everything to me.'" Creating her own sovereign identity by constructing herself as the queen's twin, Abby Martin dreams about the "two sisters" "being together out in some pretty fields, young as ever we was, and holdin' hands as we walk along. I'd like to know if she ever has that dream too. I used to have days when I made believe she did know, an' was comin' to see me." Abby's friend Mrs. Todd mystifies Mrs. Martin's fantasy. Masking the economic reality, she remarks, "'Don't it show that for folks that have any fancy in 'em, such beautiful dreams is the real part o' life? But to most folks the common things that happens outside 'em is all in all.'"[79] Sarah Orne Jewett insists, then, that though women might identify with the queen, the "womanization" of the age she represented too often erased the harsh realities resulting from "gorgeous illusions" about queenly womanhood. Thus Jewett deconstructs the "gorgeous" economic illusions that made the British monarchy possible by establishing her own democratizing imaginative powers as the prototype of sovereignty.

In a similar vein, Mary Bradford Whiting critiques Ruskin's "Of Queen's Gardens" by examining the class implications of his use of the queenly trope to define women. In an article written for the *Social Pioneer,* Whiting points out how important it is to recognize that Ruskin explicitly admitted that "Of Queen's Gardens" was written for upper-class girls and for the "undistressed middle-classes." "In these times of widespread monetary depression it is the rule and not the exception for women to take their share with men in the struggle for existence," Whiting argues, and "therefore we have to consider Ruskin's Ideal from the outside." In other words, because most women help support their families financially through their own labor, Ruskin's ideal woman is "something entirely out of the range of their experience."[80] Indeed, Whiting deplores the fact that Ruskin elides his elitist intentions.

Whiting compares Ruskin's approach to the Woman Question with the old tradition of having younger princes "put out of the way" so that the king could rest easy about attempts to unseat him. "We could hardly expect a few millions of women to immolate themselves in order that the fortunate remainder might reign as queens! And yet without some such proceeding, Ruskin's ideal will be for ever unattainable." Could a "country flourish where there were more queens than subjects?," Whiting asks, and goes on to question Ruskin about the role he gives "those women who are compelled to suffer and strive and labour, who are not and cannot be guarded like hot-house flowers, or worshipped like queens. . . . Is woman less pure and holy when she is obliged to leave her throne and descend into the arena" to work and provide for herself and others dependent upon her? Though she may "strive, and labour, the ideal woman is still more majestic than queens,"[81] Whiting concludes, making a powerful argument for the subject status of women as the opposite of the disempowered yet privileged designation of "queen."

I have tried to show here that both male and female Victorian writers' master narratives represent the queen and her various powers in ways that attempt to negotiate the culture's confused, burdensome gender ideologies and the accompanying "feminization" of the age. I have also examined the ways in which Victoria seems to trade places with her literary competitors in the contest for representational authority. This preview of Victoria's venture into literary representation, and of several writers' explicit or implicit appropriations of the queen for the purpose of defining gender, subjectivity, sovereignty, and writerly authority, will now enable us to focus more extensively on the conflicted, often intense representations of Queen Victoria produced by Charles Dickens, Elizabeth Barrett Browning, and Margaret Oliphant.

III

"From the Humblest of Authors to One of the Greatest": The Queen and Dickens's Failure of Masculinity

We are obliged to hold a Levee for all comers, every day when we are not travelling—and labour very hard indeed, I do assure you. The Queen and Prince Albert can scarcely be more tired—for ours is a perpetual Drawing Room. Our crown, too, is not a Golden one, except in opinion.

Charles Dickens, Letter to Lady Holland

THE FOCUS OF THIS chapter is the textual manifestations of Charles Dickens's desire to domesticate the queen and authenticate his virility, while at the same time contravening the dominant sex roles that made Her Majesty so threatening to him. I suggest that as an author Dickens felt constrained by Victorian sex roles that prevented him from writing in an even more idiosyncratic style and excluded him from explicitly representing Victorian sexuality. With regard to Victorian sex roles, Dickens clearly identified with his fictional heroines, and contemporary literary critics described him as a "feminine" writer. Yet Dickens's savvy employment of the serialized novel and his bellicose treatment of his publishers seemed to be, in part, "the Inimitable's" way of proving his aesthetic and economic mastery. If he experienced himself as a failure of masculinity—in writing "feminine" novels in which the queen in the house displaces the hero as the point of interest and site of power—Dickens also brilliantly used this femininity to disguise the way he had mastered the material machinations of his profession. In particular, Dickens's

representations of his relationship with the gender-deviant Queen Victoria—which are by turns sarcastic, competitive, condescending, and
dutiful—are a provocative means by which to examine his conflicted
constructions of gender, sovereignty, and literary authority. To begin
with, Dickens imaged Queen Victoria as explicitly implicated in his professional success or failure. For example, when angry with Dickens for
declining the opportunity to meet fellow author Maria Edgeworth, Basil
Hall accused the newly famous writer of possessing "a great fancy for
wagging your tail." Dickens responded defensively, explaining that he
was in the first stages of writing a new story and that all his energies had
to be devoted to it because of the "difficulty of settling down into the
track I must pursue." He added that even "If the Queen were to send for
me at such times, I wouldn't go to her."[1] Although the inference is that
Dickens's profession is more important than the monarch's, this brash
statement implicitly acknowledges that Queen Victoria is the ultimate
British authority figure. Conversely, the queen paid a dubious compliment to this man of the age by naming one of her Skye terriers "Boz,"
indicating, perhaps, the kind of tail-wagging obeisance she expected
from the author who fancied wagging his own tail. It should also be
noted, however, that according to one of her former servants the monarch "possess[ed] and value[d] greatly an original unpublished manuscript
of Charles Dickens."[2]

Dickens performed his own tail wagging when he explicitly referred
to his profession as a royal one. Triumphantly touring America, the famous thirty-year-old author boasted to Daniel Maclise, "Imagine Kate
and I—a kind of Queen and Albert—holding a Levee every day (pro-
claimed and placarded in newspapers) and receiving all who choose to
come." When Dickens wrote of the same trip that "The Queen and
Prince Albert can scarcely be more tired—for ours is a perpetual Drawing Room," he remarked that "Our crown, too, is not a Golden one,
except in opinion."[3] Though the Inimitable subliminally compared his
profession with the queen's, his statements also indicate that he realized
that in some ways hers was the inimitable profession. Although he pic-
tured his own career as superior, he was also well aware that the monarch
had a higher profile, more money, and more financial security than he
did. As Dickens knew from firsthand experience, even though an author
might, at times, seem to possess more cultural capital than the monarch,

the author's "Golden" crown, unlike the queen's, always depended on the whims of the public. By contrast, her profession and the legal tender known as the "crown" were the referents to which all Victorian identities were anchored.

Dickens actively sought to strengthen the socioeconomic position of the Victorian male writer, who in most cases relied solely upon his writing for a living. Piqued that so many of his colleagues had fallen on hard times because of the financial insecurity of their profession, Dickens helped to establish the Guild of Literature and Art. By providing financial help to authors who were no longer popular or who faced family emergencies, this organization allowed the writer to continue to identify himself as an author and to sustain the albeit unstable benefits of that professional association. As with his aggressive activism in the matter of copyright law, Dickens's efforts to help authors who were down on their luck also substantiated his own cultural significance and success while fortifying the writers' social position as a special, necessary class of citizen whose influence was essential to the culture.

On a number of occasions, the Guild requested Her Majesty's aid. In 1851, for instance, Dickens wrote to the queen's aide Colonel Phipps to invite Victoria to a comedy being staged to help needy authors, "I venture to hope that Her Majesty and His Royal Highness will view the project with favour; because I share the general knowledge of their consideration for Letters and Art." By strategically referring to Prince Albert's active patronage of the arts, Dickens intimates that if the royal couple responds positively to his request, they will vicariously enjoy the artist's special status. This becomes even clearer in Dickens's closing remarks when he invokes national pride and links it to the nation's writers: "In the name of it's author, and of all the authors and artists united in this endeavour to render a lasting service to their order, *and therefore to England,* I beg to entrust you with our loyal appeal to Her Majesty" [4] (my emphasis).

But while he recognized the need to appeal to the crown in order to expand the writers' cultural and economic capital, in his relations with the queen Dickens also insisted upon mystifying himself and his profession. Thus in 1848 Dickens wrote to his actor friend Macready about the possibility of meeting the young queen after a play. "I had doubts," he wrote, "of my being glad to receive the Queen, even if she were content to be so received." He then remarked that after having "considered the matter," he was "quite clear that as I have never been to Court, or presented myself before her either in my public capacity or as a private gentleman, it would not be becoming or agreeable to me to claim her recognition on such an occasion."[5] Extraordinarily fastidious about his own status as it compares with the queen's more stable, aristocratic rank, in what amounts to a turning of the tables on his superior, the famous author indicates that he will not condescend to encounter her face to face, even if she expresses an interest in meeting him. Hence, Dickens self-consciously uses the "cut," an important Victorian mechanism for maintaining one's social status—in this case, Dickens's sense of himself as a "gentleman." One wonders, however, what he was trying to prove by insulting the world's most powerful sovereign in such a self-aggrandizing way.

This was not the only time Dickens cut the queen. The preeminent author repeatedly refused Victoria's invitations to meet or perform for her. He was, after all, "the author whose name Queen Victoria was soon told 'will hereafter be closely associated with the Victorian era.'"[6] But Dickens's display of sophisticated indifference to the queen's invitations was not wholly the result of his self-confidence. He must have felt some anxiety when he wrote to a friend in 1857, "The wildest legends are circulating about town, to the effect that the Queen proposes to ask to have the Frozen Deep at Windsor. I have heard nothing of it otherwise, but slink about, holding my breath."[7] On 20 June of the same year, he wrote again about the queen's desire to see *The Frozen Deep,* saying, "I am anxious to let you know what has since passed about it with the Queen."[8] Apparently, bowing to royal protocol, the queen decided not to accept Dickens's invitation to see a play he was helping to produce so as to secure subscriptions for a memorial to the late writer Douglas Jerrold. Instead, the middle-aged Victoria suggested that he bring the play to Buckingham Palace.

Dickens's response was characteristically finicky. Protesting too much, he wrote, "I should not feel easy as to the social position of my daughters at the Court under such circumstances." He then countered her invitation with an offer to set aside a private night for the queen to attend the play. In a letter to Burdett Coutts, he explained, "I added that . . . if she could not act upon my suggestion, we would, however much I might desire to avoid it, go to the Palace." After the queen had seen the play, Dickens name-dropped to John Forster, "My gracious sovereign was so pleased that she sent round begging me to go and see her and accept her thanks. I replied that I was in my Farce dress, and must beg to be excused. Whereupon she sent again, saying that the dress 'could not be so ridiculous as that,' and repeating the request. I sent my duty in reply, but again hoped her Majesty would have the kindness to excuse my presenting myself in a costume and appearance that were not my own. I was mighty glad to think, when I woke this morning, that I had carried the point." [9] Clearly in this exchange Dickens views the potential tete-à-tete as a contest between the female sovereign and the male writer over who possesses more authority and cultural capital. Taking pleasure in the fact that the queen repeatedly "begs" to see him, Dickens positively gloats when he recalls the way he "won" his "point." His "point," of course, had little to do with his being in costume. It did have to do with his desire that she recognize him for who he was out of costume—no less than the greatest writer of the age. In that regard, his communiqué implies that he is the celebrity and she merely a provincial devotee.

The queen wrote about this embarrassing impasse in her journal of 4 July 1857, and, given Dickens's behavior, she prepared a subtle but potent rejoinder. It was almost as if she responded to Dickens's magisterial self-importance by invading his own terrain, specifically requesting Colonel Phipps to pass on her literary critique of the play in which Dickens had performed. "The Queen," Colonel Phipps explained to Dickens,

> commanded me particularly to express her admiration of the piece itself—not only on account of its interest and striking situations, or of the very superior way in which it is written, but on account of the high tone which is preserved in it. There was every temptation to an Author to increase the effect of the play by representing the triumph of the Evil, but it was particularly pleasing to Her Majesty to find a much higher lesson taught in the Victory of the better and nobler feelings—and of the Reward—the only one he could obtain—to Richard, in his self-content before his death. [10]

An amateur at best, Victoria assumes that her royal opinion is important to the professional playwright and cast members. Indeed, the tone of her complimentary letter is condescending. Implicitly encouraging the proud actor/writer to act like the unselfish character he played in the drama, the queen is confidently assured of her own superior status. To add inadvertent insult to unintentional injury, she suggests that the "Author" writes a better play when he is less concerned about magnifying himself and his ideas and more concerned to express a moral point. Considering how Dickens had proudly refused to meet her after the performance, this could not have gone over well with him.

In his account of the same event, Robert Wilson, one of the queen's memorialists, notes Dickens's ill-mannered behavior toward Victoria. "So delighted was the Queen with the performance that she sent round a kind message to Dickens asking him to come and see her and receive her thanks personally." Wilson's interpretation of the author's refusal to meet the queen is most apt. "It had been her desire in the early days of her married life to make his acquaintance personally, but the touch of false pride which marred Dickens's character, and rendered him morbidly sensitive as to 'patronage,' prevented their meeting."[11] "Patronage," of course, implies that, compared with the author, the queen was in a superior position socially and economically. And in fact Dickens's correspondence with the queen suggests that he subliminally felt that in order to meet the queen, he would have to submit to being a failure of masculinity for at least the few minutes he was with Her Majesty. In any case, his hesitancy to meet Victoria seems to have had as much to do with his insistence upon not obeying her "who must be obeyed" as it did with any other reason for demurring, such as professional or class pride.

After Dickens's enormous success with *A Christmas Carol,* the queen once again asked to meet him, and Dickens again played the prima donna, acting as though he were the royal monarch and she the petitioner. In his description of the affair, Dickens manifested his ambivalence toward the queen as well as his pleasure in outmaneuvering her without having to take the consequences.

> *I was put into a state of much perplexity on Sunday. . . . the Queen is bent upon hearing the* Carol *read, and has expressed her desire to bring it about without offence; hesitating about the manner of it, in consequence of my having begged to be excused from going to her when she sent for me after the* Frozen Deep. *I parried the thing as well as I could; but being asked to be prepared with a considerate and obliging answer, as it was known the request would be preferred, I said, "Well! I supposed Col. Phipps would speak to me about it, and if it were he*

> *who did so, I should assure him of my desire to meet any wish of her*
> *Majesty's, and should express my hope that she would indulge me by*
> *making one of some audience or other—for I thought an audience nec-*
> *essary to the effect." Thus it stands; but it bothers me.*[12]

Here again Dickens regards the situation as a combative one, and he does not seem very concerned about the precedent of *The Frozen Deep.* Repeating his earlier behavior, the author insists on setting conditions for the meeting. Contesting the queen's obvious political power with cool pride, Dickens refuses to respond to her request until it is made by her highest court retainer, Colonel Phipps. The suggestion that she be merely part of "some audience or other" is insulting in its studied indifference. We suspect, too, that Dickens's being "bother[ed]" by the unresolved situation has more to do with his own anxieties about his prestige than it does with any concerns about discourtesy to the queen.

It was not until just before his death that Dickens finally deigned to meet the monarch, who had by then been waiting to meet him for twenty-two years. The popular author was almost caustic in his anticipation of the impending meeting. Observing that "my Sovereign desires that I should attend the next levee," Dickens commanded his correspondent not to "faint with amazement if you see my name in that unwonted connection."[13] When the world-famous author finally stooped to meet the world-famous sovereign, the two celebrities exchanged their cultural capital: Dickens pontificated about political matters—in particular, class issues—while she gave the famous author *More Leaves,* which bore the inscription: "From the humblest of authors to one of the greatest."[14] When Victoria made this presentation, she was fully aware of her books' popularity, and Dickens, of course, viewed himself as an authority on class issues. Thus it might be said that they manifested their appropriation of the other's profession: Dickens usurped the queen's state power, while, no less wily, the queen annexed his literary authority.

Like other male authors, Dickens also resorted in his early days to sexualizing the female monarch in order to dilute her power and magnify his own. In his characteristic overdetermined manner, he attempted to appropriate a great deal of private cultural capital in his jokes about the young queen's marriage. For example, spreading the scuttlebutt he had heard about the queen, the young author gleefully reported that in one street song Victoria protested her subjects' dislike of Albert by vamping,

"Prince Hallbert he vill always be / My own dear Fancy Man." In the same letter, the author described an extended gag in which the English prototype, John Bull, was catechized about his feelings about the queen's betrothal. The joke refers with obvious sexual innuendo to the dowry—sausage—Albert brings to the marriage. Bull expresses his displeasure that the British people must spend "thirty thousand pound per annewum [*sic*]" for "German Sassages—fresh as imported Sir from Saxe Humbug and Go-to-her," when they could more easily afford the English variety.[15] In a convoluted way, perhaps, by repeating this salacious joke, Dickens takes pleasure in recognizing that he himself is closer to representing the British people than is the extremely young, now compromised (because sexually domesticated), constitutionally mandated female representative. He also enjoys imagining the queen in a sexually subordinate position in marriage.

Dickens also perpetrated a protracted gag about being infatuated with the queen, another mechanism by which to sexualize and depose Victoria. On 11 February 1840, Dickens wrote to Walter Savage Landor that "Society is unhinged here, by her majesty's marriage" and "I am sorry to add that I have fallen hopelessly in love with the Queen, and wander up and down with vague and dismal thoughts of running away to some uninhabited island with a maid of honor, to be entrapped by conspiracy for that purpose." Landor did not understand the joke and asked their mutual friend Forster, "What on earth does it all mean?"[16] But Dickens carried on excessively with the gag. On 12 February of the same year, he jokingly confided to Forster that he was "lost in misery" and had tried to pull himself out of his despondency by reading *Oliver, Pickwick,* and *Nickleby* in preparation for writing his new book. But he impudently remarked that it was "all in vain," for

> *My heart is at Windsor,*
> *My heart isn't here;*
> *My heart is at Windsor,*
> *A following my dear.*[17]

In ironic purple prose worthy of Micawber, in the same letter Dickens described his passion for the queen:

> *The presence of my wife aggravates me. I loathe my parents. I detest my*
> *house. I begin to have thoughts of the Serpentine, of the regent's-canal,*

*of the razors upstairs, of the chemist's down the street, of poisoning my-
self at Mrs. _____'s table, of hanging myself upon the pear-tree in
the garden, of abstaining from food and starving myself to death, of being bled for my cold and tearing off the bandage, of falling under the feet
of cab-horses in the New-road, of murdering Chapman and Hall and
becoming great in story (SHE must hear something of me then—perhaps sign the warrant: or is that a fable?), of turning Chartist, of head-
ing some bloody assault upon the palace and saving Her by my single
hand—of being anything but what I have been, and doing anything
but what I have done.*[18]

Among other things, this passage illustrates Dickens's longing to expand
his new and still insecure celebrity status by entering places he has not
been, including the ranks of the famous and socially superior. The parenthetical matter is as telling as the main text, for the author begs to be
recognized as the extraordinary man he is, both personally and professionally. It is the queen (in the house), the sign of British identity, to
whom he naturally looks for that acknowledgment. It is almost as though
he thinks of himself as a failure (of masculinity) without the recognition
"SHE" could give him. The extravagant descriptions of the lure of self-
annihilation exaggerate rather than erase his subjectivity, yet they also
suggest that he must look outside himself to authenticate his identity.
That this authentication comes from a woman only increases his sense of
failure, yet the passage acknowledges—and it must do so sarcastically—
that the queen is the ultimate embodiment of individual and national
sovereignty. Obtaining the pubescent queen's sexual favor, however, is
the only way the writer can conceive of the female monarch sanctioning
his noble profession. Thus, in this almost hysterical passage, Dickens subliminally realizes that, in spite of his being a male genius and no matter
how much he sexualizes her, the queen is the source of his cultural
capital.

Persevering in this jest, Dickens wrote to T. J. Thompson that
"Maclise and I are raving with love for the Queen." And, like other male
writers, he had no compunction about metaphorically entering the
queen's private quarters. "On Tuesday we sallied down to Windsor,"
Dickens writes of a jaunt with Maclise, and "prowled about the Castle,
saw the Corridor and their private rooms—nay, the very bedchamber
(which we know from having been there twice) lighted up with such a

ruddy, homely, brilliant glow . . . that I . . . lay down in the mud at the top of the long walk and refused all comfort." He concluded that "now we wear marriage medals next our hearts and go about with pockets full of portraits which we weep over in secret." He then begged to know if there was any way that he could become a "Gentleman at Arms," for "I must be near her." The suggestion that he had twice been in the queen's bedchamber before her marriage implicates his tongue-in-cheek desire to "be near her." Here again, he cannot imagine being near Victoria in any other but a sexual way; but the whole reason for making a joke of the queen is that she possesses the ultimate cultural, political, and socio-economic power that he would like to appropriate. Indeed, in slapstick fashion, Dickens admitted to Maclise that the queen stood in the way of his professional success. As the Inimitable jokingly complained of his royal infatuation, "I am utterly miserable and unfitted for my calling. What the upshot will be, I don't know, but something tremendous I am sure." [19]

Dickens's prolonged prank hardly came across to others as a joke. Walter Savage Landor, as we saw, was puzzled by Boz's outlandish behavior. Apparently, too, Her Majesty's attendants knew of Dickens's mocking infatuation for the queen, and at least one of Victoria's house servants took it seriously. Signing himself "one of her Majesty's servants," the author of *The Private Life of the Queen* wrote:

> *The great author, while still early in his career, conceived the most passionate attachment for Her Majesty, the girlish beauty which she retained unimpaired for very many years after her marriage, and her sweet grace having made the deepest impression on Dickens. He went everywhere he was likely to be able to see her, and in a most touching letter to Mr. Thompson . . . he poured out his love for the Queen, not as his Sovereign, but as a woman. In this same letter he described how he had spent days and weeks in the neighbourhood of Windsor, hiding among the trees in the Park and lounging about her favourite drives so that he might sometimes catch a glimpse of her.* [20]

Given the date of this memorial, surely the queen had some knowledge of Dickens's comic "gorgeous illusion" of eloping with her and becoming her lord and master. I have been unable to discover any record of her response to this knowledge. But in a real sense, she, in all of her longevity, had the last laugh on the supreme comic writer of the age, who preceded her in death.

Later, in an essay in *All the Year Round,* which Dickens edited, an anonymous writer, quite possibly Dickens himself, describes a dream in which he openly carries on an affair with the queen. In an impressionistic disquisition on the dream state, the essayist writes:

> *I have, however, another recurring dream, which leads me through a variety of places, dimly and indistinctly shadowed, but of which the connecting link is no less a person— or rather personage— than our most gracious Sovereign Queen Victoria. Awful to relate, that amiable lady, whom I have but casually seen from afar, is, in my dream, amazingly in love with me. It seems, according to the dream, that I met her Majesty, when she was walking all by herself in a wood. There and then the mutual attraction (I hope it is not traitorous to record that it is mutual) began, and I always, in a new dream of the kind, recur to the first meeting, and then to each successive meeting. In each new dream I am agitated with all sorts of hopes and fears. Will the Queen deign to remember me? Shall I have an interview with her? Sometimes I have the interview: sometimes I only see my beloved lady from a distance. On all these occasions I am tormented by an idea that Prince Albert is jealous of me. Sometimes I am at a grand royal fête, which sometimes takes place in a palace, sometimes in an island. Numbers of persons are at the fête, and, on these occasions, Prince Albert appears, and does me the honour to be remarkably jealous.* [21]

As with Dickens's mock crush on the queen, the male dreamer's chief anxiety concerns the question of whether the queen will treat him as an equal and recognize him in public, thus authenticating his sovereign subjectivity and relinquishing her own. The author of this passage also vacillates between feeling mastery over his sovereign and fear that she will not recognize him. Implicitly expressing the underlying fear of emasculation that has already had its effect on the prince, the dreamer seeks equality ("mutual attraction") with the Queen in the meeting in the woods, where conventional rites/rights of rule (hers) and obeisance (his) hold no sway. As a result, the sexualization of the queen destabilizes her authority and refers it back to the dreamer, the male writer. Seeking to master the female sovereign by replacing Prince Albert in her affections, the writer figures Victoria as a commodity that circulates between men. Nevertheless, the dreamer's royal acquisition hints at his persisting anxiety, for becoming the new prince consort would simply reproduce Prince Albert's subjectivity, which veered between kingly authority and insignificance. It should be noted, too, that in mockingly fearing that his dream might be treasonous to the crown, the author manifests the classic antagonism between royalty and writer discussed by Susan Stewart.

As I suggest elsewhere, in *Aurora Leigh* and *David Copperfield* Elizabeth Barrett Browning and Dickens depicted the struggle to achieve artistic mastery in terms of mastering one's gender anxiety. I would also submit that both writers felt constrained by overdetermined Victorian definitions of sexual difference. Yet, caught in the bonds of gender, both writers brilliantly manipulated Victorian gender ideologies in order to establish their aesthetic achievements. I would suggest that Dickens's longing to be the opposite sex indicates his desire for more creative, expansive, flexible means of identifying the (writerly) self. But though he longs to be the queen (in the house), Dickens ends up resisting and co-opting the queen's dominance as he insists upon the special nature of the male creator as culture's legislator.[22]

Dickens's contemporaries caught on to his subliminal desire to be female, for in at least two instances Victorian literary critics referred to him as having an effeminate writing sensibility. "Who, it may be asked, takes Mr. Dickens seriously?" literary critic Fitzjames Stephen asks, linking his lack of seriousness with the feminine:

> As there are reproaches which can be uttered by no one but a woman or a child, there are accusations which can only be conveyed through a novel. . . . The most wonderful feature in Mr. Dickens' influence is the nature of the foundation on which it stands. Who is this man who is so much wiser than the rest of the world that he can pour contempt on all the institutions of his country? . . . Freedom, law, established rules, have their difficulties. They are possible only to men who will be patient, quiet, moderate, and tolerant of difference in opinion; and therefore their results are intolerable to a feminine, irritable, and noisy mind, which is always clamouring and shrieking for protection and guidance."[23]

Richard Hold Hutton expressed a similar view in his review of the author, asserting that "the type of Dickens' genius is, in many respects, feminine. Like most women's genius, it is founded on the delicate powers of perception alone. . . . There is no intellectual background to his pictures; and in this respect, he resembles the numerous authoresses of modern English fiction."[24] In both reviews, the male critic defines feminine writing as subordinate to more masterful, original masculine writing. The ideological supposition is that the male writer can draw on both intellect and emotion and that the intellect appropriately tempers the emotion. The female writer, on the contrary, can draw only on her feelings, however exquisite they might be. Thus both reviewers associate Dickens's desire to change Victorian society with feminine impatience and naiveté; they also interpret his cultural critique as womanish querulousness. But in making these gendered analyses of fiction writers, the two critics inadvertently acknowledge that there is nothing really inherent in gender, for those positions can so easily be mimicked by the opposite sex. And there was no greater Victorian mimic than Dickens.

Before examining the ways in which Dickens mimicked gender and sexualized masterful writing in *David Copperfield,* I would like to look at how the author described the limitations of gender in *Dombey and Son,* for in this novel, as in *Copperfield,* Dickens explicitly refers to the failure of masculinity and the enthronement of the proper queen in the house as a kind of desiderata. Sent away to school at the Blimbers in Brighton, little Paul Dombey spends more time reading the wallpaper than he does studying the classical curriculum. Indeed, Brighton is as much a rest cure for the fragile child as it is the beginning of his formal education. As the narrator says of the sickly, passive boy, "He was intimate with all the paperhanging in the house; saw things that no one else saw in the patterns; found out miniature tigers and lions running up the bedroom walls, and squinting faces leering in the squares and diamonds of the floorcloth."[25] Like the madwoman in Charlotte Perkins Gilman's "The Yellow Wallpaper," Paul Dombey psychologically turns his face to the wall, and, ultimately, rather than descend into permanent madness, he simply ceases to exist.

Many have noted that the patient in "The Yellow Wallpaper" goes mad because the rest cure was a way to enforce dominant nineteenth-century expectations of women. Similarly, I suggest that Paul Dombey turns his face to the wall because his father is forcing him to fit into a dominant nineteenth-century masculine mold, one that envisioned the male as aggressive, inhumane, and economically ruthless. Impatient for the boy to grow into the "'Son' of the Firm" as a "grown man," the senior Paul Dombey reacts more favorably to the economic implications of the phrase "Dombey and Son" than he does to the familial nuances. Thus, when Dr. Blimber repeatedly asks Paul Sr., "Shall we make a man of him?," little Paul responds, "I had rather be a child," and then adds that he just wants to stay with his sister Florence. I read this as Paul's resistance to being "forced and crammed"[26] into the Victorian ideal of manhood, the *homo economicus,* who is best represented in his unfeeling, automaton father.

Perhaps in some ways Paul Dombey represents Dickens's own restlessness with gender expectations. Throughout the writing of *Dombey and Son,* Dickens complained of needing some tranquility. For example, in a letter to Madame de la Rue, he wrote of going abroad in order to escape his feelings of "incessant restlessness, uneasiness, and uncertainty." What he needed, he told another correspondent, was a place to "write [*Dombey and Son*] peacefully." Dickens may in fact have longed to escape the overdetermined expectations that the man should perform all remunerated labor and support the economic excesses of his indolent spouse and children. This is the counterpoint to "The Yellow Wallpaper's" portrait of the brand-new mother overwhelmed by the overdetermined cultural expectation that women should exist only in the domestic sphere. Dickens himself felt smothered when he attempted his own self-prescribed rest cure. What the great author found was that his dream of a leisurely interlude in Switzerland drained him of the creative energy he needed to write. Without the bustle of London, Dickens wrote, "*My* figures seem to stagnate." Thus, like Gilman, who noted that in order to recuperate from the debilitating effects of the rest cure she had to return to "work," for work was "the normal life of every human being," Dickens too needed his profession in order to be a sovereign self.[27]

In order to mitigate social expectations for gender roles, in *Dombey and Son* Dickens merges the sex roles, with the queen in the house taking over as figurehead of her husband's profession. Dickens recognizes that the figurehead, like Queen Victoria, has powerful avenues for regulating the culture. Indeed, Florence, who throughout the novel is rejected because she is a failure of male issue, gently usurps Paul Jr.'s role as protagonist of the novel named for him. In doing so, she redeems her own failure of masculinity—as well as her brother's—while she miraculously decreases the senior Paul Dombey's overdetermined virility. Though she does not actually head the company her brother Paul was meant to direct, she makes sure that her father drops out of the sovereign position in the business. Essentially, she oversees its collapse, as the terms "husband and wife" replace "father and son" as economic and spiritual symbols of the age. And, though her husband Walter replaces Dombey's over-the-top masculinity with a more feminized version, it is still Florence who is in control, for Walter is merely a cipher. If Dickens is concerned about who has cultural capital, in this case Florence is the proper pinnacle, or capital, of the culture. Thus, as with the Victorian sovereign, in feminizing the age Florence decapitates the father's law and insists that the failure of masculinity, represented in the capitalist title of the firm "Dombey and Son," is the only salvation for the culture.

David Copperfield is a novel that is both terrified of and attracted to the possibility of masculine failure and the potential of the queenly figurehead. U. C. Knoepflemacher and Margaret Myers have suggested that David yearns for and tries to achieve a feminine side of himself, and there is much evidence to support this view. But the novel also consistently views the feminine as the cause of the loss of masculinity. The text's repetition of the ominous phrase "No boys here" is only the most explicit expression of misanthropy. David's initial speculation as to "Whether I shall turn out to be the hero of my own life"[28] responds to that ominous phrase. Revolving around the gendered implications of the term "hero," David's question implies deeper questions about the culture's structuring of gender: Will this protagonist, for example, be overthrown by the heroine in the same way both Paul Dombeys were? Or, put another way, will the fictional queen in the house, who (because of Queen Victoria's actual reign) is associated with domesticity and submission as well as with dominance and rule, depose the rightful male sovereign in the novel? And how will the protagonist—if he gets to be male—ensure the triumph of his masculinity? The answers are as conflicted and compelling as the interchanges between Dickens and Queen Victoria and deserve some discussion.

From the very first chapter, the hero of *David Copperfield* struggles against the text's volatile desire for the failure of male issue. In the initial sentences of the novel, the narrative explicitly wrangles over what sex the unborn protagonist/future author will be. Although the reader assumes that the autobiographer is male, the narrative voice expends a great deal of energy on the expectation that he will be a female. The castrating Aunt Betsey categorically demands that Clara Copperfield give birth to a girl. She is disappointed, of course, but once the adolescent David appeals to her charity, she does everything in her power to impose on him the norms for feminine behavior. Insisting that David live up to the standard of his absent, in fact nonexistent, sister—the girl he should have been— Aunt Betsey urges Copperfield to "Be as like your sister as you can." In response, David muses hopefully that "I might take equal rank in her [Aunt Betsey's] affections with my sister Betsey Trotwood." [29] Steerforth, too, refers to David with the feminine nickname "Daisy," and, wondering if David has a sister, expresses his desire to meet her.

If it is assumed that David should have been a girl, it is also taken for granted that he will never achieve his sister's queenly perfection—unless, that is, he immerses himself in a queenly woman like his non-existent sister or, better yet, becomes her. As Joseph Bristow suggests, "nineteenth-century misogyny sometimes has at its heart a male desire not to have, but to be a woman." [30] By marrying Agnes, David Copperfield comes closer to achieving the subliminal aspiration to be the queenly female the novel flirtatiously portends he will be. In fact, though Copperfield's ego is anything but feeble, curiously, by the end of the novel, the male protagonist seems to have been decapitated by his female idol. Thus, in a way, the novel comes full circle. Ending where it began, when David finally marries Agnes, he becomes in a sense the sister/queen in the house the text initially expected him to be. One of the things Dickens seems to be saying here is that Victorian "gorgeous illusions" about the feminine, submissive "queenly" woman would always refer, in part, to the real queen, whose actual cultural power was the very symbol of the failure of masculinity. Thus, queenly Agnes and David's non-existent queenly sister are insistent, portentous emblems of David's failed manhood.

Dickens's solution to the culture's desire for and fear of the two-faced queenly woman is to have David appropriate and overrule Agnes, his queen in the house. At the same time, she in effect oversees his masculine failure and feminizes his interior and exterior worlds. To be the chief representative author of the age, Dickens could not actually enforce the rule "No boys here." For the same reasons, he could not refuse to obey the queen or the queenly heroine. The novel, then, is a battle of the sexes covered over by a dream of the harmonious melding of the genders. In this paradigm, Dickens's conscious display of Agnes as spiritual icon is reinforced by the suggestion that this queen of the house is, like the female monarch, a foreboding if indispensable presence. If David's sense of his authoritative profession relies upon the reader's viewing him through his second self—Agnes—Dickens also ensures that the reader will recognize her domination as only an interregnum, and will thus understand that she is really only an imitation of rightful masculine precedence.

Though Dickens vigorously interrogates gender construction, *David Copperfield* implies that he is overwhelmed by a Dombey-like cultural expectation that the male author's "favorite child" (his epithet for *David Copperfield*) be a boy after all. To prove that he is a boy, the protagonist must take up the pen in order to access the penis. In fact, it seems that only when he uses his profession to write his life can David be assured of being a man. Yet desiring, and in fact needing, the perquisites of both genders in order to be the Inimitable author, and in order to overcome the rigid, unimaginative confines of a binary gender system, Dickens repeatedly represents the return and overthrow of the binary system Victorian men were caught in and which they tried to repress. This conflicted pattern appears in the merged characters of Mr. Dick/King Charles and, to a lesser extent, Dr. Strong/Jack Maldon.

The half-wit Mr. Dick is a feminized, unsuccessful writer who, because of his failure of masculinity, acts as a moral mediator for the capitalist culture from which he has escaped. Inhabiting and guiding the domestic sphere, he is the queen in the masculine Aunt Betsey's house. Trying to decipher the nature of Mr. Dick's daft writing, David, the future author, asks Aunt Betsey, "Is it a Memorial about his own history that he is writing, aunt?" Betsey's extraordinary response sheds light on the generic (autobiographical) character of Dickens's text: "Yes, child," Betsey replies. "He is memorialising the Lord Chancellor, or the Lord Somebody or other—one of those people, at all events, who are paid to *be* memorialised—about his affairs."[31] A labyrinthine insider's joke, the punch line, of course, is that Mr. Dick's name is the diminutive of Dickens's own.

But there is more than comedy in Charles Dickens's obsessive double inscription of his own name in Mr. Dick's when that minor character manifests his obsession with King *Charles,* a name he literarily cannot get out of his head. A Dickensian ur-self, King Charles cannot be controlled, for he constantly overthrows Mr. Dick and overrules his memorial to an unnamed, renowned Victorian contemporary. Indeed, Mr. Dick cannot finish the text he labors over because his psychological obsession with Charles I's beheading produces a grisly, literal form of writer's block— with the writer's head (read: masculinity) on the chopping block, as it were. Aside from explicitly linking literary authority with sovereignty and masculinity, this seemingly minor but elaborate part of the narrative seems to connect the male writer's anxiety about his own potency with Dickens himself, for his name (and fame) is an anagram of the deposed King Charles and Mr. Dick. If so, then the suggestion is that the writer's persona is naturally gender divergent—inhabited by both the masculine and feminine.

In order to be the successful author that Mr. Dick is not, then, Dickens's alter ego must prove his masculinity. Yet in having to prove that he is male—isn't the whole novel a male rite of passage?—David is assured only that such proof is not innate or natural. In other words, the emasculated King Charles side of his subjectivity demonstrates his masculine fortitude and mettle by repeatedly overcoming his decapitation, insisting that, as the chief representative of the culture, he owns and *is* his culture's capital. In this portrayal of gender acquisition, then, it is almost as if the penis has less to do with masculine identity than does the sheer imaginary act of asserting over and over again that one is male. Representing masculinity as failure (decapitation) that keeps reproducing and overthrowing that failure, the author of *David Copperfield* memorializes his own imaginative powers in order to succeed within a representational system that ensures his emasculation.

Every time he successfully completed and sold a novel, each one a professional erection of his masculinity, Dickens avoided the possibility of feminization. But as we know from his letters, the psychic cost of repeating that act was enormous. Anticipating Freud, Dickens recognized that the text incorporates the writer's gender anxieties. As Aunt Betsey says of Mr. Dick's royal alter ego, "He connects his illness with great disturbance and agitation, naturally, and that's the figure, or the simile, or whatever it's called, which he chooses to use." [32] Dickens was explicitly aware that he had transposed his own initials in the name David Copperfield, and I would suggest that his portrayal of Mr. Dick's psyche encourages the reader to examine the text as a psychological allegory. Surely, too, the author was at least indirectly conscious of the association between his own name and the names "Mr. Dick" and King Charles; more probably the association was deliberate. Indeed, one of the slang phrases that referred to "dick" (and there were many), is particularly relevant to my argument that Dickens viewed the queen as an anomalous figure who had to be taught to recognize rightful male authority. The colloquialism "that happened during the reign of Queen Dick" underlines Dickens's own comparison of himself and his wife to the prince and queen during the author's tour of America. In his peculiar self-flattery about the overwhelming American response to his tour, Dickens both is and is not "Queen Dick," as he analogizes his authority with Victoria's sovereignty but genders himself as male, like the impotent Albert. As the term "dick" came to denote the phallus in the nineteenth century, the eighteenth-century colloquialism "in the reign of Queen Dick" consolidated the English Constitution's vexed definition of a reigning female monarch in remarkably concise form. Revolving around the key term "dick" and its deeply inflected meanings, Dickens's own constitution of literary authority vis-à-vis a queen's sovereignty compresses the relationships between King Charles, Mr. Dick, Mr. Strong, and Charles Dickens/David Copperfield. The phrase "that happened during the reign of Queen Dick" was used to refer to an absurdity, the reign of a queen presumably representing the height of nonsense. That "dick" came to have phallogocentric applications in addition to its being a diminutive form of a male given name—which was part of Dickens's own surname—adds significant implications to a seemingly minor part of the plot. The title of Dickens's short story "The Story of Richard Doubledick" suggests that Dickens was very conscious of the double meanings of "dick." Even if he did not adopt the slang usage of "dick," which was being used in English military circles by about 1860,[33] it could very well have been circulating in the language he would have heard on the London streets he so obsessively traversed. In any case, if Dickens was not aware of the slang term "dick," he prophetically associated the future meaning of the term and consolidated other rich connotations with his own (failure and mastery of) masculinity.

The psychological allegory of the triad of Mr. Dick, King Charles, and David Copperfield is certainly abstruse, and I do not pretend that my analysis comprehends all of the nuances of this uncanny representation of the writer's gender-divergent psyche. I do suggest that the "figures" of the failed writer Mr. Dick and his alter ego King Charles replicate Copperfield's relationship with Agnes. In both relationships, the culture's categorical description of gender roles leads to unstable, surprising performances of gender. The overdetermined site of gender also results in extreme states of subjectivity, either of selflessness (Agnes) or self-seeking (David). These excessively gendered subjectivities absolutely depend on as well as engulf their opposite. The engendering of these Victorian subjects is further complicated by the feminization of the age, chiefly represented by the queen but also implicated in the increasingly feminized profession of the writer. Thus, the male writer found himself in a situation in which he had to pay homage to the feminized sphere while simultaneously engendering himself as masterful—ergo masculine—artist.

When the feminized Mr. Dick failed to capture the public's imagination, Dickens repeated his ironic statements that without Queen Victoria's recognition he was a failed writer and a failure of masculinity. David and Dickens were extremely fond of Mr. Dick, and I would suggest that they could not attain cultural capital without him. I suspect, too, that Dickens truly needed to envision himself as having all of the best characteristics of the so-called female writer. His inclusion of the failed writer Mr. Dick in the story of the successful writer, David, allowed him humorously to allegorize his own complex psychic conflicts about the interrelations of his performance of gender with his material, aesthetic success. A passage describing Mr. Dick's "allegorical . . . disturbance" indicates David's admiration for his feminized counterpart. It is also, however, a ruthless portrait:

> *Every day of his life he had a long sitting at the Memorial, which never made the least progress, however hard he labored, for King Charles the First always strayed into it, sooner or later, and then it was thrown aside, and another one begun. The patience and hope with which he bore these perpetual disappointments, the mild perception he had that there was something wrong about King Charles the First, the feeble efforts he made to keep him out, and the certainty with which he came in,*

and tumbled the Memorial out of all shape, made a deep impression on me. What Mr. Dick supposed would come of the Memorial, if it were completed; where he thought it was to go, or what he thought it was to do; he knew no more than anybody else, I believe. Nor was it at all necessary that he should trouble himself with such questions, for if anything were certain under the sun, it was certain that the Memorial never would be finished.

It was quite an affecting sight, I used to think, to see him with the kite when it was up a great height in the air. What he had told me, in his room, about his belief in its disseminating the statements pasted on it, which were nothing but old leaves of abortive Memorials, might have been a fancy with him sometimes.[34]

Constructing feminine writing as "abortive" without the consummate, virile, shaping powers of the masculine (Mr.) Dick, Dickens inextricably links the writing process and identity formation with gender. He also recognizes that one's gender designation is necessarily associated with one's ability to obtain cultural and economic capital. Figuring Mr. Dick as an emasculated foil, Dickens implies that David's efforts at authorship are masculine and therefore masterful. In a later passage, David enumerates the masculine qualities that ostensibly gave rise to his success: "perseverance," "patient and continuous energy," "punctuality," "order, and diligence." If this list (a stark contrast to David's description of Mr. Dick's writing habits) can be taken as Dickens's representation of his own keys to success, then clearly the shape and completion of the finished product are central to his aesthetic credo. Unlike Mr. Dick, whose discourse is "not a businesslike way of speaking," Dickens's efforts are also not "abortive" because he "disseminates," that is, markets, his very self to the reading public, thus mastering (capitalizing on) rather than being subordinated to the capitalist system. Lavished with his culture's acclamation and capital, David will never say of himself, as Mr. Dick—or for that matter, Agnes—does, that "Dick's nobody!"[35]

Intuitive, emotional, illogical, and mad, the stereotypically feminized Mr. Dick is a failed and thus economically unsuccessful writer because he becomes the queen/alter ego Copperfield portends to be in the first chapter of the novel. Given that during the writing of *Dombey and Son* Dickens sought a restful haven in Switzerland, it might be argued that Dickens, like Paul Dombey Jr., desired, like Dick, to dwell in a feminized, domestic site where he could be free of the demands of the market. By combining King Charles and Mr. Dick to create his own name—and I include "King" in Dickens's identity formation—Dickens manifests a yearning to be the feminized, emasculated self. That self, like Mr. Dick, must be dominated by an authoritative woman like Betsey Trotwood or David's imaginary sister. Yet, like Queen Victoria, this domineering woman must acknowledge that she is wisely guided by her failed male companion (Prince Albert/Mr. Dick). Decapitated but tenaciously virile, King Charles is the ultimate sign of the failure and recuperation of masculinity, and his is the likely figure to haunt the failed/feminized writer Mr. Dick.

The cycle of the incessant return of the repressed King Charles, and Mr. Dick's continuous efforts to expunge him from his text, indicate that in Dickens's allegory the scene of engendering and the scene of writing are messy, ongoing, and unstable. In a way, then, Dickens suggests that David is successful because he incorporates femininity without being engulfed by it. Successfully mimicking without really copying the features of queenly womanhood, David also constitutes masculine sovereignty as an indefatigable, if tenuous, entity whose superiority is always implied in a feminized interregnum, which itself acknowledges that the male is the norm from which the female departs. David learns to manipulate the ruptures in his culture's rigid constructions of gender: Multiplying images of failed masculinity, he manages his own gender divergence through the act of representation. In this backhanded compliment to the feminized age, then, Dickens acknowledges and assimilates the power of his effete mentor Mr. Dick, his nonexistent sister, his muse Agnes, and his monarch, Queen Victoria, but even more importantly he represents them as copies or copiers of his own original, lawful authority.

To reiterate, then, although Dickens's own subjectivity needed to be unstably gendered in order for him to succeed as an author, his portrayal of the writing profession incorporates the notion that the writer must be accompanied by a queen who engulfs, unmans, and feminizes him. But though this queen by her very gender initiates his failure of masculinity, she will always be haunted by the certain reemergence of the masculine sign of domination—the king. If in a feminized age this sign of power is always decapitated, the decapitation itself figures the king's inherent, recurring right to rule. Thus, in this complicated and conflicted portrayal of the male writer, Dickens constructed a feminized authorial subjectivity that gave him vast amounts of cultural capital. But, like Prince Albert, he also subliminally taught the dominant, queenly heroine that the failure of masculinity—represented in King Charles and made successful by Charles Dickens's transformations of the letter—would continuously recycle itself after being castrated.

As noted earlier, one of those recapitulations is to be found in the characters of Dr. Strong and his amanuensis Jack Maldon. Dr. Strong is incapable of mastering his young wife or of completing the only book he might ever author, a dictionary. Since young Copperfield acts as Strong's amanuensis before establishing his own authorial fame, his ineffectual employer serves as a cautionary tale of potential failure. Indeed, like Mr. Dick, Dr. Strong represents the effete self David could have become. In his sham claim to authorship, Dr. Strong obsessively writes a magnus opus or definitive text—the dictionary. Given Dickens's convoluted, often Joycean flair for puns, perhaps the first syllable of *dict*ionary suggests a connection between Mr. Dick and Strong. In any case, if the dictionary gives meaning to words and is the doctor's life's work, this dictionary literally defines Dr. Strong's life. But just as Mr. Dick's memorial is a travesty, Strong's presumption of an enduring reputation as a man of letters is laughable. Like Mr. Dick's memorial, the dictionary will never be finished; in reality the project amounts only to "cumbrous fragments" which the Doctor "always carried in his pockets, and in the lining of his hat." [36] Empty symbols, his head and phallus cannot do the work of the writer, nor can he satisfy his young wife's yearning for love.

As a literalist with no feeling for the ambiguous, Dr. Strong defines his wife as a companionable appendage with no inner life of her own. But where David memorizes and memorializes the feminine psyche—thus earning the right to rule it—Strong fails the test. At the height of Annie's need for him, when her cousin Jack tries to seduce her, Dr. Strong remains oblivious to the hidden meanings of her lack of words because he is so insistent on expounding his own lists of words to her. While he "read[s] aloud some manuscript explanation or statement of a theory out of that interminable Dictionary," she looks on with "Penitence, humiliation, shame, pride, love, and trustfulness." [37] At the moment of crisis, as ineffectual and emasculated as Mr. Dick, Strong belies his name: With no strong sexual desires of his own, he cannot recognize them in his wife. Nor is he able to enact the role of king to her queen.

The overly virile Jack Maldon—who is thus also a failure of masculinity—also fails to negotiate the feminization of the age properly. He, too, recapitulates the decapitation of the would-be male king. It should be recalled that when Betsey loses her small fortune, Agnes suggests that David work on the dictionary as a secretary to Dr. Strong. Before he begins copying, David clears up the confusion caused by Dr. Strong's former amanuensis and sexual rival. "I found Mr. Jack Maldon's efforts more troublesome to me than I had expected," David says, "as he had not confined himself to making numerous mistakes, but had sketched so many soldiers, and ladies' heads, over the Doctor's manuscript, that I often became involved in labyrinths of obscurity."[38] Like Mr. Dick, then, Maldon cannot write; instead of the headless King Charles invading his text, Maldon is overcome by images of "'ladies' heads." While Maldon and Dick represent the sexes as headless bodies or bodiless heads, Dr. Strong has lost his head over his wife. Thus, all of these would-be writers are unmanned (read: decapitated) by the feminization of the age and their own inability to master unstable Victorian gender roles.

In contrast, David learns to be the head of the house and the foremost writer of the house of England by submitting to and suavely subverting the queen in his house. If the feminized age decapitates/emasculates him, he will, like King Charles, always return. Mediating extreme forms of (failed) masculinity, David engenders himself as the strong Bloomian writer who can be misread but never erased. Reading, expunging, and writing over Maldon's masculine overwriting of the emasculated Strong, David shows that he is already the all-powerful omniscient author, for the future successful writer perceives the copyist Maldon's sexual plot against the would-be writer Strong, who is completely unaware of such extravagant, masculine sexual urges. Presumably, in taking over the project of writing, David erases Maldon's sexually graphic graffiti and reinscribes the meanings of Dr. Strong's corrupted text. Similarly, David negotiates manhood by mastering the "labyrinth of obscurity" (shorthand for language itself), placing Strong's effete sexuality and Maldon's blundering masculinity a safe distance away from himself. Dickens's fictive self-portrait strongly suggests that David will not remain a copyist like Mr. Dick, Dr. Strong, or Jack Maldon, because he achieves true masculine authority that properly incorporates the queenly woman.

Thus Dickens's *Kunstlerroman* portrays Victorian society as one in which most people are just copies or copiers of a few original (male) geniuses who really know how to negotiate the gender instability inherent in a culture that viewed gender as binary and that was thus doubly feminized with its female queen and feminized subject. In this context, it is well to remember that Dickens referred to himself as the Inimitable, and his fervent support of the copyright laws indicates his desire to outlaw any cheap imitations or piratings of his work. As Dickens shows, Copperfield is no copyist. His is a tale in which the masculine, authoritative, originary self masters the pen, assumes the penis, and penetrates the meaning of the culture, which, as the *Kunstlerroman* solipsistically asserts, is himself. Thus, if to Dickens the profession of writing incorporated the task of mastering one's gender designation while also successfully mediating the actual precariousness of Victorian gender performance under a queen, Dickens also masters the instability of sex roles by engendering the relationship between the reader and writer. Figuring the rite of reading as passively feminine, Dickens represents writing as a virile, energetic domination of the word. Imposing on but concealing from the reader the role of passive, submissive self, the authority figure David genuflects before the feminized self and writer only in order to construct them as blank pages on which to prove his own power to pen.

The power to pen translates into the power to represent one's culture, and Dickens certainly viewed himself as England's chief representer and critic, a position that would necessarily have put him in conflict with the queen's symbolic position. Indeed, the *Kunstlerroman,* which really comes into existence during the life and reign of Queen Victoria, assumes that the artist is the touchstone of the most treasured values and laws of the age. In Dickens's *Kunstlerroman,* the most important universal truth the author writes about is the process of the making of his gender. Having portrayed himself as a true and originary self, a touchstone, David becomes the hero who establishes himself as the embodiment of the spiritual wealth of his culture. Dickens must conceal the labyrinth of obscurity or shorthand in which such logic results: that the author's successful performance of his gender imposes economic rights. In other words,

David Copperfield assumes that those capable of authentically representing the spiritual and aesthetic wealth of their culture deserve their culture's economic wealth. Not only does the pen equal the penis, but the man with the biggest pension as well.

Not that David should boast or describe his prowess. Rather, Dickens implies that David is a successful writer because he refuses to describe the practical nature of writing: "It is not my purpose, in this record, though in all other essentials it is my written memory, to pursue the history of my own fictions. They express themselves, and I leave them to themselves. When I refer to them, incidentally, it is only as a part of my progress." If David were to refer to his profession in any further detail, he would erase his representation of himself as patriarch-prophet inspired by his female muse and expose himself as masculinist, elitist profitmaker. Copperfield's longest discussion of his profession starts with the direct statement that "I have been very fortunate in worldly matters; many men have worked much harder, and not succeeded half so well." But he attributes all of his financial and personal success to Agnes: "How much of the practice I have just reduced to precept, I owe to Agnes, I will not repeat here. My narrative proceeds to Agnes, with a thankful love."[39] As I argued earlier, Queen Victoria employed the same strategy to cover over the discrepancies of being a masterful sovereign and submissive, queenly wife. Attributing all of her public successes to Albert's masculine guidance, Victoria never attempted to explain why she was such a successful sovereign after her husband's death. In a real way, then, both Dickens and the queen became exceptional professionals at this sort of Victorian spin doctoring.

Dickens discursively performed this same negotiation of gender divergence in his advertisement for the cheap edition of his novels. In a bit of puffery, he described his ambitions for his literary offspring and softened the aggressive character of those ambitions by situating the reader and the text in the feminized private sphere. Implying that reading is a failure of masculinity because it is a domestic pleasure, Dickens insinuated that his books can be treated like familiar friends, rather than business partners:

> *It had been intended that this CHEAP EDITION, now announced,*
> *should not be undertaken until the books were much older, or the Au-*

thor was dead . . . To become, in his new guise, a permanent inmate of many English homes, where, in his old shape he was only known as a guest, or hardly known at all; to be well thumbed and soiled in a plain suit that will be read a great deal by children, and grown people, at the fireside and on the journey; to be hoarded on the humble shelf where there are few books, and to lie about in libraries like any familiar piece of household stuff that is easy of placement: and to see and feel this— not to die first, or grow old and passionless, must obviously be among the hopes of a living author, venturing on such an enterprise.[40]

In this domestic scene, the author is such a familiar guest in the reader's home that he becomes, like Agnes, practically invisible. Thus both reader and writer feel comfortable in their thoroughly domesticated relationship. By feminizing this relationship, Dickens disguises the fact that his is an "enterprise," after all, one to be pursued not for domestic pleasures but for pecuniary rewards. Capitalizing "Author," Dickens capitalizes on his cultural authority and simultaneously erases the commercial trajectory of his trade by depicting the discursive scene as an interregnum from the cares of the capitalist, masculine public sphere. In fact, the unspoken consequence of his aspiration to be a household god— like the queen in the house and like Queen Victoria—is that he does indeed gain the financial rewards associated with such domination. When Dickens imagines that there are few books on his readers' shelves besides the ones he authors, it is a subliminal means of perpetuating his economic and cultural capital. Desiring nothing less than that his be the only book the English home might contain—even replacing Shakespeare and the Bible?—Dickens figures himself as the greatest Author of all time because, throughout all time, feminized men, women, and children (when they have time in their economically dominated lives), will read only his works.

Dickens persistently claims that he and his works will outlast the feminized realm. Like the emasculated King Charles, he will recover his supreme place in the ranks of future generations of men. But this brilliant writer at least subliminally knew that it was not that simple. The psychological underpinnings of the Mr. Dick/King Charles connection, with all of their gender instability, along with other characters' longings to be another sex, or at least have access to the range of experience of another sex, indicate that Dickens was deeply imprinted with his culture's anxieties about gender, just as was the queen. He could not explicitly depict these anxieties, but he manifests them in graphic psychological displays of gender deviance, divergence, and repression. And in Dickens's novels, letters, and other ephemera, the queen (in the house) acts as one of the focal points of those psychological displays.

IV

Womanizing Sovereignty:
Queen Victoria and the
Victorian Queen of Poetry

*I have written so much that I shall have to go like Her
Majesty, in two or three carriages today, I see.*

Elizabeth
Barrett
Browning,
Letter to
Mary Russell
Mitford

IN DECEMBER 1871, after Elizabeth Barrett Browning's death, *Scribner's
Monthly Magazine* referred to her as the "Queen of Poetry."[1] Barrett
Browning had crowned herself Queen of Poetry years earlier, in her
theorization of poetic sovereignty. This chapter looks at Barrett Browning's views of Queen Victoria and of queenliness and examines how her
"gorgeous illusions" construct the sovereign self and literary authority. I
argue that Barrett Browning's view of herself as the Queen of Poetry
depends explicitly on her master narrative about the womanization of the
Victorian age, which itself is implicitly bound up in Queen Victoria's
rule. In Barrett Browning's poetry, both "womanization" and "queen"
have conflicted trajectories, "queen" referring to the subordinate, domestic angel in the house as well as to the powerful ruling monarch. Barrett Browning's vision of the "womanization" of the age rests on the idea
that the female poet must incorporate in her body (of work) the degradation of the "brawling," "calculating" age. Yet by grounding herself in
that degradation, the female poet who imprints the material reality with
the ideal becomes, in Barrett Browning's system, the most exalted queen.
These trajectories can be seen in the epic poem *Aurora Leigh,* in her occasional pieces about Queen Victoria at her accession ("Victoria's Tears,"

and "The Young Queen") and her marriage to Prince Albert ("Crowned and Wedded"), and in her correspondence with Mary Russell Mitford, which includes many references to Victoria.

In 1836, the young poet Elizabeth Barrett met the famous author Mary Russell Mitford, with whom she corresponded until Mitford's death in 1854. The epistolary genre provides an informal entry into the aesthetic views of the two women, especially in their exchange of opinions about nineteenth-century women writers such as Felicia Hemans, Letitia Landon, Joanna Baillie, Maria Edgeworth, George Sand and others. The letters also contain Barrett Browning's and Mitford's observations on local and national gossip and their views of current events, including Queen Victoria's activities, both public and private. Given Barrett Browning's many references to the queen, her statement in a letter to Mitford that there "is much in her that interests me,"[2] turns out to be more than the preliminary to an exchange of gossip, although it is that too. In fact, Barrett Browning's frequent commentaries on Queen Victoria allow her to define her literary credo and form her own poetic, sovereign persona in contradistinction to and parallel with the female monarch's profession.

On 24 March 1842, Mitford wrote to encourage Barrett Browning in her "queenly" aspirations:

> *My love and my ambition for you often seems to be more like that of a mother for a son, or a father for a daughter (the two fondest of natural emotions), than the common bonds of even a close friendship between two women of different ages and similar pursuits. I sit and think of you, and of the poems that you will write, and of that strange, brief rainbow crown called Fame, until the vision is before me as vividly as ever a mother's heart hailed the eloquence of a patriot son. Do you understand this? and do you pardon it? You must, my precious, for there is no chance that I should unbuild that house of clouds; and the position that I long to see you fill is higher, firmer, prouder than ever has been filled by woman. It is a strange feeling, but one of indescribable pleasure. My pride and my hopes seem altogether merged in you.*[3]

In this aesthetic genealogy, Mitford transfers her own mantel of poetic authority to Barrett Browning and anoints her the woman poet of the age. "I have got to think your obscurity of style, my love, merely the far-reaching and far-seeing of a spirit more elevated than ours, and look at the passages till I see light breaking through, as we see the sun shining upon some bright point . . . in some noble landscape." [4] Clearly, Mitford is not talking about woman's "position" as queen in the house; she has bigger, more public ambitions for her friend and protégé. As one professional female poet addressing another, Mitford dares to speak of the "rainbow crown called Fame" and views it as a kind of aesthetic legacy passed down through aesthetic mothers—Mitford and the other Romantic women writers she and Barrett Browning evaluate in their letters to each other.

Barrett Browning aspired to fulfil Mitford's prophecy, and she succeeded. In a letter thanking Mitford for extravagant praise of her poetic sensibility, Barrett Browning convolutedly replied: "nothing wd be left to the faculty of my logic, than the miserable inference . . . that by some mortal casualty, instability, or imperfection, common to the strongest of the earth-kings & earth-queens, . . Miss Mitford had so far beyond sight over-rated, hyper-exalted, praised above measure said Elizabeth Barrett . . . in any segment of degree!" With this modest demurral, Barrett Browning reinscribes the sublime province within which Mitford has placed her, implying that the poetic call is a royal one far above mere "earth-kings & earth-queens," whose powers are mundane and evanescent. The Queen of Poetry, she intimates, has more comprehensive powers with which to represent the material and the ideal.

Barrett Browning's own poetics enshrine the "noble," "elevated" calling of the poet. She earnestly believed that the lionized Wordsworth "deserve[d]" his royal poetic "crown," [5] and she admired "Queen Joanna" Baillie, "said by Mr. Kenyon to Papa to be, the deepest thinker for a woman, he ever met with!" [6] When she entered the ranks of her beloved Wordsworth and Baillie, Barrett Browning gained the "rainbow crown called Fame" that Mitford had envisioned for her; indeed, she was commonly referred to as a "queen" by contemporary literary critics. On 1 January 1850, the *International Magazine* noted that she was "the greatest poet of [the queen's] own sex." Ten years later *The New York Times* called her "womanly not in being 'lachrymose and egotistical,' but as Queen Elizabeth was, asserting herself impetuously and with 'loyal directness.'" Even as late as 1871 *Scribner's Monthly Magazine* made the queenly connection when it referred to Barrett Browning as the "Queen of Poetry." [7]

Barrett Browning's description of her chosen profession is also explicitly patrician. In *Aurora Leigh,* of course, she associates her fictional living artist with female sovereignty when she playfully crowns herself a poet, refuses to give up her sovereignty for the love of a man, and says, "I stood upon the brink of twenty years, / And looked before and after, as I stood / Woman and artist." [8] In a letter to her poet-husband Robert Browning, Barrett Browning figures her very essence as discursive and that discursiveness as sublimely—royally—munificent, for, she implies, discourse, like the female body and mind, is endlessly procreative: "I mean fully when I say, that I have lived all my chief *joys,* & indeed nearly all emotions that go warmly by that name & relate to /me>myself personally, in poetry & in poetry alone. Like to write? Of course, of course, I do. I seem to live while I write—it is life, for me. Why what is to live? Not to eat & drink & breathe, . . . but to feel the life in you down all the fibres of being, passionately & joyfully. And thus, one lives in composition surely . . . not always . . . but when the wheel goes round & the procession is uninterrupted." [9] With this notion that the poet only "lives in composition," the Queen of Poetry links art with the "fibres" of her own body, a womanized, queenly entity that incorporates physical as well as spiritual being. Linking true or "living art" with the female body, Barrett Browning believes that in order "to record true life," the poet must incorporate both the material and ideal manifestations of the sovereign profession (much as the theory of the king's two bodies does).

To the Queen of Poetry the true poetic profession produces "sovereign impressions" that outlive the materiality of the poet's subject (both content and audience), because the poet actually impresses the subject, forming a material relationship with the reader. "A work without unity is a defective work," she explains, "& . . . a work which leaves no sovereign impression, cannot have unity. The reader's impression is the transcript—may it not be called so?—of the author's conception—or rather of the poet's—since the principle refers essentially to works of the imagination. Should there not be a sovereign impression?" [10] Here Barrett Browning implies that the transaction between the poet and the reader is like that between a forceful, sovereign being and a passive subject who is literally imprinted by the sentiments of the printed page. The reader becomes a graphic representation of the author's consummate imagination as the poet's mind—and body—actually etch themselves onto the tabula rasa of the reader's soul. Barrett Browning goes even further and asserts that only the poet has the true sovereign power to make such an impression on other people because that impression is created by the literary imagination.

In contrast to the poet's imaginative impressions, the queen's image on the mint or on postage stamps is merely the material manifestation of secular sovereignty and therefore an inferior facsimile of the female poet's imagination. Almost obsessive in her use of the image of the queen's imprimatur, Barrett Browning once wrote to Mitford, "I like the abstract idea of a letter—I like the postman's rap at the door—I like the queen's head upon the paper—and with a negation of queen's heads (which doesn't mean treason) I like the sealing wax under the seal and the postmark on the envelope."[11] Barrett Browning's enjoyment of the queen's stamp and the treason-like stamping out of that stamp playfully indicates her strong identification with and rejection of Queen Victoria's sovereign power, as well as her understanding of the writer's representative ability for treasonous offense. As she sees it, Queen Victoria's authority is only a material manifestation of female sovereignty that can be erased with the earthly monarch's demise or with the inevitable obsolescence of the objects her official image adorns.

Barrett Browning's own aesthetic sovereignty, by contrast, (the letter inside the envelope) will be transmitted long after the queen's head (stamp) is used and cancelled. Like Corelli, Eliot, and Carlyle, Barrett Browning sees the products of her own literary imagination overruling any cultural artifacts associated with the queen. Barrett Browning proves her superiority to the monarch by imaginatively depicting the material representations (stamps and money) of the queen's power as fleeting impressions of temporal sovereignty associated with the mundane transactions of writing and representation. In contrast, though the poet's imaginative representations in letters and poems can only be transmitted via the queen's literal and figural stamp of approval, Barrett Browning shows that the letters transmitted between writer and reader carry the true sovereign impression. Thus the poet graphically illustrates how her work has a more "sovereign impression" than do Victoria's material emblems of authority.

Again using the minted sovereign to theorize female sovereignty and the womanization of the age, Barrett Browning discusses with Mitford the relative aesthetic merits of their work. "And so you ring me down on the counter as a better coin than yourself? and I fall flat & light by the side of you, dishonored by her Majesty's proclamation!" [12] Here again the "Queen of Poetry" alludes to the monarch as the inherent authority figure standing behind all material, political, or public transactions, and she ultimately rejects Queen Victoria's powers in order to establish her own sovereign poetic authority. This deposition occurs in another letter in which she uses Victoria's monetary significance to prove her own truer sense of queenly grace. Sending money to the impoverished Mitford, Barrett Browning teases, "And now my beloved friend, you will not be angry at any word I have written, or at the impertinent pretensions of the yellow double of our sovereign lady the queen. I have the right of love,—have'nt I? to take such liberties . . & I may use it to the end of my life." [13]

In all of these passages, Barrett Browning associates herself with both the queen's "yellow double" (the minted sovereign or coin of the realm) and with the female monarch's sovereign will and magnanimous pleasure. Yet in each case, the Queen of Poetry asserts that the womanization of the age engenders a female poetic genius that is more autonomous and abundant than any "genius" the political monarch might claim. Claiming to have the queen's face value, Barrett Browning appropriates the queen's ability to be a coin of the realm when she asserts that the poet leaves the most exalted "sovereign impression." To do so, the poet and her work must be passed from "hand to hand" like legal tender. In her evocation of this esoteric master narrative, Barrett Browning must resolve the ways in which domestic women, women writers, womanization, and female sovereignty are prostituted when associated with coin.

Queen Victoria, then, is figured as a base or counterfeit coin compared to the poet's more precious metal. This is not to say that Barrett Browning did not have a conflicted view about the queen. It is my guess that she recognized that the whole notion of sovereignty she was using to define the poet had its source in the legal concept of the political sovereign. In fact one could argue that Barrett Browning undermines her own radical politics to the extent that she uses the elitist category of "queen" within which to locate the true poet. Perhaps this is why many of Barrett Browning's references to the queen border on invective. Her unattractive allusions to the queen may, in addition, be graphic subliminal images that illustrate the female poet's difficult task of creating a sovereign—and culturally acceptable—space for herself. Thus when Barrett Browning castigates Victoria's as political, inept "vulgar sovereignty," she manifests not merely professional rivalry.[14] She also exhibits frustration with the professional possibilities open to women, especially considering the kind of overdetermined critique they would inevitably receive despite their advantageous positions.

In any case, a little disconcerted by her feelings toward the queen, Barrett Browning admitted to Mitford, "Dont you see what a straight I am in? How can loyalty & republicanism be brought together 'into a consistency.'" It appears that Barrett Browning admired the young Victoria but at the same time often found her personal and public politics reprehensible. In fact, in "The Young Queen," Barrett Browning reveres the sovereign impression Queen Victoria made at the beginning of her reign. The poem pictures the awesome "shadow" cast across the country at King William IV's demise, a specter that is only exorcised because "A royal maiden treadeth from where *that* departed trod!" The Queen of Poetry pays homage to the maiden's wisdom as well as to her purity. The queen's understanding is profoundly discerning, even primordial, and Barrett Browning venerates her majesty: "Her thoughts are deep within her: / No outward pageants win her / From memories that in her soul are rolling wave on wave—."[15] Troping the "womanization" of the age, Barrett Browning depicts sovereignty as being an internal act of the imagination rather than a physical or political demonstration of power. As she asserts in "The Young Queen," the imagination is found deep within the female body, a body that is also comprehensive in its knowledge.

The young queen's comprehensive wisdom includes the poet's exquisite sensibility. Barrett Browning had been particularly affected by the fact that Victoria cried when she first learned that she was queen. In a letter to Mitford describing the impression Victoria's tears made on her, she notes that Victoria "wept not only amidst the multitudes at the proclamation, but in the silence of the dead midnight—(we heard that she cried all night before holding her first privy council, notwithstanding the stateliness & composure with which she received her councillors)." To the Queen of Poetry, the tears shed by the political queen at her accession were "beautiful & touching to think upon." In a poem commemorating those tears, Barrett Browning sees them as evidence that a discerning, "noble Queen succeeds" who will be no tyrant imposing arbitrary rule. Victoria's tears incarnate her sanctified understanding of the spiritual bond between her sovereign body and the body politic. The royal tears act as a covenant, then, showing that the queen's very "nature" is to guard her subjects' "liberties." Thus, to the Queen of Poetry, Victoria's tears, rather than any official insignia, are the imprimatur of right and righteous rule that will lead to her wearing that even more important emblem of righteousness, a "heavenly crown." [16]

As Barrett Browning suggests in "Victoria's Tears," Victoria's right rule is absolutely associated with her sensitivity to each of her individual subjects. She describes any sympathetic accord between Victoria and her subjects as a kind of sovereign impression that authenticates the queen's high position. She celebrates the fact that when the Duke of Sussex "bent his knee" before the newly crowned queen, "regardless of spectators, she threw her arms around his neck & kissed him fervently!" As Victoria's reign wore on, Barrett Browning became increasingly disillusioned with the queen. But Victoria gained stature in the poet's eyes when, at a court ceremony, she shook hands with the aging Lord Melbourne, who was in disfavor at the time. About this event, Barrett Browning remarks, "Poor queen! there may be good in her yet: and it is a merit (*for a queen*) to be cordial to a friend in adversity—!" [17]

At the same time she harshly criticized the wealthy queen's indifference toward her subjects on other occasions. She had nothing but scorn for the royal physicians' medical prescription that Victoria must be "amused from morning to night" to allay her despondency. And while reading the diary of Madame D'Arblay, second Keeper of the Robes to Queen Charlotte, Barrett Browning was disgusted with "queen's houses & queen's servants & above all of queen's condescendances & sweetnesses." If court rituals are not relaxed so that servants can be "tired, or hungry even, in the presence of Majesty," then the poet will "give her up . . . that is, her Majesty, . . & she may go the way of all crowned flesh." [18]

Barrett Browning was particularly appalled by the debacle of the Hastings affair, when Victoria, believing the false rumor that Lady Hastings was pregnant out of wedlock, insisted that the woman resign as a court retainer. The poet wondered if the queen "really *has* no feeling" and saw her remorseless behavior as a sign that she was "a mere Queen

Stone, co-regnant with King Log." [19] Barrett Browning condemned the queen's insensitivity to the individual bodies of the subjects who made up the body politic; if the Queen could not feel their pain, how could she hope to embody or represent them? Because she saw the female principle as a powerful, authoritative, shaping energy as well as an ability to imagine and empathize with others, Barrett Browning had high expectations of her queen.

The poet also used Victoria's marriage to inscribe the complex expectations she had of any female sovereign. Wrestling with the concept of "womanization" as subordination to one's spouse, Barrett Browning addressed the dilemma the young queen faced in her poem "Crowned and Wedded," written on the occasion of Victoria's marriage to Albert. Being "crowned" meant that Victoria was taking "a solemn vow" to "rule," while being "wedded" created obligations to love and obey her husband. The tension between the two duties provides the structural crux of this occasional piece. The poem begins with a long section memorializing Victoria's most recent ritual appearance before her people, the celebration of her ascension to the throne. In this ceremony, the young queen took "a princely vow—to rule—" followed by "A priestly vow—to rule by grace of God the pitiful,—/ A very godlike vow—to rule in right and righteousness, / And with the law and for the land!" [20] Focusing on the queen's sheer power, Barrett Browning shows that the female monarch ultimately moves from "princely," to "priestly" potency and then to omnipotence, or "godlike" power, each move appropriating a higher level of masculine power.

In the next twenty-four lines of the sixty-four-line epithalamium, Barrett Browning memorializes Queen Victoria's accession to power, acknowledging that a fundamental transition took place within the girl when she became queen: "She vowed to rule, and in that oath, her childhood put away: / She doth maintain her womanhood, in vowing love today." In this case, being womanized means exchanging the girl's abject dependence for the power to rule and represent her country. Her womanhood is "maintained" when she marries. Indeed, Barrett Browning views the nuptials as a means of reiterating Victoria's sovereignty and declares that the queen is "no less a queen" for marrying. But she does not ignore the domestic role of the queen in the house. Arguing that Queen Victoria's monarchical "crown" is "shallow" compared to the crown she will wear when she becomes a "bride" or "woman," Barrett Browning attempts to resolve this conflict by exhorting Albert to recognize Victoria's "uncrowned womanhood to be the royal thing!"

The conclusion of the poem reiterates the idea that Victoria's "uncrowned womanhood" cannot be subordinated to wifehood. There is no suggestion, for instance, that Victoria should or could relinquish her queenship in order to be married, in the way that she had put off her childhood to become a woman. Despite her sentimental tone, Barrett Browning strongly resists the separation of Victoria's womanhood and sovereignty into distinct spheres. In the final lines of the poem, she counsels the queen's subjects to pray, "The blessings happy PEASANTS have, be thine, O crowned queen!"[21] Barrett Browning thus reasserts Victoria's political power. Marriage for Victoria is an interval of womanly submission, not an outright renunciation of political sovereignty. As the ending of the poem suggests, Victoria's public role as monarch can never be erased even by the marriage ceremony that provides her with a different crown; nor can she be parted from her sovereign autonomy when she marries. Like the female poet's imagination, Victoria's sovereignty is integral to her very being.

It is no wonder, then, that Barrett Browning reviles the queen whenever she gives female sovereignty a bad name, whenever she passes off a counterfeit coin, if you will. She implies that the female artist's sovereignty is more secure, less tainted than that of the female monarch, who, though capable of sublime self-representation, too often leaves "sovereign impressions" that are vulgar, insensitive, gauche. Given the poet's belief that true royalty was manifest in artistic genius, she respectively honors and reviles the queen most for her dealings with poets. She mentions to Mitford, for instance, that the queen "gave two hundred pounds to Leigh Hunt, I believe, unsolicited." Saying, "That was well,"[22] she expresses her own "sovereign impression" of the queen's beneficence. Similarly, on 20 November 1844, Barrett Browning asked whether the queen would visit Mitford while staying in her neighborhood. "If she does, I shall be her more devoted subject for evermore. It will do her honour (not you!) in the eyes of the whole country. I will forgive her much—oh, so much! . . if she really does go to see you."[23] Barrett Browning repeats this wish a few months later, remarking, "If the Queen is right queenly, she will do herself the honour of going to see you from Strathfieldsay." [24]

The queen never did visit Mitford. Expressing "pity and disdain" for Victoria's insensitivity to the poet, Barrett Browning mocks the mock queen in a scathing remark. Referring to the "Poor, foolish queen," the Queen of Poetry wonders about "The Hanoverian wits, to say nothing of royal wits in general," which are "apt to have a 'divine wrong.'" Impugning even the queen's sanity, the poet laments the "world! & these kings & queens of the world! . . . these queens of England! for in France & Prussia the crowns go together with more civilization." To Barrett Browning, this insensitivity to the poet's royal genius showed that Victoria was neither capable nor deserving of representing a civilized country. As she sarcastically remarked to Mitford when she questioned Victoria's sensitivity, "You are a rebellious subject, my beloved friend, of her Majesty. 'No sensibility'!" [25] Lack of sensibility was the worst kind of "sovereign impression" as far as the poet was concerned.

But Victoria's was a double failure, for she was insensible not only to her subjects' bodies and work, but also to the poet's body of work. Barrett Browning haughtily characterizes the queen's "vulgar sovereignty" in a letter to Mitford in which she remarks that she is "probably quite right in your devination that neither gods nor goddesses made her poetical— Otherwise she wd care more for Shakespeare." Indeed, Barrett Browning cannot accept the idea that a truly sovereign soul could be untouched by the divine art of poetry. That Queen Victoria would attend the lion tamer Isaac A. Van Ambrugh's show six times at Drury Lane was appalling, considering what she could have seen at the theater. "I am sure you were polishing your dagger," she wrote to Mitford, "just when you asked me to agree with you in giving Goethe's laurel to Schiller. You might as well ask our young Queen to prefer Shakespeare to Mr. Van Ambrugh." [26]

Barrett Browning delighted in reports of the queen's aesthetic ignorance and was happy to pass on "the court news" that Victoria "confessed the other day to having never read Wordsworth's poems—upon which a Maid of honour answered quite broadly" that '*That* is a great pity—they would do your Majesty good.'" To the poet's way of thinking, the saving grace that redeemed Her Grace from total "vulgar sover-

eignty" was the queen's "womanization." In other words, the maid of
honor who reported this incident "spoke all manner of good of the
queen—called her 'earnest & genuine'—& expressed not merely personal attachment as from subject to queen, but attachment & esteem as
from woman to woman."[27] The queen's "earnest & genuine" response as
a woman to a woman was, for Barrett Browning, an intuitive, if naive,
kind of poetic sensibility that left the kind of sovereign impression that
the female poetic genius would leave.

She could not, however, forgive the queen's inability to appreciate
Barrett Browning's own genius. The apparent snub took place when
Marianne Skerrit, dresser to the queen and friend of Mitford's, was asked
to show Her Majesty Barrett Browning's memorial of Victoria's wedding, "Crowned and Wedded." Reportedly Victoria showed little interest. On learning this, Barrett Browning shot off a letter to Mitford:

> You relieved me my beloved & kindest friend by what you said . . . of
> the queen! I had inferred after my illogical fashion, from the previous
> saying, that some idol of mine with a crowned head like Wordsworth
> rather than Victoria, had scorned me from the heights of his regality.
> Now . . . if it is only Victoria . . . why I peradventure can be regal too.
> My dearest friend, I never had a thought until you put it into me that
> she wd look at verses of mine, or that looking I shd ever be aware that
> she did. Many probabilities were against the former,—all etiquettes
> against the latter! & after all your pleadings on the other side, I by no
> means feel aggrieved, to the breadth of this line _____ which my bad
> pen (by the way) has made broader than my bad temper desired to
> do—by the quodlibets of queenhood.[28]

Barrett Browning's self-conscious indifference to the queen's unsat-
isfactory observations is remarkable. For one thing, the self-serving, condescending dispatch demonstrates what a poor impression the queen's
"vulgar sovereignty" makes when compared with Barrett Browning's own
majestic genius. Showing that she is the true queen, Barrett Browning
rather quickly deposes the counterfeit queen in the only way true genius
can, by writing a royal proclamation of her own. Barrett Browning further establishes her own sovereign authority by identifying Wordsworth
as a true sovereign. Since genius is the true aristocracy, it is equals like
Wordsworth in the elite realm of artists to whom Barrett Browning looks

for the stamp of approval, not to the lowly Victoria. In asserting Wordsworth's superiority, Barrett Browning rhetorically uses her own sovereign impressions to cancel out Queen Victoria's imprimatur.

Yet Barrett Browning's very demonstration of her genius in these remarks—the maze-like intricacy and graciousness masking the caustic condemnation—also reveals the poet's own vulnerability to the response of the royal audience. One guesses that Barrett Browning's dissembling hauteur conceals some dejection. In the long parenthetical remark she claims to be unperturbed by the queen's imbecility. But the pen is mightier than the poet in this case, for the graphic line she draws to represent her anger literally underlines her annoyance that she should have to refer to the political monarch at all to justify her own authority as the Queen of Poetry. She even adds that this line is larger than she had intended. But the subliminal slip of the pen literally underlines the poet's overdetermined protests of indifference to the queen's tepid response to her poetry.

Annoyed with the queen for her unwillingness to concede the poet's sovereignty, Barrett Browning erases Queen Victoria in order to exalt herself and the profession of poetry. Indeed, in the passage quoted above Barrett Browning hints that, contrary to conventional wisdom, Queen Victoria's sovereignty could not exist without Barrett Browning's "fancy" or living art. The poet had performed just such an obliteration of Her Majesty when explicating "Victoria's Tears" for Mitford. Undermining the political monarch in order to exalt the gorgeous illusion of her own sovereignty, Barrett Browning admits to Mitford that "the Gods know that I have no peculiar admiration for her *because* of her queenship." Rather, the inspiration for the poem "was because of something beyond or under it & taken account of by *my fancy*"[29] (my emphasis). Suggesting here that the political sovereign is just a hollow, malleable form that achieves meaning only through the Queen of Poetry's imagination, Barrett Browning quite literally puts the monarch in her place.

In her poetic novel *Aurora Leigh,* Barrett Browning again uses and disabuses the queen and the "womanization" of the age to establish her own poetic sovereignty. In their relationship with the reading audience, many Victorian writers preferred to focus on the prophetic nature of art while concealing the financial transactions so central to the profession. In *Aurora Leigh,* however, Barrett Browning graphically illustrates the way all professional artists are immersed in the market and shows, also, how the woman writer is doubly compromised in having her body of work passed from "hand to hand" in exchange for profit. As Barrett Browning sees it, all Victorian women are prostitutes, no matter what class they come from. The age is a "brawling," "calculating" one, she says, and the (female) poet embodies the age. In *Aurora Leigh,* Barrett Browning places her alter ego at the center of the market—where she becomes the coin of the realm—before safely ensconcing her "Queen of Poetry" in the private sphere.[30] She thus boldly illustrates what Tamar Heller has so carefully argued, that in the market economy woman is the sign of the subject's subordination to exchange. Yet the poet's brazen representation of that subordination also endows her with an ineluctable, if unstable, power.

In a letter written in 1865, Victoria asked her daughter Vicky if she had "ever read an extraordinary poem by a lady now dead a Mrs. Browning . . . called 'Aurora Leigh'?"; it has "poetry I like in all shapes." The queen described the epic poem as "very strange, very original full of talent and of some beautiful things—but at times dreadfully coarse—though very moral in its tendency—but an incredible book for a lady to have written." In a way, in *Aurora Leigh* Barrett Browning had paid a compliment to the queen by glorifying the "womanization" of the "full-veined, heaving, double-breasted" Victorian age. This famous passage defines queenliness not only as vigorous but also as the primal, womb-like source of power. Given birth by the womanized author and age, "the men of" future times

> May touch the impress with reverent hand, and say
> "Behold,—behold the paps we all have sucked!
> That bosom seems to beat still, or at least
> It sets ours beating. This is living art,
> Which thus presents, and thus records true life."[31]

Imaged as having colossal, fructifying "paps," Barrett Browning's fictional representative of the age is closely associated with Victoria's real and symbolic fertility, symbolized in the epithets "Grandmother of Europe" and the "Mother of Nations."

Graphically illustrating her own artistic intentions in this robust bodily image, Barrett Browning implicitly acknowledges her aspirations to be the authoritative artist whose effulgent womanhood gives life and voice to this extraordinary era and whose living words will leave a powerful impression on those to come. One of the reasons why this stunning image works is that it is contemporaneous with the reign of an actual female monarch. By aligning the poet's visionary powers with a political female life-force, Barrett Browning implicitly identifies with and appropriates the power of the most authoritative woman in the world at the time. Yet, as we have seen, in order to appropriate the queen's power, the poet must also dethrone "gorgeous illusions" about Queen Victoria's counterfeit sovereignty so as to sustain herself as the sovereign representative of England. Given Barrett Browning's poetics, in which "womanization" and female sovereignty are central, if Queen Victoria had not existed Barrett Browning would have had to invent her. Barrett Browning's use of the imagery of "queenship" throughout *Aurora Leigh* illustrates this concern with her own royalty.

Barrett Browning's apologia for the womanization of the age and the womanization of poetry required the invention of a new kind of woman, one who represented herself in the guise of the age's gender norms, a positionality which, as we have seen, Queen Victoria also attempted to invent for herself. In comparing herself with the political queen, Barrett Browning's task is to normalize the profession and professions of the female author, and naturalize the sovereignty of women, without losing the domestic connotations of "queen." The poet's private letters indicate that difficulty, revealing her identification with the female sovereignty associated with independence and strength, but also showing that she strongly related to the domestic meaning of "queen." On the one hand, she takes pleasure in representing herself as a "disorderly woman and freethinking poet!" [32] But on the other she is also capable of outright sentimentality, as when she proclaims in a letter to Mitford that the "heiress is accursed above the poetess: & I will grant to you & willingly, that the happiest woman of all, hides deepest & most quietly by the hearthside of domestic duty—without an aspiration beyond." [33]

Encountering the twofold Victorian connotations of "queen," Barrett Browning's alter ego, Aurora Leigh, struggles to find a way to be both a poet and a woman. Faced with the female writer's classic double bind, Aurora believes that to be a great poet she must experience all of life. But faced with the Victorian doctrine that the proper profession for a woman was marriage, Aurora must confront the possibility that her choice of a literary career may cost her her femininity. This dilemma ultimately results in the unsatisfying ending of *Aurora Leigh,* in which Barrett Browning attempts to link Aurora's decision to marry Romney with her poetic, sovereign impressions in the same way that elsewhere she associates political sovereignty with her art. In the conclusion of the poem, Aurora relinquishes her ambitions to be a queen of poetry, for she learns that being a queen in the house is the most royal of callings and provides the highest form of individual sovereignty. The narrator portrays the lovers in terms of monarchical accession and describes how Romney enters the "presence of a queen," Aurora, to bid her a final farewell. Here Romney's love and recent blindness teach Aurora the home lesson of her true crowning achievement. Only when Aurora testifies that "Art is much, but love is more" is she able to see that though his eyes are "blind," they are "majestic eyes."[34] Hence, the Queen of Poetry recognizes her true sovereign and gives him her obeisance. Glorifying both the female poet and the woman who renounces her profession for love, *Aurora Leigh* asserts that without the "womanhood" there can be no "womanization" of the age that she so extravagantly praises. Yet, ironically, Barrett Browning also believes that Aurora must appear to renounce her poetic authority in order to authorize the "womanization" of the age.

One senses, then, that Barrett Browning was strategically aware that female sovereignty of the independent, resourceful, empowered kind could only be had by honoring (if even in the breech) female royalty of the subordinate, compliant, domestic kind. Though proud of being a "disorderly, freethinking" woman, Barrett Browning also felt the need to neutralize such claims in her writing by always magnifying the crown of "womanhood" that finds its greatest vocation in the act of submission. *Aurora Leigh* represents a Queen of Poetry who incorporates that female submission into her full-bodied, powerful, protofeminist poetics. The result is disturbing, to say the least. At best, the reader is left with hopes for an egalitarian marriage of the kind Barrett Browning experienced with Robert. By the end of *Aurora Leigh,* gone is the sheer sovereign independence we see in Aurora's first inklings that she is a potential Queen of Poetry. Gone, too, is the extraordinary protocol that defines the female poet as at once sovereign, prostitute, and prophet.

Barrett Browning, of course, pays tribute to the idealistic notion that the poet enjoys an autonomous existence, independent even of his or her audience. And assuming that the qualities of great poetry are innate, unnamable, and outside market relations, the narrator of the semi-autobiographical *Aurora Leigh* resists the thought that "holy lines" might be for "hire." Yet even when she mystifies the role of the writer, Barrett Browning consciously depicts the ways in which the poet's soul always bears the marks of her culture's "obscene" customs:

> Let who says
> "The soul's a clean white paper," rather say,
> A palimpsest, a prophet's holograph
> Defiled, erased and covered by a monk's,—
> The apocalypse, by a Longus! poring on
> Which obscene text, we may discern perhaps
> Some fair, fine trace of what was written once,
> Some upstroke of an alpha and omega
> Expressing the old scripture. . . .[35]

Though these lines argue that subjectivity is an unchanging Platonic form or holy text that has been defiled, they also suggest that the self's immersion in culture constitutes a new, variegated entity that simultaneously bears the traces of perfection—but a perfection that cannot be consummated without traces of the mundane, "obscene" world it inhabits. In this philosophy, a Queen of Poetry is the true representative of her material culture because she has been adulterated by the market economy yet still bears her soul intact. To erase the traces of her construction would be to defile her royal subjectivity even further.

What Queen Victoria was probably referring to when she described *Aurora Leigh* as "coarse" were those scenes in which women are associated with the "sovereign," meaning legal currency, rather than with the "sovereign," meaning queenly womanhood. In an age highly sensitive to such "coarse" depictions of women, Barrett Browning boldly exposes the underside of the association of women with the coin. Thus Barrett Browning agrees with Victorian feminists who argued that sexual and economic prostitution was not limited to streetwalkers but included virtually all women. Prostitution, it was noted repeatedly, was the prototypical "relationship between men and women, repeated in perhaps a more veiled and

subtle manner within the confines of genteel society." [36] Frankly depicting the way Victorian gender ideology left "obscene" traces on women,
Barrett Browning constructs her Queen of Poetry, Aurora Leigh, as the
representative of the age both in spite and because of the fact that she
is defiled by her culture's "calculati[ons]" about women. In doing so,
Aurora Leigh becomes a new kind of woman, one who refuses, as it were,
to accept the blame for being raped (one of the characters in the epic
poem is raped twice), but who chooses to bear the traces of that obscenity
publicly in order to reform the times.

Tracking the age's obscenity, Aurora vehemently protests the economic implications of Romney's first marriage proposal to her. Her description of his insensitivity focuses on the financial transactions that were
inherent in many Victorian love-matches:

> *Love, to him, was made*
> *A simple law-clause. If I married him,*
> *I would not dare to call my soul my own,*
> *Which so he had bought and paid for: every thought*
> *And every heart-beat down there in the bill,—*
> *Not one found honestly deductible*
> *From any use that pleased him!*

Saying "we keep / Our love, to pay our debts with," Aurora notes darkly
that "women of my class . . . haggle for the small change of our gold, /
And so much love, accord, for so much love, / Rialto-prices." If she married Romney, she "would not dare to call [her] soul [her] own," because
"he had bought and paid for" it. As *Aurora Leigh* shows, being a queen in
the house too often meant that the husband "might cut / [the woman's]
body into coins to give away." Aurora ends her speech with a brutal analysis of the role of the feminine in Victorian society:

> *I suppose*
> *We women should remember what we are,*
> *And not throw back an obolus inscribed*
> *With Caesar's image, lightly."* [37]

Barrett Browning blurs the mantels of prophet and prostitute by
inscribing the role of Caesar's image in Aurora's own evolving construc-

tion of herself as poet-prophet. She brazenly suggests that prostitution literally underwrites poetic prophecy:

> *What the poet writes,*
> *He writes: mankind accepts it, if it suits,*
> *And that's success: if not, the poem's passed*
> *From hand to hand, and yet from hand to hand,*
> *Until the unborn snatch it, crying out*
> *In pity on their father's being so dull,*
> *And that's success too. . . .*[38]

Here again Barrett Browning refuses to separate the "obscene" elements of the poetic profession from the "soul" of the writer. She believes that ultimately a wide readership will recognize—will buy—the truly worthwhile work. Thus entangling "success" with "popularity," she images the literary work as though it were money moving (through) the masses in a kind of market exchange. This description also implicitly depicts woman as the representative poet because she is the sign of debased exchange.

Barrett Browning even seems to take pleasure in describing the pecuniary trade-offs a Victorian woman writer must negotiate. Noting that fledgling writers not only plead for her comments on their work but also beg for money, she deadpans, "From me, who scarce have money for my needs." Barrett Browning also shows how the emerging field of literary criticism establishes itself as a profession by, at times, procuring powerful bargaining positions with the poet: "My critic Hammond flatters prettily," says Aurora, who acknowledges the expected trade-off. Whereas Hammond "wants another volume like the last," another critic "wants another book / Entirely different, which will sell, (and live?) / A striking book, yet not a startling book, / The public blames originalities."[39] Barrett Browning's descriptions of Aurora's struggles for financial success, then, merge with her more abstract, romantic evocations of poetic inspiration. Thus her epic argues that if her "trade is verse," the author cannot conceive of herself as independent of the market.

Though Aurora admits that her material needs are "vulgar," she also asserts that the female poet's coarse bodily needs engender the womanized poetic genius and the feminized age:

I had to live, that therefore I might work
And, being but poor, I was constrained, for life,
To work with one hand for the booksellers,
While working with the other for myself
And art.

Therefore Aurora does the hack work of writing for encyclopedias, newspapers, and magazines, for "In England, no one lives by verse that lives; / And, apprehending, I resolved by prose / To make a space to sphere my living verse."[40] Submitting her work to the "calculations" of the market, she consolidates her womanly sensibility, showing that the true woman will not ascend above her body or the body politic, nor will she abandon her exalted, sovereign impressions despite, and perhaps as a result of, her participation in the aggressive capitalist system. The womanized poet, then, is the prostitute with a heart of gold. Sacralizing the female poet's ascension above and within material culture, Barrett Browning authorizes her own living art by suggesting that she has paid the price—her body of work and thus she herself have been passed from hand to hand—to represent the culture with her bountiful, living art. But Aurora also turns this kind of womanizing to her account of the womanization of the age. Valorizing the woman who heroically incorporates the mercenary age within her body, Barrett Browning asserts that the female poet does hack jobs for minted sovereigns so that she can write the exalted "sovereign impressions" that will help others to transcend and ameliorate the "calculating age" in which they live.

Aurora also depicts the supposedly autonomous realm of art as saturated with the culture's representations of sexual difference. Starkly inscribing the way Victorian gender ideologies vitiate the allegedly holy state of artistic sensibility, Barrett Browning turns the palimpsestic definitions of art and the writer inside out. Uncovering the holy "hieroglyphic," Barrett Browning portrays her culture's fall from grace—and the resulting inability of the Victorian sovereign self to be visionary—as the logical result of a society that identifies women as the ultimate signifiers of economic exchange or prostitution:

Thus is Art
Self-magnified in magnifying a truth
Which, fully recognized, would change the world

And shift its morals. If a man could feel,
Not one day, in the artist's ecstasy,
But every day, feast, fast, or working-day,
The spiritual significance burn through
The hieroglyphic of material shows,
Henceforward he would paint the globe with wings,
And reverence fish and fowl, the bull, the tree,
And even his very body as a man,—
Which now he counts so vile, that all the towns
Make offal of their daughters for its use
On summer-nights, when God is sad in heaven
To think what goes on in his recreant world
He made quite other; while that moon he made
To shine there, at the first love's covenant,
Shines still, convictive as a marriage-ring
Before adulterous eyes.[41]

Addressing the culture's obsessive focus on sexual difference, Barrett Browning shows in these lines that this focus creates fragmented subjectivities who nevertheless believe themselves to be whole. Thus this poet's body of work must embody the way men are alienated from their own bodies when they view women's bodies as "offal" of which to make "adulterous" "use." The implication is that if Barrett Browning can make the male reader experience art almost corporally as the body (of work) of a female poet, perhaps her poetry can transform the body politic.

Prostitution of the female poet's goods seems to result from making her wares public. But to Barrett Browning such publicity is necessary to create a condition in which the reading audience might receive a "sovereign impression" from a queenly poet. A queenly poet, like a political queen, has no power unless she makes a strong impression on her subjects. Hence, if Barrett Browning glorifies the womanization of the age, she also clearly recognizes the economic implications for women in a culture that essentially endorsed womanizing of the more traditional type. Acknowledging the sexual implications of the passing of the female self from hand to hand, Barrett Browning boldly figures the prostitution of the female body as being central to the transmission of "sovereign impressions." In her poetics, the sovereign poet, whose conceptions are abstract and exalted, must validate those conceptions by living fully in the midst of the material world which for that very reason needs the impress of an exalted imagination even more. If the womanized age requires the female poet's submission to capitalism, then Barrett Browning must include the Victorian commodification of female sexuality within her material, abstract conception of poetry. She must also make inextricable connections between the queen's yellow double, motherhood, and authorial sovereignty.

Barrett Browning does not resolve the complex of issues surrounding gender, artistic authority, and capital, but her assessment of the material, practical realities of writing, which *David Copperfield* avoids acknowledging, constitutes a bold challenge to the representation of the male writer as patriarch-prophet. She makes this challenge by revealing how difficult it is for the woman writer to transcend the material conditions of her culture, something the male writer seems to do with relative ease. Thus, as Barrett Browning challenges stereotypes regarding women writers, she also uncovers the very manipulations of the feminine so crucial to Dickens's idealistic representation of the writing task. Unlike David Copperfield, who only gives idealized glimpses of his profession, Aurora continually exposes the practical concerns of her craft. While Dickens represents his own mastery of the age's masculine failure, what Barrett Browning reveals is that in a market system not only were all Victorians prostitutes, but women as writers and human beings became the signs of market transactions. What is remarkable is that both Barrett Browning and Dickens negotiate these gendered constructions of their profession through a poetics founded on and informed by the reign of Queen Victoria.

Implicating precisely the gender ideologies that produced the material version of the woman and woman writer as prostitute—figuring Aurora as prostitute and prophet—Barrett Browning squarely situates the poet's place in the marketplace:

> *Their sole work is to represent the age,*
> *Their age, not Charlemagne's,—this live, throbbing*
> > *age,*
> *That brawls, cheats, maddens, calculates, aspires,*
> *And spends more passion, more heroic heat,*

Betwixt the mirrors of its drawing-rooms,
Than Roland with his knights, at Roncesvalles.

Almost immediately after this call to represent the "throbbing age," Barrett Browning bodies forth "the full-veined, heaving, double-breasted Age" as a woman deeply immersed in, representative of, and inspirational to the calculating age. She explicitly associates this womanly figure with "living art, / Which thus presents, and thus records true life." This figuration of art, the woman writer, and the age itself as colossal female body literalizes the notion of touchstone and implicates the Queen of England and the queen of the house as extraordinarily potent female figures. As Aurora pronounces: "I'm a woman, sir, / And use the woman's figures naturally, / As you, the male license." [42]

Similarly, in her suggestion that modern Quixotes are Donnas (and Dulcineas) rather than Dons, Barrett Browning tilts with the sacred icons of her age. Chastising male poet-prophets like Carlyle and Tennyson for their loss of belief in the culture's vitality (read: virility), this female vates-whore asserts that in order to revive the culture these writers must attend to the ways in which a woman's mind and body are inflected by the "cheating" and "spending" that accompany prophetic "heroic heat." Barrett Browning shows that Dickens himself, the sagacious Jeremiah of his age, was no less influenced by material concerns. In fact, in another passage, she describes how Romney and Aurora avoid any discussion of their romantic love for each other by conversing on contemporary topics instead. Aurora's exchange with Romney consists of and insists on the collusions of the material and ideal: "Can Guizot stand? is London full? is trade / Competitive? has Dickens turned his hinge / A-pinch upon the fingers of the great?" [43] Rapping some literary knuckles, Barrett Browning here reveals syntactically and didactically that politics, trade, competition, love, money, and professional writing cannot be separated. Though clearly one of the supreme monitory geniuses of his age, Dickens could not own up to the fact, as Barrett Browning does, that the construction of himself as writer-prophet was the result of the economics and aesthetics of man-made law.

The dominant Victorian ideology that constructed woman either as angel in the house (the regulator of the spirit of the law), or prostitute (the outlawed sexual difference of the feminine), implicitly aligns that incongruity with the constitutional law that figured women as at once contingent (outside but subordinate to the law) and omnipotent (as queen, the incarnation of the law). In *Aurora Leigh* and epistolary descriptions of the queen's material image, Barrett Browning recognized that the fully embodied female sovereign was embedded in material culture at the same time that she represented the ideal letter of the law. Indeed, Barrett Browning showed that while a queen represents the nation-state's economic well-being, cultural treasures, and political fortunes, those representations, like the writer's vigorous, carnal body of work, assume their power only in being passed from hand to hand.

V

"The Grandest Trade of All": Professional Exchanges between the Queen and Margaret Oliphant

Politics are the occupation and profession of the royal worker, as literature is of the writer—the grandest trade of all, and the most exciting.

Margaret Oliphant, *Queen Victoria: A Personal Sketch*

OF ALL VICTORIAN writers, Margaret Oliphant is perhaps the most matter-of-fact about the failure of masculinity in the Victorian age. Typically, it is the woman who occupies the center of energy and labor in Oliphant's writings, and, like the men in Oliphant's own life (her father, husband, brother, and sons), males either abandon their economic responsibilities or fulfil them inadequately. This personal observation becomes political in Oliphant's view that England's few queens regnant appeared at critical historical junctures when the nation's destiny had been compromised by impotent, feckless, or debauched male rulers. Oliphant focuses much of her biographical work on historical British queens and on the preeminent Victorian working woman, Queen Victoria. In addressing the feminization of work in the nineteenth century, she upgrades the Victorian estimation of women's work, while blurring the boundaries between women's public and domestic lives. By representing her trade as a pedestrian but worthy endeavor, and constructing herself as an authority on the "profession" of queenship, Oliphant increases her own authority to represent the culture. This is not to say that the personal and professional exchanges between the queen and Oliphant were always complimentary. Indeed, they were not. But though as an amateur writer the queen impinged on Oliphant's professional territory, for the most part Oliphant was able to avoid the antagonistic exchanges Dickens and Barrett Browning had with their queen over cultural authority.

The sheer abundance of Oliphant's literary output is a testament to a long career of hard work. As her publisher's "general utility woman," [1] Oliphant penned 267 articles, books, and reviews for *Blackwoods* alone. On average, in one year she produced two novels, ten published articles, one short story, and a volume of nonfiction. [2] Altogether, "she wrote ninety-eight novels, fifty or more stories, four hundred articles and numerous travel books and biographies," an astonishing feat by any standard. [3] The explanation for this voluminous output rests, of course, in the fact that Oliphant became the sole provider for her own two sons, her nieces, a nephew, and a profligate, alcoholic brother. She explains frankly that writing became "my trade" because "it was necessary for me to work for my children." Recalling the decision to consider herself a tradesperson rather than an artist, Oliphant describes having made a "pretence to myself that I had to think it over, to make a great decision, to give up what hopes I might have had of doing now my very best, and to set myself steadily to make as much money as I could, and do the best I could for the three boys." After coming to this momentous resolution, Oliphant "refused no work that was offered to" her. [4]

Perhaps more than any other Victorian writer, Oliphant persistently alluded to financial worries whenever she discussed her "trade." Her autobiography is filled with snippets about financial crises, the necessity to work, and the amount of money she was spending or, usually, overspending. Referring to her life as one of "infinite labour," Oliphant noted that though her publishers were "good and kind in the way of making me advances," they were never "very lavish in payment." Despite the financial crapshoot, Oliphant was gratified that even if the way she produced her means of support was not "the noblest way," nevertheless, "I could work." Indeed, she never took "much thought for the morrow" because she had so much "faith in my own power to go on working." [5]

As many scholars have noted, the downside of having to view her profession as a "trade" was that Oliphant gave up the possibility of literary greatness. At times she seemed embarrassed that she was not a luminary like George Eliot and loathed "contemptuous compliments" about her " 'industry.' " "When people comment upon the number of books I have written," she commonly responded "that I should like at least half of them forgotten." But though Oliphant was defensive about being over-worked and underappreciated, she never apologized for her focus on making money. After she had outlived both of her sons, Oliphant freely admitted that financial considerations were a major factor in her decision to complete her autobiography. After the death of her sons, she wrote, she was "consciously" writing her autobiography for the public, "with the aim (no evil aim) of leaving a little more money," yet she felt "all this to be so vulgar, so common, so unnecessary, as if I were making penny-worths of myself." [6]

As a result of the financial straits she constantly negotiated—so apparent in her relations with the queen—Oliphant, more even than Barrett Browning, could not construct the writing profession in the ide-alized ways that became so prevalent in the Romantic period and that culminated in the Aesthetic Movement. Of her own works she wrote, "I am afraid I can't take the books *au grand serieux*. Occasionally they pleased me, very often they did not." "Bewilder[ed]" by "elaborate ways of forming and enhancing style, and all the studies for that end," Oliphant could only think of her trade as "my perfectly artless art," and she lam-pooned contemporary writers who had the luxury of viewing their work as an art rather than a trade. Describing a letter Ruskin had written to his friends, Oliphant pulled no punches: "He is 'about to enter on some work which cannot be well done except without interruption,' he says, and therefore begs his friends 'to think of me as if actually absent from England, and not to be displeased though I must decline all correspon-dence!' " With irreverent disregard for the venerable art critic, Oliphant remarked that the letter "would throw you into fits of laughter" and that it was "positively sublime." [7]

Just as Ruskin reinforced his own authority by writing about queen-ship, so, too, did Oliphant benefit from her representation of female sov-ereignty, but, unlike Ruskin, her evaluation never strayed from the ma-terial. Given the course of her career, it is hardly surprising that the often insolvent Oliphant personally felt the full weight of Victoria's economic centrality to the culture. As Oliphant well knew, the queen's cultural au-thority could set an author up for life or leave her penniless. Finding herself in financial straits in 1860, the author asked her publisher, Black-wood, to apply for a royal pension on her behalf. When his request was refused, Oliphant wrote, "I am sorry her Majesty does not think it worth while to exert her royal bounty on my behalf."[8]

The novelist, however, got a better response after she wrote positive reviews of the queen's authorial attempts. As far as I can tell, the two women first expressed their mutual regard in an exchange of letters in 1868, when Oliphant wrote an anonymous critique of the queen's *Leaves from the Journal of our Life in the Highlands* for *Blackwoods Magazine.* The queen's attendant Theodore Martin wrote the following request to Oli-phant about "the Queen's little book," which "Her Majesty would be well pleased to have reviewed by you for the Magazine," adding, "If you feel yourself justified in speaking well of it, I am very sure you will add to the very warm feeling which was produced by your beautiful paper on General Grey's volume."[9] Since Oliphant had already praised *The Early Years of His Royal Highness the Prince Consort,* which the queen very pos-sibly helped to write, Martin asked the writer to critique Victoria's first publicly acknowledged attempt at authorship. Of course Martin subtly requested that Oliphant puff the piece, for clearly he wanted Oliphant to judge the book only if she could give it a rave review. Whether or not Victoria had anything to do with this request is unknown, though it seems likely, as Martin was working under the queen's direction.

Oliphant did produce the required puffery for *Leaves* in a review entitled "The Queen of the Highlands," in which she described the queen as containing the "centre of all human interest—an individual mind and heart." Apparently Oliphant received some kind of payoff for the review, for eight months later she received "a hundred totally unex-pected pounds," and described the money as rare "luck" resulting from "royal grace and favour." Assuming that the queen was behind the gen-erous reward, Oliphant wrote to a friend, "Curiosity, however, mingles with my rapture. Are pensions of this kind generally paid in the lump once a-year? It is very good of the Queen—if she has anything to do with it."[10] As Merryn Williams suggests, the queen had everything to do with it, for Blackwood had intimated to Oliphant that if she wrote a good review for the queen it might be possible for her to get a Civil List pen-sion, which she did in fact receive with Disraeli's endorsement.[11]

In acknowledging her need for the money she earned from the re-

view that figured the queen as the sine qua non of representational authority, Oliphant implicitly admitted the subordinate status of her own
author-ity. Unlike Dickens, Oliphant was very interested in what the
queen could do for her, for while Dickens sought to bring Victoria to
her knees, Oliphant was not above flattering her sovereign for her own
benefit. It cannot be ignored that writing the queen's biography and re-
viewing her writing gave the novelist actual entry into the queen's life
and opened Oliphant to the professional perquisites that would result
from a personal relationship with Victoria. Indeed, Oliphant considered
ways to use the monarch's name to further her professional ambitions, as,
for example, when she pondered the possibility of editing a "new paper"
under "the patronage of the Queen." "The idea has just shot across my
mind, and I don't know if anything could be made of it, or if even that
patronage could be secured." [12]

But one becomes grateful for Oliphant's concern with money when
comparing her accounts of queenliness with Ruskin's. Drastically rewriting the abstract representation of woman as queen found in "Of Queen's
Gardens," Oliphant analyzes the political power of the real queens of
England. Rather than focusing on the spiritual powers of women as metaphorical queens submissive to a priori masculine authority, Oliphant
forces the reader to look at the material conditions of women's lives. This,
of course, was a subject of great significance to Oliphant, since, as she
explicitly maintained, material conditions were the basis for her having
to enter a profession as well as for her materialist enactment of that career.
Embedded in Oliphant's materialist point of view was the belief that
women were, in general, undermined by the culture's imperative that
men financially support and politically guide the so-called inferior sex. In
Oliphant's experience, the construction of masculinity in Western culture was a failure. Accordingly, she believed that she herself, as well as the
queen, proved women's ability to survive and succeed despite the material
failures of men.

These subversive ideas are apparent in Oliphant's rhetorical switch
in mid-text from history to herstory. In *Historical Sketches of the Reign of
George Second,* for example, Oliphant completely ignores George the Second himself in order to concentrate a long chapter on his remarkable
wife, Queen Caroline, who, according to Oliphant, was the real power
behind the throne. A woman who displaced a sitting but effete male king,

Caroline (like Oliphant) successfully took over the reins of power when the rightful male authority actually and metaphorically decamped. Oliphant uses Caroline's specific case as an opportunity to extrapolate about women's professional qualifications. Unlike other fields that women have entered, "The historian cannot regard" English queens "with the condescending approbation which critics in every other branch of science and art extend to women," for "in very absolute contradiction to all conventional theories," women "are great monarchs, figures that stand fully out against the background of history in the boldest and most forcible lines." Queen Caroline, she argues, was "even a greater contradiction to every ordinary theory which ordinary men frame about women" because she "proved the art of government to be one of the arts within a woman's powers."[13]

In *Historical Sketches of the Reign of Queen Anne,* Oliphant shows the same fascination with the queen's admirable performance despite all odds or expectations. She begins the first chapter with the suggestion that "It pleases the fancy to step historically from queen to queen, and to find in each a climax of national greatness knitting together the loose threads of the general web." As Oliphant interprets history, during the reigns of Anne and Elizabeth "the country was trembling between two dynasties, scarcely yet recovered from the convulsion of great political changes." In this state of affairs, "nothing but the life of the sovereign on the throne stood between it and unknown rulers and dangers to come. The deluge in both cases was ready to be let loose after the termination of the life of the central personage in the state." In the midst of political chaos, Queen "Anne's life and her times, like those of Elizabeth, were to her contemporaries the only piece of solid ground amid a sea of evil chances."[14]

Similarly, Oliphant represents Victoria as returning the monarchy to its noble tradition after years of disastrous male leadership. Oliphant views Victoria's immediate predecessors with extreme disdain, referring to them as "A crowd of unrestrained young men, . . . whose debts had continually to be paid, and whose lives shocked" the British people. The author concludes that, if continued, this "sad decadence" of "the Royal House" would "have ruined any royal stock." In utter contrast to "such representatives of royalty as these," Oliphant graphically represents "the appearance of a young woman upon the eager and curious world." "Everything was possible to so young and untried a creature, a mere girl, not much over childhood." "The Maid of England stepped forth, bringing with her all the lessons of self-abnegation and high patriotism, and that perfection of moral training, which a woman's education was fitted to give." Oliphant claims that though Victorians discerned the "contrast of extreme youth, simplicity, and inexperience with the position and duties thus suddenly devolving upon the young Queen," none "anticipated the marvellous changes that were coming in with her, the new ideal, which was almost a revelation of what a monarch ought to be."[15]

Oliphant associates this "queenliness" with the artist's cultural role. If in *The Reign of King George the Second* there is no chapter on the king, there are whole chapters devoted to "The Poet" and "The Novelist" who were representative of his reign. Likewise, in *Historical Sketches of the Reign of Queen Anne,* Oliphant includes a number of chapters on notable personalities of the time, with the last three chapters devoted to Jonathan Swift, Dr. Addison, and Daniel Defoe. Conversely, in *The Victorian Age of English Literature,* Oliphant locates the meaning of the period's writers within the parameters of Victoria's reign. For example, the first chapter is entitled "Of the State of Literature at the Queen's Accession, and of those whose Work Was already Done."[16] The modern field of English literature has taken for granted an inherent connection between the life span of English monarchs and the literature produced within those spans, an assumption that figures the monarch and writer as cultural icons as well as the supreme owners of cultural capital. But it should be noted that in her vast critical work historicizing English literature, Oliphant helped to establish this seemingly inherent connection, a connection that increased the value of her own writing as it also manipulated the fiction of royal personages to raise the devalued status of women.

Oliphant was particularly focused on the working woman. To her, the "ideal" monarch was always industriously at work for the good of her people. She exulted triumphantly that "the young lady upon the throne" was no clinging vine but rather a vigorous ruler who "was getting through an amount of business daily which only those acquainted with the manifold anxieties of official life could fully estimate." Refusing to conceal the mental and physical exertions that typify women's labor, Oliphant described the "details" of Victoria's "serious and steady work." She relished the fact that during "one public crisis" in 1848 "28,000 despatches were received at the Foreign Office alone, all which passed through the Queen's hands." She also noted that aside from her rigorous daily schedule, the queen was "liable to be called upon at any moment, should any political crisis or commotion of State arise either at home or abroad."[17]

One of Victoria's servants corroborates Oliphant's view of the queen as an indefatigable worker: "No greater delusion exists," he says, "than that the Queen at any period of her life ever indulged herself in idleness." Victoria, he writes, was trained from childhood on "to work, work, work."[18] The matronly monarch herself emphasized the burdensome requirements of her position vis-à-vis the author's when she told Oliphant in conversation that "I also work hard."[19] Oliphant points out that so much did the young Victoria's mind take to the "trade" of ruling that she "put all ideas of marriage out of her head." Defying conventional expectations of women, this novelist's "gorgeous illusion" about the queen is that Her Majesty "was too busy enjoying her wonderful new trade, going into every detail of it, reading every paper, curious, eager, taking full advantage of every novelty in her way, and especially of the novelty of doing what she liked and guiding herself by her own will alone."[20]

Defining work as part and parcel of pursuing a trade and being a mother, Oliphant argues that the "disciplined and dutiful," "independent and sagacious" married queen had more understanding of "foreign politics" because "the happiness and progress of her own family" was "so involved in them." Victoria is "the first officer of the State, . . . the Sovereign of the country" whose "purity and dignity through all the vicissitudes of human life," include "loving, wedding,[and] bearing children."[21] Victoria's pregnancies are not embarrassing, if necessary, reminders of her sexual difference vis-à-vis patriarchal law, but rather signifiers of the absolute connection between the queen's gender and her expansive state powers. Thus Oliphant disputes the Victorian assumption that a woman could not simultaneously pursue a career and fulfil the obligations of being a wife and mother.

Since Victoria's power is essentially based on her intimate familial associations, Oliphant suggests, this "great sovereign" can "enter her cabinet and sit down to the serious work of State with a distinct exhilaration in her mind and more perfect disposition for her work, because her letters that morning have brought the news that an infant in a distant palace yesterday for the first time walked alone!"[22] Queen Victoria's gender actually makes her a stronger monarch than any man could be, Oliphant argues, overturning Victorian conventions that asserted the solipsistic narcissism of maternity. Oliphant's notion that the queen's home life is an integral part of the life of the nation brilliantly makes any other position on the subject appear absurdly untenable.

She also specifies the ways in which Victoria firmly ruled the men around her, quoting, for example, a lengthy memo from Victoria to Lord Palmerston that clarifies what "it is she expects from the Foreign Secretary." The first requirement is that "he will distinctly state what he proposes in a given case." Then, "Having once given her sanction to a measure," the queen demands "that it be not arbitrarily altered or modified by the Minister." Finally, she insists that she "be kept informed of what passes between him and the foreign Ministers before important decisions are taken" and that she receive dispatches "in sufficient time to make herself acquainted with their contents before they are sent off." Oliphant writes sardonically that it "cannot be supposed that this could be a very palatable document to an all-powerful Minister." To Oliphant's mind, the failure of the minister's masculinity in the presence of the female monarch "is a vindication of the Queen's position as having really a part in great public affairs, instead of being merely a puppet of State."[23]

Perhaps the most invigorating aspect of Oliphant's "gorgeous illusion" about the queen is her scornful dismissal of the notion that Victoria was Albert's puppet. As she sees it, after being widowed, the queen's independence became even more necessary and admirable. As an example, Oliphant quotes a Cabinet Minister who remarked that the queen "Never kept us waiting" even in her time of bereavement, adding the information that the widowed queen "resumed her place in the Council" and "took her place at the head of the Cabinet." Oliphant also takes special care to counter Victoria's own assertions that Albert was the true monarch. "[H]ere arises a remarkable question, which no one, so far as we are aware, has ever entered into": why "the object of the Queen's life was to convince the world that all that was worthy in the first twenty years of her reign was the doing of the Prince Consort." This is merely generous hyperbole, "beautiful" "self-abnegation," says the biographer: "Had we taken her Majesty at her word . . . we should have looked for nothing but complete breakdown, and a season of helpless misery and distraction" after the prince's death. "If she owed all to her husband, as her Majesty has over and over again told us, to what has she owed it that her great career has gone on undiminished?" In fact, Oliphant continues, Victoria's "wise, enlightened, and large-minded course of action has gone on developing and growing more important through her solitary years."[24]

Oliphant clearly edited her public view of Victoria's grief for the sake of the rewards of royal patronage, as we see when we compare her published remarks to those she made in private. In one of her letters, for example, Oliphant writes bitterly, "I doubt whether nous autres poor women who have had to fight with the world all alone without much sympathy, can quite enter into the 'unprecedented' character of the Queen's sufferings. A woman is surely a poor creature if with a large happy affectionate family of children around her, she can't take heart to do her duty whether she likes it or not. *We* have to do it, with very little solace, and I don't see that anybody is particularly sorry for us."[25] Oliphant's unconcealed resentment is not difficult to understand when we recall that she too had lost a husband at a young age and raised a large family singlehandedly.

It is no wonder, then, that when Blackwood asked Oliphant to do a review of Victoria's *Leaves,* Oliphant tartly responded that she would do so "on condition that I am not to be asked to tackle the holy Albert again." After receiving the manuscript for review, Oliphant wrote, "Would that it was consistent with loyalty to make fun of it! It would be ten times easier than any other mode of treatment." Years later the author wrote to Blackwood again, complaining of the "rubbish" (*Leaves*) Victoria insisted on having printed.[26] And in perhaps the most satirical comment a professional writer could make about a privileged amateur, Oliphant bitingly remarked that the queen "may be going in for novels yet if she is to get a review in Blackwood every time she takes pen in hand."[27] Always astute, Oliphant lays bare in this passage the queen's silly airs and barely concealed aspirations to be considered a member of Dickens's, Barrett Browning's, and Oliphant's trade. Her remarks also indicate her awareness that a writer's criticism of the monarch historically constituted treason and that she was unwilling, therefore, to make such comments publicly.

If, then, as Elizabeth Jay suggests, Oliphant's sketch of royal life "displays the biographer's own criteria for evaluating the life of a professional woman,"[28] the ruthlessness of her private correspondence stands in stark contrast to the studied public sycophancy. Clearly she was disgusted by Victoria's obsessive and prolonged mourning and, it seems, over-compensated for the queen's embarrassing ten-year lapse by writing publicly in overdetermined rhetoric about Victoria's professionalism during that time. The author's private letters show that Oliphant expected the queen to respond to Albert's death with resilience, womanly strength, and professionalism—the same qualities that had guided the widowed author through her own family crises. Oliphant's doubleness toward the queen indicates how much she was willing to trade for the right to claim sisterhood with the monarch. Nevertheless, both her public and private stances illustrate Oliphant's shrewd understanding of the double bind women faced, for which she maligned the queen. Indeed, considering that double bind, duty to work may have motivated Victoria's seemingly unnatural devotion to mourning. In fact, this extraordinarily forceful woman's grief expressed itself with the same energy and dedication that she gave to her work. In that sense, Victoria certainly worked a double shift, for she intensively labored to fulfil her roles as grieving widow and powerful, matriarchal sovereign. Her very visible absence from public life also represented the nation's convoluted mourning for the failure of Albert's masculinity. His death only made it more obvious that it was a woman who wore the crown, and that female authority continued in spite of the death of a politically minded husband or the failures and displacements of many male prime ministers. Since the culture required it, Victoria had to have it both ways to a royal extreme: fiercely expressing her devotion to and dependence on her departed spouse, the queen regnant also demonstrated an ardent belief in her regal perquisites. No one would tell *her* how to respond to her personal grief.

In that regard, too, if the novelist's descriptions of Victoria as a professional woman allowed Oliphant to authorize her own profession, Victoria made Oliphant work for that representative power. The queen apparently viewed the right to represent her life as carrying vast cultural capital, and she did not easily cede that power. Asked to write chapters about Victoria's domestic life to be included in Robert Wilson's *Life and Times of Queen Victoria,* Oliphant formally requested authorization to do so. She also asked permission to view personal materials that would help her to write these sections, inquiring "whether there are any private records to which I might be permitted access in consideration of the importance of the subject and its very great interest to the public." Knowing that her request presumed upon their friendship, she added, "I hope that the Queen would place so much confidence in me as to believe that any such material would be used with modesty and discretion."[29]

Disregarding the professional biographer's need to authenticate information, Victoria would not make her private materials the subject of any writer's close scrutiny, not even that of a friend. Sir Edwards firmly replied to Oliphant that "H M regrets that she is unable to comply and I am to add that there are no private records or particulars that could be placed at your disposal for the purpose referred to." In this situation, the queen's control over representation clashed with Oliphant's, and Victoria's authority took precedence over the author's. Oliphant, however, went ahead and wrote the chapters for the *Life and Times of the Queen*. As she had archly admitted earlier in her career, "I like biography. I have a great mind to set up that as my future trade and tout for orders. Do you know anybody that wants his or her life taken?"[30] In a way, in the end, Oliphant's representative powers won out, for the novelist showed that she did not need the queen's permission to "take" her "life." Indeed, writing a biography of the queen gave Oliphant representational power because it was a chance to authorize her own conception of the queen's subjectivity not only for Victorians but for future generations as well.

In another unsettling transaction between the monarch and the novelist over the rights to representation, Oliphant wrote to Sir Henry Ponsonby that *Scribner's Magazine* had asked her to do a piece on the queen. Subtly requiring that the crown acknowledge her professional expertise, Oliphant coyly remarked that though her own instinct was "entirely against it," "my correspondents say that my doing it would keep it out of hands perhaps less awful." The queen was just as cagey in asserting her professional superiority. After consulting Victoria's wishes, Ponsonby gave Oliphant permission to write the piece, but he remarked, seemingly in passing, that "As you refer to the articles in the Graphic most of which every one read with much interest, there were as you know one or two errors, that is to say the reproductions of stories of the Queen's childhood which were fictions." He politely added that "These were trifles, but it might be as well to avoid similar quotations in future publications. I merely give you these hints for your guidance."[31] For all of Ponsonby's tact, this exchange let Oliphant know that she was not the final arbiter on the life of Queen Victoria.

The friendship between the queen and the novelist seems always to have revolved explicitly around their authorship and implicitly around their respective degrees of professional authority. When Oliphant died in 1897, the obituaries noted both the personal and professional nature of the relationship between the two women. The *Daily Mail* editorialized that "Mrs. Oliphant's last letter was written to the Queen, who was deeply affected by the news of her death." The *Chronicle* noted that "The Queen admired her work, and accorded Mrs. Oliphant many marks of royal favour. It was stated . . . that she would have preferred Mrs. Oliphant as her biographer to any other living writer." According to *The Pall Mall Gazette,* Oliphant shared "friendly relations with her Majesty, of whom she was a great favourite, and who, it is said, had every one of Mrs. Oliphant's books read aloud to her." Likewise, *The Star* declared that Oliphant's "books are believed to have given more pleasure to the Queen than those of any lady writer of fiction of her reign." [32]

At the same time, as was true of her relationships with Dickens and Eliot, the queen evidently deemed it the highest of compliments to give an author her own published works. In 1886, Victoria sent Oliphant copies of the two Highland journals with a note from Ponsonby that read in part, "Her Majesty desires me to say that she is well aware how humble her efforts are at Authorship, but as a true Scotchwoman The Queen ventures to send them to you." A few weeks later, Victoria wrote to thank Oliphant for her kind remarks about the journals, saying that the comments "gratify me very much as coming from so distinguished a Writer as yourself." Returning to her own profession, she also explained why she had not been able to read Oliphant's latest work: "My time is alas! so much taken up that I have not time to read much; indeed often for weeks together, I can only read Despatches," adding that nevertheless she looked "forward to the pleasure of reading your last work" as soon as she had "a little leisure." [33] In a few strokes of the pen, then, the queen reiterated the superiority of her own field of representation while also illustrating her successful incursion into the less important field in which Oliphant worked, one meant only for leisurely moments.

Oliphant returned the ostensible compliment. As W. W. Tulloch wrote in 1897, the last year of Oliphant's life, "Traces of weariness are, I think, to be found in her otherwise bright and happy Jubilee articles." Coinciding with the queen's Jubilee, Oliphant's approaching death allowed her, in Tulloch's words, to "take a long, lingering survey of her own life as well as of that of the Queen." Deeply affected by "the contrast between her own circumstances as she lay there dying and those of the Queen going forth on her triumphal progress to meet the cheers of her people," Tulloch wrote, "Five days before her death [Oliphant] wrote some lines about herself which she said she would like to see printed after her Jubilee verses, already published in the June *Blackwood*." [34]

Apparently, in perhaps the final words she wrote about her trade, Oliphant insisted on an implicit comparison between her lines about the queen's Jubilee and the lines she had written about her own death, a request that intimated the belief that her own life was as important as the queen's. Those lines about her impending death were found on a piece of note paper and contained Oliphant's own critical evaluation. "This verse," the note reads, "which is probably mere dogrel [*sic*] came into my mind in the afternoon of 21 June" as "a last message only to the humble and poor in spirit." The verse itself follows:

> *On the edge of the road I lie I lie*
> *Happy and dying and dazed and poor*
> *Looking up from the vast great floor*
> *Of the infinite World that rises above,*
> *To God and to Faith and to Love, Love, Love*
> *What words have I to that World to speak*
> *Old and weary and dazed and weak*
> *From the very low to the very high*
> *Only this and this is all*
> *From the fresh green soil to the wide blue sky*
> *From Greatness to Weariness, Life to Death*
> *One God have we on Whom to call,*
> *One great bond from which now can fall*
> *Love below which is life and breath*
> *And Love above which sustaineth all.* [35]

Oliphant's poetic tribute to the queen in her verse on Victoria's Jubilee situates the professional woman in the streets. But the crowd of

well-wishers who await Victoria's procession through the roadway mag-
nifies Her Majesty's superior significance. In a climactic moment, sensing
that their queen is about to appear, the crowds tremble in expectation:

> *The streets that sound like the sea*
> > *When the tumult of life is high,*
> *Now, in a murmur of voices free,*
> *Hum and ripple and rustle and stir,*
> > *Straining each eye to see—*
> *To gaze and to watch and to wait for Her*
> > *Whose subjects and lovers they be.*

As it becomes one unified body politic, the noisy crowd falls eerily silent:
"The great heart of the multitude / Hold[s] its breath as it waits for Her, /
One being in all the crowd." The "one being" might also represent the
merging of the commoners with their adored royal representative. At any
rate, "Quiver[ing]" with almost erotic pleasure, in Oliphant's tribute
Victoria's loyal subjects respond to her appearance in the street with
"One voice" as they ecstatically shout, "The Queen! the Queen! the
Queen!"[36]

In Oliphant's farewell verse, the road on which her subject pauses
seems relatively untravelled and out of the way, while majesty and glory
adorn the road (with its throngs of faithful subjects) that awaits the queen.
The queen's progression will be triumphal, manifesting her authority and
professional craft before the multitude, who look to her for their identity.
Unlike the queen, who hears the shouts of the adoring masses, the subject
of the first poem is a lone vagrant—a literal pedestrian. Yet, as Oliphant
figures herself, unhailed and prostrate on an insignificant roadway, she is
nonetheless privileged to look up and receive the approval of the divine.
Thus, in a way, Oliphant offers herself a transcendent reward for having
accepted a terrestrial trade and reputation. That approval seems to be for
both her personal and professional life, for she asked that this poem be
publicly juxtaposed with her poem about the queen, suggesting that the
two poems, the two women, and the two professions were worthy of
comparison. By intermingling her life's work with the queen's in these
two poems, Oliphant also vicariously partakes of the bountiful praise
given by Victoria's subjects in the Jubilee tribute. Ultimately, however,
the Almighty's approval of Oliphant in her last poem supersedes the fan-

fare of the mortal crowd. For all her professed humility, then, Oliphant's final poem suggests that God himself is the ultimate literary critic.

It was not the first time that Oliphant had subliminally compared the roles of writer and queen in her literary works. In the stringently unsentimental comic novel *Miss Marjoribanks,* the novelist created two female characters—one an artist and the other a self-styled "queen"— who invoke themselves as forceful sovereigns and associate their authority with their respective professions. Beside this comparison, Oliphant set up a motif of the failure of Victorian masculinity in an age in which, via the accession of a queen regnant, both the public and private spheres became explicitly, if ambiguously, feminine. Repeatedly using the metaphor of royalty to describe the protagonist, the narrator of *Miss Marjoribanks* creates a quasi-metatext that subliminally encourages the reader to critique "queenliness" as well as the individual protagonist who would be queen.

That protagonist is nineteen-year-old Lucilla Marjoribanks, who, upon her return to Carlingford after having been away at school, exhibits a "sovereign intelligence." Having studied "political economy," Miss Marjoribanks returns to her widowed father's house and shrewdly forces him to "abdicate" all responsibility for the household. After overthrowing her father, Lucilla prepares for her "reign" and establishes her "inner court and centre of her kingdom" by deposing the next most important in command at the house, the cook. Referred to as "the prime minister," the cook is also "dethroned." In the recital of her "duty" and "the object of [her] life" to "always" be "a comfort to papa," Lucilla barely conceals the fact that, passing over her father's "ancient régime," under her "new regime" this young sovereign does exactly as she pleases.[37]

Lucilla's self-appointed task is to bring about "a great work in Carlingford" by "develop[ing]" the town "from chaos into order and harmony." Acting as the symbol and focal point of social, spiritual, economic, and political meaning in Carlingford, Lucilla puts on a weekly "Thursday Evening," to bring the townsfolk together in a cultural rite. At these carefully choreographed affairs, Lucilla sets up a "temporary throne" from which she displays her "genius." In addition, as "the head of society" in Carlingford, Lucilla provides "for the wants of her subjects." Ten years later, still unmarried and approaching thirty, Lucilla starts the "second period of her career." At this point she takes on the role of electioneer, leading Mr. Ashburton's campaign for MP from

Carlingford. Repeatedly protesting that she does not understand politics, Lucilla remarks that "I am sure I wish I had a vote . . . but I have no vote, and what can a girl do? I am so sorry I don't understand politics." One of the townspeople responds to this coyness, "You have influence, which is a great deal better than a vote . . . and they all say there is nobody like a lady for electioneering—and a young lady above all." [38]

If politics is about power, then Lucilla is a political animal of the highest order for whom having "control of society" was "a great thing." Upon moving into her "second career," she "had come to an age at which she might have gone into Parliament herself had there been no disqualification of sex." Clearly Lucilla is an example of the supremely capable woman who is thwarted by restrictive societal conventions. "Conscious that her capabilities were greater than her work," Lucilla knows that "She was a Power in Carlingford . . . ; but still there is little good in the existence of a Power unless it can be made use of." In one of her most bitterly comic depictions of woman's plight, Oliphant remarks of Lucilla that "though she said nothing about a sphere," she was still "in that condition of mind" when the "ripe female intelligence, not having . . . a nursery and a husband to manage, turns inwards, and begins to 'make a protest' against the existing order of society, and to call the world to account for giving it no due occupation." [39]

When Lucilla's father dies, the town assumes that Lucilla will "abdicate at once." But "even though retired and in crape, the constitutional monarch was still present among her subjects; and nobody could usurp her place. . . . Such an idea would have gone direct in the face of the British Constitution." Lucilla has "no intention of sinking into a nobody, and giving up all power of acting upon her fellow-creatures." Instead of marrying the MP whose campaign she directed, Lucilla ends up marrying her bumbling cousin and convinces him to help her run a "House of Mercy" in a nearby town. Not entirely philanthropic, her motives include expanding her base of power. Fantasizing about "a parish saved, a village reformed, a county reorganised," Lucilla imagines "a triumphant election at the end, the recompense and crown of all, which should put the government of the country itself, to a certain extent, into competent hands." [40] Miss Marjoribanks is certainly not thinking of her husband— or of the MP she put into office—as having the "competent hands," but of herself as the political force behind the scenes.

Lucilla consolidates her power by bringing in two lower-class local artists, the Lake sisters, to entertain at her Thursday soirées. Rose Lake, a graphic artist, takes her profession seriously and views it as a way to achieve a degree of sovereignty not usually associated with her class and gender. "An artist is not just like other people," she says to Lucille, and concludes "It is everybody's duty to leave him undisturbed." A believer in art for art's sake, Rose asserts that "An artist can do many things that other people can't do. We have an exceptional position." When her sister Barbara complains that Lucilla Marjoribanks has shamed Rose by using her as an ornament at the Thursday social gatherings, the artist defiantly exclaims that "We are a family of *artists*. We are everybody's equal, and nobody's equal. We have a rank of our own."[41]

But like Oliphant herself, Rose has to put "an end to [her] Career" and become a "little martyr and heroic victim to duty" in order to take care of her family. Like Lucilla, she has to revise her career goals. When the two meet again ten years later, Rose tells her, "I am not so sure about the moral influence of Art as I used to be—except High Art, to be sure." But though it appears that Rose comes down in the world while Lucilla's stock rises, the narrator makes it clear that even the compromised artist has the power to control representation. Moreover, the narrator metaphorically links this power to the authority inherent in monarchy. In a defining moment, as Rose walks down the posh Grange Lane where Lucilla lives, she "regard[s] the world with that air of frank recognition and acknowledgment which Rose felt she owed as an artist to her fellow-creatures." Viewing the goings-on of Lucilla's ostensible domain, Rose transforms Lucilla's subjects into her own through the sheer representative power of her art. "They were all good subjects more or less," she thought, "and the consciousness that she could draw them and immortalise them gave her the same sense of confidence in their friendliness, and her own perfect command of the situation, as a young princess." The narrator continues, "Rose, too, walked erect and open-eyed, in the confidence of *her* rank, which made her everybody's equal." Oliphant implies here that though Lucilla's genius is "prompt" and "too much for the young artist" Rose, Lucilla's is, nevertheless, a "facile genius."[42]

While the women battle over who has the greater representative power, the men of the town fail to do much of anything. Undermining the British Constitution's view of female sovereignty, in Oliphant's acerbic novel failure is inherent in the masculine rather than the feminine position. As the sovereign who "abdicates" his social position to his daughter, Dr. Marjoribanks reveals his own impotence when he compares his daughter with his nephew: "what a great loss" he thinks "it was to society and to herself that Lucilla was not 'the boy.'" By contrast, his nephew Tom "had carried off the family honours, and was 'the boy' in this limited and unfruitful generation," and was "never likely to do anything to speak of, and would be a poor man if he were to live for a hundred years." Viewed sardonically as ineffectual and obtuse about the politics of the social realm, men are ordered about by the true sovereigns, women. Consistently referring to men as "they" or "*them,*" the narrator constructs the masculine sex as a group of lesser, alien beings who cannot do without the guidance of women. As Dr. Marjoribanks realizes after the "semi–abdication into which he had been beguiled," "The female element, so long peacefully ignored and kept at a distance, had come in again in triumph and taken possession, and the Doctor knew too well by the experience of a long life what a restless and troublesome element it was."[43]

Echoes of Victoria's reign can be heard in this statement. But if women are in the ascendant in the new age that Oliphant's novel describes, the female artist acts as a check on the monolithic royal aspirations of the queen's alter ego. Thus Oliphant indicates the complex unevenness of the age's feminization as well as her own authority in helping to bring it about. Never quite overthrowing the queen, the female artist nevertheless retains a degree of representative power that the queen can never achieve. I would argue that Oliphant's specific statements about Victoria's literary abilities enact the dynamic found in *Miss Marjoribanks.* The two seem to spar at times over their representational authority, but Oliphant always maintains the female professional artist's inalienable possession of a level of power over representation unequaled by the queen. Thus, like Rose, she acknowledges Queen Victoria's "genius" over a particular domain of representation without losing confidence in her own rank.

Oliphant writes of Victoria's first book, *The Early Years of His Royal Highness the Prince Consort,* that it "possess[ed] in one way a power like that of genius, a power almost of creation in its perfect simplicity and truth." The queen's choice of subject matter, her domestic life with

Albert, "was worthy of a poet." Oliphant's explicit reference to Victoria's writing "genius" carefully conveys esteem for the queen while implicitly suggesting, with the qualifications "like that of" and "almost," that the queen's literary power will never measure up to that of a *real* writer, like Oliphant herself, who is the final arbiter in such matters. The suggestion seems to be that Victoria's achievement of "genius" is an uncanny, one-of-a-kind thing not to be produced again. In fact, Oliphant apparently views Victoria as a primitive artist a là Henri Rousseau, one whose genius rested in honesty and pristine, innocent intuition. "Nature," she notes, "has given her a pretty simplicity of utterance, . . . the language preeminently of the happy and guileless young Englishwoman of her own era, in whom feeling and sentiment were supreme, and intellectualism of every kind was still sometimes gently, sometimes severely, discouraged." As Oliphant sees it, it is the monarch's artlessness that marks her writing so unmistakably. Though her royal attendants were shocked that the queen desired to publish her diary, it became obvious that the "pages so overbrimming with personal feeling, such as few persons in any condition of life and no sovereign had ever attempted to express so freely," would make as "simple and sincere a claim upon the sympathy of her people."[44]

The professional writer, however, makes it very clear that an amateur writer like the queen has only one chance at genius. Remarking that "We will not say that the 'Leaves from the Highland Journal' were equally impressive," Oliphant suggests that "Such a story as her Majesty had to tell can be but once told." Though there were still some "glamour" and "wonderful touches of natural feeling" to be found in the Highland journals, yet, according to Oliphant, "it would have been better had the one unique performance been left as the only one." Asserting her own prerogative to judge stylistic matters, Oliphant candidly exposes Victoria's deficiencies in this area, noting that she "is no student of style, nor does she ever, we imagine, ponder and wait for the best word." "We will not pretend to claim for the Queen any purely literary gift," Oliphant pronounces, implying that there are degrees and kinds of genius associated with the power to represent.[45] Clearly Victoria's genius, like Lucilla Marjoribanks's, is of a "prompt" and "facile" type, unlike the artist's sovereign genius of "immortalising" the subject. Though Oliphant also refers to her own "artless art," she set things straight when a naïf like the queen aspires to literary greatness. And she does so without the kind of veiled assaults that Dickens and Barrett Browning made on the queen.

This, in fact, is what is so refreshing about Oliphant's critique of the Highland Journals—that the author sees her profession as equally important to Victoria's without denigrating either woman. She writes with sincere admiration, "there have been Queens as great as any man who ever sat upon a throne. It is perhaps the *rôle* in which we should least look for excellence, but it is one in which it is most usually found." Refuting the conventional wisdom that the throne was a masculine arena, she continues, "There is something in the position of sovereign which seems to develop and call forth the qualities of a woman beyond that of any other occupation." And though "The number of reigning women has no doubt been very limited," it is "curious to note how kindly the feminine mind takes to the trade of ruling whenever the opportunity occurs to it." [46]

Oliphant includes herself within the realm of legitimate sovereign power when she asserts that "Politics are the occupation and profession of the royal worker, as literature is of the writer—the grandest trade of all, and the most exciting." [47] An extraordinary intellect stands behind this statement. Its ambiguity—is it the royal worker or the writer who practices the "grandest trade of all"?—creates a relationship between queen and writer that is at once competitive and cooperative. Both are consummate professionals in their respective fields and this balance brings with it a certain dynamic mutual authority as well as a generosity of spirit: Female authority is so abundant that there is more than enough to go around. Thus, without condescending to or disparaging Victoria, Oliphant ingeniously amplifies the female writer's authority without taking anything away from the queen's professional expertise.

In judging the queen's literary talent, Oliphant sees it from a broad cultural perspective that allows her to magnify rather than minimize her own share in cultural capital. "[I]n the eyes of a person whose trade it is to write, . . , the Queen cannot be called a connoisseur. Like most people deeply occupied, Darwin, for instance, she reads novels largely; but, also like Darwin, is not so much concerned about the quality of them or their claim to be called literature." Associating the queen's work and reading pleasure with the reading habits of one of the chief Victorian male scientists, Oliphant implies that a queen is a professional in a field of study like any of the other professions. Understanding that the cultural work of representation must occur in many fields, Oliphant does not demand that the queen do the same cultural work the writer does, reasoning that it cannot "be claimed for the Queen with any truth that she is a patron, or critic, or authority in literature. This is not the turn of her genius." The female monarch is not so much interested in reading books per se as in "that science of life to which all the human combinations possible, the variations of race, the multitudinous drama of family history, are an absorbing study."[48]

Oliphant's description of the scientific nature of Victoria's "reading" matter anticipates the postmodern understanding of texts. "Her occupation in this world is with men and women. . . . She reads those human books and regulates them in their places with instinctive exactitude and knowledge; they are of more importance than the other kind of books to which we appropriate that name."[49] Enlarging the meaning of "reading" to include analysis of the world and human beings as texts, Oliphant's representation of the queen's profession presumes that "reading" *is* the fundamental skill necessary to cultural work, a skill taught and exemplified by professional readers and writers such as Oliphant herself. In fact, Oliphant tropes the writer and the queen as the consummate reproductive agents of culture itself. Thus Oliphant's "gorgeous illusion" is that both the sovereign and the sovereign self are women of letters, who read and are read and who are potent agents of culture. Unlike Dickens and Barrett Browning, Oliphant had no need to depose the monarch in order to establish her own authority. Rather, without trading places with Victoria, Oliphant assumes the complexity of representation and the resulting need for many representative agents.

This democratic stance does not stop Oliphant from recognizing that in a monarchical system the subjects of the kingdom will look to the monarch as the chief subject of representation. In that regard, Oliphant is canny about what gives Victoria her authority, and that is something that neither Oliphant herself nor any other professional Victorian writer could claim. Oliphant matter-of-factly states that the queen can require the British reader's empathy, interest, and submission to her authority simply because she is a queen who is willing to represent her personal life, her vulnerability, and her feminization to her subjects. "She came to her people" as "she had gone to the poor woman on Deeside, with hands held out, appealing to their kindness. 'Weep with me,' was the outcry of her heart." The "world responded with an answering outcry of sympathy which was full also of amazement and pity and love. For who else had ever so laid bare her heart?"[50] Oliphant concludes, "who else had the right, the privilege to" expect so much from her readers?

With almost ruthless discernment (pace, Princess Di), Oliphant dissects the authority a feminized monarch can achieve when she is willing to exhibit her feelings. Unlike any other Victorian author, including Oliphant herself, the queen was "secure . . . and never doubting, of the interest, the sympathy, the affection of all." But Oliphant also shrewdly recognizes that Victoria's genius rested in the fact that she herself believed in the fiction of royalty and her own representation of it. "Sometimes there is the highest truth in that fiction of royalty which says, '*My* people,' when a monarch has the heart and courage to believe and trust to it." Oliphant knows that the queen could depend upon the "gorgeous illusions" of her subjects with greater certainty than any other professional, including the writer, who increasingly asserted his superior cultural importance in this era. Astutely independent in her deference to Victoria's unique professional position, Oliphant admits that "the Queen reckoned upon her kingdom with such a certainty as is more persuasive than any argument. She knew that all hearts would acknowledge her claim. This required a great trust, a great faith in her people; but it was fully justified."[51]

Oliphant's willingness to accept Victoria's unique representational position is inextricably bound up in her endorsement of the queen's professionalism and her amalgamation of that profession with her own. After all, as a professional creator of fiction, Oliphant relied as much as the queen did on the subject's faith in fiction. By critiquing and elegizing the particular gorgeous illusion of Victoria's womanly professionalism, Oliphant helped to deconstruct the culture's debilitating fictions about women's helplessness. She also pointed out how, too often, Victorian men became failures in fact and fiction because the culture could not conceive of a way for men and women to succeed at the same time in the same spheres. She thus acknowledged that the kind of representation the female monarch professionally carried out was as important to the culture as were the representations created by Victorian writers. To Oliphant's mind, the queen filled a singular, predetermined space already set aside for her to represent, one that did not need to be seen by writers as a competitive field of representation. Not meant to be "an artist, nor one fitted to take the laurels of literature or produce any excelling work of that description," Victoria was, instead, "illustrious" in "the art of reigning—a greater craft and a more difficult than those by pen or pencil." "[W]hen there is trouble at home or tumult abroad, then this lady, who in other matters pretends to no knowledge beyond that of an ordinary woman, rises above the everyday level, and takes a place which Shakespeare would never have attempted to fill." Thus, "hold[ing] no merely formal place as head" of England, Queen Victoria represented the British people in ways no writer could. "Strenuously stand[ing] for peace, for order, for law, altogether just, altogether disinterested, having no advancement to look for, no risking of losing office,"[52] a queen's work, according to Oliphant, was to *be* her people's "gorgeous illusion." Though the queen's aesthetic tastes were pedestrian, just as Oliphant's profession was pedestrian, the royal trade was, like the writer's, representation itself. Implicitly inscribing her own generosity and dynamism in her reading of the queen, Oliphant's homage to Victoria recognizes that this female monarch was a gorgeous fiction to her people, a powerful representation that neither great nor pedestrian writers need try to surpass.

There were perhaps as many Queen Victorias as there were British subjects—more when one considers the non-British population to whom she was also an important representation of authority. Given her "representation of excess,"[53] Victoria could be and was used for almost all political purposes. My own use of the queen is surely as political—and as conflicted—as those of the Victorian writers I analyze. I recognize, for example, that my class politics are interrogated by my fascination with the position of Victorian women in general and of this queen in particular, just as my gender politics are magnified and articulated through this fascination. That the Victorian writer was also fascinated by the chief representative of the culture should come as no surprise. As I have tried to show, the Victorian age's disturbing constructions of gender cannot be considered extraneous to the exchanges that took place between this queen and Victorian professional writers.

As the supreme symbol of authority, the queen inhabited a site at which British cultural capital was exchanged, contested, and represented. Problematic and troublesome, Victoria Regina generated a certain heat in Victorian writers concerned not only with their professional trade but also with the trade-offs they had to make in order to assume mastery simultaneously over gender roles and literary authority. As the variety of "gorgeous illusions" about female sovereignty vis-à-vis women's so-called natural duties suggest, commentaries on Victoria's reign always incorporated overdetermined anxieties about her gender. These "gorgeous illusions" about Victoria also show how central she was to British concepts of subjecthood, just as they indicate Victorians' conflicted feelings about their queen's long-lived, robust selfhood. Given many male writers' metaphorical representations of the Victorian age as emasculated, it seems reasonable to conclude that these same writers experienced an identity crisis as long as a woman ruled their country. The tensions aroused by the accession and sixty-three-year reign of a female sovereign, in a culture in which power and privilege were the province of the male sex, provide fertile ground for future studies of the pressures created by the "gorgeous illusion" of sexual difference. The various ways in which women writers responded to Victoria's queenly power—their sympathy, emulation, criticism, and competition—also call for further study.

Notes

Works frequently cited in the notes are identified by the following abbreviations.

A&L *Autobiography and Letters of Mrs. Margaret Oliphant.* Ed. Mrs. Harry Coghill. 1899. Reprint, Leicester: Leicester Univ. Press, 1974.

LCD *Pilgrim Edition of the Letters of Charles Dickens.* 8 vols. Oxford: Clarendon Press, 1965–1995.

EBB/MRM *Letters of Elizabeth Barrett Browning to Mary Russell Mitford, 1836–1854.* Ed. Meredith B. Raymond and Mary Rose Sullivan. 3 vols. Winfield, Kans.: Wedgestone Press, 1983.

NLS National Library of Scotland

QV Margaret Oliphant. *Queen Victoria: A Personal Sketch.* London: Cassell, 1900.

RA QVJ Royal Archives, Queen Victoria's Journals

QVS Adrienne Munich. *Queen Victoria's Secrets.* New York: Columbia Univ. Press, 1996.

RA Royal Archives

Introduction

1. *QVS*, 2.
2. Thompson, *Queen Victoria;* Langland, *Nobody's Angels,* 66; *QVS,* 2; Helsinger, Sheets, and Veeder, "Queen Victoria and 'The Shadow Side' "; Homans, "Queen Victoria's Highland Journal."
3. Casteras, "The Wise Child," 183; Homans and Munich, eds., *Remaking Queen Victoria,* 2, 5, 6.
4. Homans, " 'To the Queen's Private Apartments,' " 6–7.
5. Dickens, *Little Dorrit,* 145–65; Gagnier, *Subjectivities,* 10; "Performance of Obvious Duties," *The Queen, The Lady's Newspaper,* 5 Jan. 1867, 3.
6. Munich, "Queen Victoria, Empire, and Excess," 278.
7. C. Bullock, *Queen's Resolve,* 11–12.
8. Ibid., 14, 45.
9. One of the people, "Queen of Queens," 6–7.
10. Ibid., 8–9.
11. Ibid., 11–12.
12. "Father's Prayer Answered"; Ward, "Song for the Jubilee," 216.
13. "Queen's Address to the Volunteer Army."
14. H. S. Bullock, "The King Comes!," 265–66.

I. "In the Reign of Queen Dick": Legal Fictions and the Constitution of Female Sovereignty

1. Laqueur, *Making Sex,* 149.
2. Fredeman, "Introduction: 'England Our Home, Victoria Our Queen,'" 8; *Illustrated London News,* 26 Jan. 1901, 101; *QV,* 138.
3. Featured in K. Martin, *Crown and the Establishment,* 59; Gernsheim and Gernsheim, *Queen Victoria,* 74.
4. L. F. Austin, "Our Notebook" and "Queen Victoria," *Illustrated London News,* 26 Jan. 1901, 100.
5. Poovey, *Making A Social Body.*
6. John Locke, *The Second Treatise of Government,* ed. Thomas P. Peardon (Indianapolis: Bobbs-Merrill, 1952), 17, quoted in Mary Poovey, *Uneven Developments,* 76; Corrigan and Sayer, *Great Arch,* 12.
7. Blackstone, *Commentaries,* 1: statute nos. 218, 224.
8. More, *Latin Epigrams of Thomas More,* 172.
9. Pratt, "Women, Literature, and National Brotherhood," 30.
10. Gagnier, *Subjectivities,* 6.
11. Vaihinger, *Philosophy of "As If,"* 84, xli, 12, 83, 57, 62.
12. Blackstone, *Commentaries,* 1: statute no. 422.
13. Ibid., 1: statute nos. 442, 445.
14. Gagnier, *Subjectivities,* 8.
15. Blackstone, *Commentaries,* 1: statute no. 41.
16. Trimmer, *Fabulous Histories,* 147.
17. Patten, "George's Hive," 38.
18. Blackstone, *Commentaries,* 1: statute nos. 244, 246.
19. Bender, *Imagining the Penitentiary,* 35, 37; letter to Victoria, Princess Royal, 24 Mar. 1858, *Translations of Extracts of Letters from Albert,* 190, RA Y190/10.
20. Blackstone, *Commentaries,* 1: statute nos. 23, 123.
21. Maitland, *Collected Papers,* 3: 211, 210, 280.
22. Ibid., 3: 245.
23. Ibid., 3: 250, 251.
24. Ibid., 3: 251–52, 269.
25. Blackstone, *Commentaries,* 1: statute nos. 39, 7, 9.
26. Disraeli, *Sybil,* 49–50.
27. Bradlaugh, *Impeachment of the House of Brunswick,* 154, 160.
28. RA QVJ, 25 May 1880.
29. Letter to Queen Victoria, 28 Jan. 1874, RA L13/159.
30. Bagehot, *English Constitution,* xxxvi–vii.
31. Fox, "A Political and Social Anomaly," 637.
32. Old England, "This Country Must Be Governed," 6, 8, 17.
33. A friend of the people, "Letter to the Queen on the State of the Monarchy," 7.
34. Ibid., 7, 9, 6.
35. One of Themselves, "Address to the People," 2, 18.
36. One of Her Majesty's Most Loyal Subjects, "Letter to the Queen, On her Retirement," 10, 12–13.
37. Ibid., 17.

38. Ibid., 43–44, 67, 78.
39. W. Anderson Smith, quoted in Killham, *Tennyson and "The Princess,"* 105–106.
40. Quoted in Langland, *Nobody's Angels,* 65.
41. Corelli, *Passing of the Great Queen,* 8–9, 83, 7–8.
42. Ibid., 11, 12, 13, 16.
43. Ibid., 30–31.
44. Ibid., 18–19, 20.
45. Queen Victoria's statement quoted in Helsinger, Sheets, and Veeder, "Queen Victoria and 'The Shadow Side,'" 68–69; "Franchise for Women," *The Queen, The Lady's Newspaper,* 6 Apr. 1867, 263.
46. "Political Persons," *The Queen, The Lady's Newspaper,* 6 Apr. 1867, 263; Bodichon, "Authorities and Precedents," 65, 69.
47. Swiney, *Cosmic Procession,* 54, xi, 59.
48. Poovey, *Making A Social Body.*
49. Homans, "Powers of Powerlessness," 249.
50. Gay, *Bourgeois Experience,* vol. 3: 300; *National Memorial to His Royal Highness the Prince Consort,* 94.
51. Grey, *Early Years of His Royal Highness the Prince Consort,* 230.
52. *Queen Victoria in Her Letters and Journals,* ed. C. Hibbert, 152.
53. RA QVJ, 9 June 1842; *Queen Victoria in Her Letters and Journals,* ed. C. Hibbert, 103.
54. *Gentlewoman's In Memoriam,* In Memoriam no., Jan. 1901, 31.
55. Quoted in Thompson, *Queen Victoria,* 38.
56. Strachey, *Queen Victoria,* 161.
57. C. Bullock, *Queen's Resolve,* 154.
58. O'Doherty, "On Prince Albert's Birthday," *Fraser's Magazine* 22, no. 129. (Sept. 1840): 382.
59. Ibid.
60. Strachey, *Queen Victoria,* 285–86.
61. Ibid., 289–90.
62. Grey, *Early Years,* xxii.
63. Ibid., 255, 256, 227.
64. Ibid., 255.
65. Ibid., 256.
66. Ibid., 257.
67. Quoted in Helsinger, Sheets, and Veeder, "Queen Victoria and 'The Shadow Side,'" 1: 68–69.
68. RA QVJ, 24–25 June 1837, 1 July 1837, 22 June 1838.
69. Quoted in Longford, *Victoria R. I.,* 105, 106, 133.
70. Grey, *Early Years,* 144.
71. RA QVJ, 20 June 1845.
72. Homans, "Powers of Powerlessness," 245.
73. RA QVJ, 18 Dec. 1839.
74. Quoted in Helsinger, Sheets, Veeder, "Queen Victoria and 'The Shadow Side,'" 1:66.
75. Quoted in Homans, "Queen Victoria's Highland Journal."
76. Quoted in Thompson, *Queen Victoria,* 55.
77. *QV,* 62.

II. The Royal Crown and the Laurel Crown: Gendering Sovereign Subjects and Professions

1. Parrinder, *Authors and Authority,* 21.
2. Cannadine, "Context, Performance and Meaning of Ritual," 133, 121.
3. One of Her Majesty's Most Loyal Subjects, "Letter to the Queen, On her Retirement," 16.
4. Ibid., 14.
5. Ibid.
6. Ibid., 60, 61, 62.
7. Strachey, *Queen Victoria,* 398–99.
8. Ibid., 401.
9. One of Her Majesty's Servants, *Private Life of the Queen,* 70, 71.
10. Ibid., 69.
11. Gernsheim and Gernsheim, *Queen Victoria,* 261, 264; Kaplan, *Dickens,* 549.
12. Richards, *Commodity Culture of Victorian England,* 71, 86, 92; Fredeman, "'She Wrought Her People Lasting Good,'" 224.
13. Richards, *Commodity Culture of Victorian England,* 2, 14, 163; McClintock, *Imperial Leather.*
14. Braddon, "Good Hermione," 53, insert nos. 1, 2.
15. Ibid., 53, insert no. 2.
16. Strachey, *Queen Victoria,* 417, 194–95.
17. St. Aubyn, "Queen Victoria as an Author," 128–129.
18. One of Her Majesty's Servants, *Private Life of the Queen,* 168.
19. Vallone, "The Princess and the Authoress"; Shelley, "A Defence of Poetry," 737–38.
20. Gagnier, *Subjectivities,* 32.
21. Sutherland, *Victorian Novelists and Publishers,* 94.
22. Poovey, *Uneven Developments,* 103.
23. Gallagher, "George Eliot and *Daniel Deronda,*" 43.
24. Not only the Victorian writers themselves but also current feminist writers recognize this historical process. See, for example, Nancy Armstrong, *Desire and Domestic Fiction: A Political History of the Novel* (New York: Oxford Univ. Press, 1987); Langland, "Nation and Nationality," 25.
25. *QVS,* 158; and Homans, "'To the Queen's Private Apartments,'" 2.
26. Heller, *Dead Secrets,* 70, 66, 72.
27. See Homans, "'To the Queen's Private Apartments,'" 1–41; Nadel, "Portraits of the Queen," 169–191; and Casteras, "The Wise Child," on this topic.
28. Casteras, "The Wise Child," 182.
29. See Froula, "Gender and the Law of Genre," 155–64, on this topic.
30. Augustine Birrell, *Seven Lectures on the Law and History of Copyright in Books,* quoted in Stewart, *Crimes of Writing,* 10, 12; see also Stewart's discussion on pp. 10–16.
31. See my discussion of the male Victorian's fear of emasculation in *Consuming Fictions,* 46–47.
32. Montrose, "'Shaping Fantasies,'" 31–64; Munich, "'Capture the Heart of a Queen,'" 23–44.
33. O'Toole, "A Full, True, and Particular Account," 592.
34. Foz, "Fishing scene in Windsor Park," featured in Jones, *Cartoon History of the Monarch,* 110.

35. Quoted in Thompson, *Queen Victoria,* 43.
36. Staker, ed., *Waiting for World's End,* 347.
37. Strachey, *Queen Victoria,* 49, 53.
38. Platt, *Queenly Womanhood,* 1, 115.
39. Ibid., 154.
40. Ibid., 157, 129, 131, 132.
41. Carlyle, *Collected Letters,* vol. 3: 245.
42. Quoted in Parrinder, *Authors and Authority,* 109.
43. Carlyle, *On Heroes,* 193.
44. Said, *Beginnings,* 83.
45. Houston, *Consuming Fictions,* 46−47.
46. Letter to Robert Mitchell, 24 Oct. 1814, in Carlyle, *Collected Letters,* vol. 1: 32.
47. Letters to John A. Carlyle, 15 Feb. 1840, 16 Apr. 1839, and to Jean Carlyle Aitken, 11 Mar. 1869, in Carlyle, *Collected Letters,* vol. 12: 48, vol. 11: 86−87; see also Sanders's discussion of Carlyle's view of the Queen in "Carlyle's Pen Portraits of Queen Victoria," 217.
48. Gilbert, "The Female King," 865; *Works of Alfred Lord Tennyson,* vol. 1: 1−2.
49. Ricks, "The Princess and the Queen," 133−39.
50. Tennyson, *The Princess, Works of Alfred Lord Tennyson,* vol. 3: 12−13.
51. Ibid., 178, 174.
52. Ruskin, "Of Queen's Gardens," 129.
53. Ibid.; "Of King's Treasures," 54.
54. Henderson, *Swinburne,* 48−49. Adrienne Munich also discusses Swinburne's parodies of the Queen in *QVS,* 176−77.
55. One of Her Majesty's Servants, *Private Life of the Queen,* 126.
56. Haggard, *She,* 255.
57. Ibid., 5, 255.
58. Ibid., 256, 295.
59. Ibid., 288.
60. Corelli, *Passing of the Great Queen,* 40−41.
61. Rossetti, "Our Widowed Queen," *Complete Poems,* vol. 3: 284.
62. Ibid., 284−85.
63. "By the authors of 'Our Queen' and 'Life of General Gordon,'" *Queens of Literature of the Victorian Period,* 185.
64. Quoted in Thompson, *Queen Victoria,* xvi.
65. 12 January 1868, *Selections from George Eliot's Letters,* 341.
66. Wolff, *Sensational Victorian,* 19.
67. Braddon journal entry 23 June 1897, *Diaries.*
68. Braddon, *During Her Majesty's Pleasure,* 167.
69. Braddon, "Good Hermione," 1, 3.
70. Ibid., 2−3.
71. Ibid., 3, 23.
72. Ibid., 7, 8, 23.
73. Ibid., 7, 8, 41.
74. Ibid., insert E, 68.
75. Ibid., 68, insert 69.
76. Jewett, "Queen's Twin," 146−47, 155, 147.

77. Ibid., 162, 163.

78. Ibid., 156, 160.

79. Ibid., 163, 164, 165.

80. Whiting, "LILIES," 174, 175.

81. Ibid.

III. *"From the Humblest of Authors to One of the Greatest"*: The Queen and Dickens's Failure of Masculinity

1. Letter to Basil Hall, 28 Jan. 1841, *LCD*, 2: 196–97.

2. One of Her Majesty's Servants, *Private Life of the Queen*, 126, 127.

3. Letters to Daniel Maclise and to Lady Holland, 22 Mar. 1842, *LCD*, 3: 154, 151.

4. Letter [21] Mar. 1851, *LCD*, 6: 325.

5. Letter 3 July 1848, *LCD*, 5: 357.

6. Kent, *Authentic Record of the Public Banquet Given to Mr. Charles Dickens*, quoted in Kaplan, *Dickens*, 503.

7. Letter to Miss Burdett Coutts, 3 Feb. 1857, *LCD*, 8: 273.

8. Letter to Miss Burdett Coutts, *LCD*, 8: 356.

9. Letters 20 June 1857, 5 and 6 July 1857, *LCD*, 8: 357, 366.

10. Letter to Dickens, 5 July 1857, *LCD*, 8: 366n.

11. Wilson, *Life and Times of Queen Victoria*, 3: 381–82.

12. Letter to John Forster, [30 Mar. 1858], *LCD*, 8: 540.

13. Wilson, *Life and Times of Queen Victoria*, 3: 383.

14. St. John Nevill, *Life at the Court of Queen Victoria*, 9.

15. Letter to Richard Monckton Milnes, 1 Feb. 1840, *LCD*, 2: 16–17.

16. 11 Feb. 1840; F, 2, viii, 155, *LCD*, 2: 23n.

17. [12 Feb. 1840], *LCD*, 2: 24.

18. Ibid.

19. [13 Feb. 1840], *LCD*, 2: 25–26, 29.

20. One of Her Majesty's Servants, *Private Life of the Queen*, 126–27.

21. "A Physician's Dreams," 136–37.

22. Houston, "Gender Construction and the *Kunstlerroman*," 213–36; in chapter three of *Consuming Fictions*, I also discuss the Inimitable's desire to be female.

23. Stephen, "Mr. Dickens as a Politician," 1857, quoted in Lenard, *Preaching Pity*, forthcoming.

24. Hutton 1858, quoted in Lenard, *Preaching Pity*, forthcoming.

25. Dickens, *Dombey and Son*, 234.

26. Ibid., 150–51, 210, 234.

27. Letters to Madame de la Rue, 17 Apr. 1846, H. P. Smith, 22 Apr. 1846, and John Forster, 13 Aug. 1846, *LCD*, 4: 533, 540, 612–13; Gilman, *Charlotte Perkins Gilman Reader*, 20.

28. Knoepflmacher, "From Outrage to Rage," 75–96; Myers, "Lost Self: Gender in *David Copperfield*," 120–32; Dickens, *David Copperfield*, 1.

29. Dickens, *David Copperfield*, 174, 185.

30. Bristow, "Coventry Patmore and the Womanly Mission," 136.

31. Dickens, *David Copperfield*, 175.

32. Ibid.

33. Dickens, "Story of Richard Doubledick." "Dick" referred to "Dictionary," that is, to "fine words," in Britain from 1870 and in America from 1860. From 1660, the phrase "that happened in the reign of Queen Dick" meant "any absurd old story." From 1870, "swallow the dick" meant "to use long words" without knowing their meaning. "Up to dick," from around 1870, meant "artful"; "dick in the green," from 1805, meant "inferior" and "weak"; "Dick's hatband"—which links the failed writing of Mr. Dick and Mr. Strong—meant strange or "queer." "Dicked in the nob," from 1820, meant "silly" or "crazy." Thus Dickens presciently and brilliantly intertwined in one word the writerly relationship between the authoritative writer David and the inferior writers Strong and Dick. He also alluded to the strangeness of authority residing in the narrative of a Queen Dick, if you will. Partridge, *Dictionary of Historical Slang*, 254–255.

34. Dickens, *David Copperfield*, 185.

35. Ibid., 517, 185, 558.

36. Ibid., 204. See also note 33 on the meaning of "dick's hatband."

37. Ibid., 210–211.

38. Ibid., 447.

39. Ibid., 589, 517–518.

40. "Advertisement in Athenaeum for the Dickens Editions," March 1847, quoted in Sutherland, *Victorian Novelists and Publishers*, 35.

IV. Womanizing Sovereignty: Queen Victoria and the Victorian Queen of Poetry

1. Quoted in Donaldson, *Elizabeth Barrett Browning*, 119.

2. 31 [*sic* for 29?] Feb. 1840, *EBB/MRM*, 1: 183.

3. Quoted in L'Estrange, *Life of Mary Russell Mitford*, 2: 243.

4. 21 Mar. 1842, *EBB/MRM*, 1: 364–65; 1 Feb. 1838.

5. Letter to M. R. Mitford, 9 Dec. 1842, *EBB/MRM*, 2: 114.

6. Letter to M. R. Mitford, 9 Oct. 1841, *EBB/MRM*, 1: 283.

7. Quoted in Donaldson, *Elizabeth Barrett Browning*, 51, 83, 119.

8. Browning, *Aurora Leigh* (Chicago: Academy), 37.

9. 20 Mar. 1845, quoted in *Letters of Robert Browning and Elizabeth Barrett Browning 1845–1846*, 1: 42.

10. Letter to M. R. Mitford, 24 Mar. 1842, *EBB/MRM*, 1: 370.

11. 24 May 1843, *EBB/MRM*, 2: 231.

12. [16?] Oct. 1843, *EBB/MRM*, 2: 330.

13. 20 Apr. 1844, *EBB/MRM*, 2: 406.

14. Letter to M. R. Mitford, [16?] Jan. 1844, *EBB/MRM*, 2: 375.

15. 22 July 1837, *EBB/MRM*, 1: 41; Browning, *Seraphim and Other Poems*, 324–325.

16. Letter to M. R. Mitford, 22 July 1837, *EBB/MRM*, 1: 40–41; Browning, *Seraphim and Other Poems*, 329, 330–331.

17. Letters to M. R. Mitford, 22 July 1837 and 21 May 1842, *EBB/MRM*, 1: 41, 416.

18. Letters to M. R. Mitford, 7 Dec. 1843 and 23 Nov. 1842, *EBB/MRM*, 2: 357, 86.

19. Letters to M. R. Mitford, 11 July 1839 and 27 Sept. 1839, *EBB/MRM*, 1: 137, 156.

20. *Poetical Works of Elizabeth Barrett Browning*, 343.

21. Ibid.

22. 25 Apr. 1842, *EBB/MRM*, 1: 400.

23. *EBB/MRM*, 3: 22.

24. 22 Jan. 1845, *EBB/MRM*, 3: 63.

25. Letters to M. R. Mitford, 28 Jan. 1845 and 21 Nov. 1842, *EBB/MRM*, 3: 64–65, 2: 86.

26. Letters to M. R. Mitford, 31 [*sic* for 29] Feb. 1840 and 7–12 Mar. 1839, *EBB/MRM*, 1: 183, 113.

27. Letter to M. R. Mitford, 2 May 1845, *EBB/MRM*, 3: 104–105.

28. 13 Apr. 1842, *EBB/MRM*, 1: 394.

29. 21 Nov. 1842, *EBB/MRM*, 2: 86.

30. I also discuss the motif of prostitution in "Gender Construction and the *Kunstlerroman*," 213–36.

31. 1 Mar. 1865, *Queen Victoria in her Letters and Journal*, ed. Hibbert, 188; letter to Vicky, 6 May 1863, *Letters of Queen Victoria to her eldest daughter*, quoted in Longford, *Victoria R. I.*, 306; Browning, *Aurora Leigh*, 164.

32. Forms of *queen* occur thirteen times, of *royal*, six times, of *majesty*, three times, of *king*, thirteen times, of *crown*, twenty times in *Aurora Leigh*; see *An Elizabeth Barrett Browning Concordance*, 3: 1285, 1389, 1402, 1313, 1158; letter to Anna Jameson, 2 Feb. 1857, quoted in Browning, *Aurora Leigh: Authoritative Text*, 342.

33. 27 Sept. 1842, *EBB/MRM*, 2: 34.

34. Browning, *Aurora Leigh*, 335, 341, 351.

35. Browning, *Aurora Leigh*, 27.

36. Walkowitz, *Prostitution and Victorian Society*, 70.

37. Browning, *Aurora Leigh*, 62, 123, 127.

38. Ibid., 165.

39. Ibid., 79.

40. Ibid., 87.

41. Ibid., 266.

42. Ibid., 163, 164, 316.

43. Ibid., 246, 130.

V. "The Grandest Trade of All": Professional Exchanges between the Queen and Margaret Oliphant

1. Oliphant, *Annals of a Publishing House*, 2: 475.

2. Trela, ed., *Margaret Oliphant*, 18, 21.

3. Jay, "Freed by Necessity, Trapped by the Market," 135.

4. *A&L*, 4, 67, 125, 126.

5. Ibid., 6, 129, 126, 106.

6. Ibid., 131, 5, 75.

7. Ibid., 86, 219.

8. Ibid., 169.

9. Theodore Martin, letter to Oliphant, 30 Jan. 1868, NLS MS 23210.

10. "Queen of the Highlands," *Blackwoods Magazine* (Feb. 1868): 243; Letter to Mrs. Tulloch, 3 Oct. 1868, *A&L*, 220.

11. Williams, *Margaret Oliphant*, 91, 92.

12. Letter to Mr. Craik, 29 Jan. 1881, *A&L*, 294.

13. Oliphant, *Historical Sketches of the Reign of George Second*, 1, 2.

14. Oliphant, *Historical Sketches of the Reign of Queen Anne*, 1–2, 4.
15. *QV*, 1, 2–3.
16. *Victorian Age of English Literature*, 1.
17. *QV*, 72, 70.
18. One of Her Majesty's Servants, *Private Life of the Queen*, 215.
19. Quoted in Colby and Colby, *Equivocal Virtue*, 237.
20. *QV*, 42.
21. Ibid., 138, 136, 68.
22. Ibid., 129.
23. Ibid., 88.
24. Ibid., 118, 115, 119, 139.
25. Letter to Blackwood, 8 Aug. 1867, quoted in Williams, *Margaret Oliphant*, 90–91.
26. Letter to Blackwood, n.d., 1867, quoted in Williams, *Margaret Oliphant*, 91; letter to Blackwood, quoted in Colby and Colby, *Equivocal Virtue*, 268 n51.
27. Letter to Blackwood, n.d., quoted in Colby and Colby, *Equivocal Virtue*, 117.
28. Jay, *Mrs. Oliphant*, 256.
29. Letter to Sir Fleetwood Edwards, 20 Mar. 1896, RA PPVic. 1896/14345.
30. Letter to M. Oliphant, 28 Mar. 1896, RA PPVic. 1896/14345; letter to Miss Blackwood, 11 Oct. 1861, *A&L*, 176.
31. 9 Nov. 1881 and 13 Nov. 1881, RA PPVic. 1881/11773.
32. Obituaries from *Daily Mail*, 30 June 1897; *Chronicle*, 28 June 1897; *The Pall Mall Gazette*, 28 June 1897; *The Star*, 28 June 1897, NLS MS 23211.
33. Letters to M. Oliphant, 28 Feb. 1886 and 2 Mar. 1886, NLS MS 23210.
34. Tulloch, "The Reader: Mrs. Oliphant."
35. Oliphant, Lines upon her impending death, NLS MS 23210, no. 217.
36. "22nd June 1897," *A&L*, 435–36.
37. Oliphant, *Miss Marjoribanks*, 44, 33, 111, 179, 260, 50, 48, 51, 81, 72.
38. Ibid., 44, 103, 99, 239, 265, 267, 332, 338, 346, 342, 338, 340, 373.
39. Ibid., 394–95.
40. Ibid., 420–21, 435, 497.
41. Ibid., 251, 117.
42. Ibid., 335, 336, 433, 163–64, 252.
43. Ibid., 400, 122, 125, 73.
44. *QV*, 122, 123.
45. Ibid., 124, 122.
46. Ibid., 142; Oliphant, *Historical Sketches of the Reign of George Second*, 1.
47. *QV*, 70.
48. Ibid., 140, 142.
49. Ibid., 140.
50. Ibid., 124.
51. Ibid.
52. Ibid., 142.
53. Munich, "Queen Victoria, Empire, and Excess," 269.

Bibliography

"Advertisement for the Dickens Editions." *Athenaeum* March 1847. Quoted in J. A. Sutherland, *Victorian Novelists and Publishers*. London: Athlone Press, 1976.

All the Year Round. 3 Dec. 1859.

Authors of "Our Queen" and "Life of General Gordon." *Queens of Literature of the Victorian Period*. London: Walter Scott, 1886. National Library of Scotland Bf.8.2.

Bagehot, Walter. *The English Constitution*. London: Henry S. King, 1872.

Bender, John. *Imagining the Penitentiary: Fiction and the Architecture of Mind in Eighteenth-Century England*. Chicago: Univ. of Chicago Press, 1987.

Blackstone, William. *Commentaries on the Laws of England*. 2d ed. 2 vols. Chicago: Callaghan, 1872.

Bodichon, Barbara L. S. "Authorities and Precedents for Giving the Suffrage to Qualified Women." *The Englishwoman's Review* no. 2 (Jan. 1867): 63–75.

Braddon, Mary. *Diaries*. 25 vols. Robert E. Wolff Collection. Harry Ransom Humanities Research Center at The University of Texas at Austin.

———. *During Her Majesty's Pleasure*. London: Hurst and Blackett, 1908.

———. "The Good Hermione: A Story for the Jubilee." 1886. Robert E. Wolff Collection. Harry Ransom Humanities Research Center at The University of Texas at Austin.

Bradlaugh, Charles. *The Impeachment of the House of Brunswick*. Boston: William F. Gill, 1875.

Bristow, Joseph. "Coventry Patmore and the Womanly Mission of the Mid-Victorian Poet." In *Sexualities in Victorian Britain,* ed. Andrew H. Miller and James Eli Adams, pp. 118–39. Bloomington: Indiana Univ. Press, 1996.

Browning, Elizabeth Barrett. *An Elizabeth Barrett Browning Concordance*. Comp. Gladys W. Hudson. Vol. 3. Detroit: Gale Research, 1973.

———. *Aurora Leigh*. Chicago: Academy Chicago, 1989.

———. *Aurora Leigh: Authoritative Text, Backgrounds and Contexts, Criticism*. Ed. Margaret Reynolds. New York: W. W. Norton, 1996.

———. *The Letters of Elizabeth Barrett Browning to Mary Russell Mitford, 1836–1854*. Ed. Meredith B. Raymond and Mary Rose Sullivan. 3 vols. Winfield, Kans.: Wedgestone Press, 1983.

———. *The Letters of Robert Browning and Elizabeth Barrett Browning 1845–1846*. Ed. Elvan Kintner. Vol. 1. Cambridge: Harvard Univ. Press, 1969.

———. *Poetical Works of Elizabeth Barrett Browning*. 12th London ed. New York: Thomas Y. Crowell, n.d.

———. *The Seraphim and Other Poems*. London: Saunders and Otley, 1838.

Bullock, Charles, ed. *The Queen's Resolve: And Her "Doubly Royal" Reign*. London: Home Words Publishing Office, 1901. National Library of Scotland MS S.146.L.

Bullock, H. Somerset. "The King Comes!" In *The Queen's Resolve: And Her "Doubly Royal" Reign,* ed. Charles Bullock, pp. 265–66. London: Home Words Publishing Office, 1901. National Library of Scotland MS S.146.L.

Cannadine, David. "The Context, Performance and Meaning of Ritual: The British Monarchy and the 'Invention of Tradition,' c. 1820–1977." In *The Invention of Tradition,* ed. Eric J. Hobsbawm and Terence O. Ranger, pp. 101–64. Cambridge: Cambridge Univ. Press, 1983.

Carlyle, Thomas. *On Heroes, Hero-Worship and the Heroic in History.* Boston: Ginn and Co., 1901.

———. *The Collected Letters of Thomas and Jane Welsh Carlyle.* Ed. Charles Richard Sanders and Kenneth J. Fielding. Vols. 1, 3, 11, 12. Durham: Duke Univ. Press, 1970–1985.

Casteras, Susan P. "The Wise Child and Her 'Offspring': Some Changing Faces of Queen Victoria." In *Remaking Queen Victoria,* ed. Margaret Homans and Adrienne Munich, pp. 182–199. Cambridge: Cambridge Univ. Press, 1997.

Chronicle. 28 June 1897. National Library of Scotland MS 23211.

Colby, Vineta, and Robert A. Colby. *The Equivocal Virtue: Mrs. Oliphant and the Victorian Literary Market Place.* N.p.: Archon Books, 1966.

Corelli, Marie. *The Passing of the Great Queen.* London: Dodd, Mead, 1901.

Corrigan, Philip, and Derek Sayer. *The Great Arch: English State Formation as Cultural Revolution.* London: Basil Blackwell, 1985.

Daily Mail. 30 June 1897. National Library of Scotland MS 23211.

Dickens, Charles. *David Copperfield.* Ed. Nina Burgis. Oxford: Clarendon Press, 1981.

———. *Dombey and Son.* London: Penguin, 1970.

———. *Letters of Charles Dickens.* Ed. Madeline House and Graham Storey. Vol. 2, 1840–1841, Pilgrim edition. Oxford: Clarendon Press, 1969.

———. *Letters of Charles Dickens.* Ed. Madeline House, Graham Storey, and Kathleen Tillotson. Vol. 3, 1842–1843, Pilgrim edition. Oxford: Clarendon Press, 1974.

———. *Letters of Charles Dickens.* Ed. Kathleen Tillotson. Vol. 4, 1844–1846, Pilgrim edition. Oxford: Clarendon Press, 1977.

———. *Letters of Charles Dickens.* Ed. Graham Storey and K. J. Fielding. Vol. 5, 1847–1849, Pilgrim edition. Oxford: Clarendon Press, 1981.

———. *Letters of Charles Dickens.* Ed. Graham Storey, Kathleen Tillotson, and Nina Burgis. Vol. 6, 1850–1852, Pilgrim edition. Oxford: Clarendon Press, 1988.

———. *Letters of Charles Dickens.* Ed. Graham Storey and Kathleen Tillotson. Vol. 8, 1856–1858, Pilgrim edition. Oxford: Clarendon Press, 1995.

———. *Little Dorrit.* London: Penguin, 1985.

———. "The Story of Richard Doubledick." In *The Seven Poor Travellers.* London: Sisley's, n.d.

Disraeli, Benjamin. *Sybil, or: The Two Nations.* 1845. Reprint, Baltimore: Penguin, 1954.

Donaldson, Sandra. *Elizabeth Barrett Browning: An Annotated Bibliography of the Commentary and Criticism, 1826–1990.* New York: G. K. Hall, 1993.

Edwards, Fleetwood. Letter to Margaret Oliphant. 27 Mar. 1896. Royal Archives PPVic. 1896/14345.

Eliot, George. *Selections from George Eliot's Letters.* Ed. Gordon S. Haight. New Haven: Yale Univ. Press, 1980.

"A Father's Prayer Answered: Traced from the Cradle to Our Queen's." London: Hatchards, 1887. National Library of Scotland MS 4.86.

Fielding, K. J., and Rodger L. Tarr, eds. *Carlyle Past and Present: A Collection of New Essays.* London: Vision, 1976.

Fox, William Johnson. "A Political and Social Anomaly." *Monthly Repository,* n.s., 6, no. 69 (Sept. 1832): 637–42.

Fredeman, William E. "Introduction: 'England Our Home, Victoria Our Queen.'" *Victorian Poetry* 25, nos. 3–4 (1987): 1–8.

——. "'She Wrought Her People Lasting Good': A Commemorative Exhibition in Color of Artifacts Associated with Queen Victoria." *Victorian Poetry* 25, nos. 3–4 (1987): 223–41.

Friend of the people. "Letter to the Queen on the State of the Monarchy." London: Simpkin, Marshall, 1838. National Library of Scotland MS 3.1137.

Froula, Christine. "Gender and the Law of Genre: Joyce, Woolf, and the Autobiographical Artist-Novel." In *New Alliances in Joyce Studies,* ed. Bonnie Kime Scott, pp. 155–64. Newark, Del.: Univ. of Delaware Press, 1988.

Gagnier, Regenia. *Subjectivities: A History of Self-Representation in Britain, 1832–1920.* New York: Oxford Univ. Press, 1991.

Gallagher, Catherine. "George Eliot and *Daniel Deronda:* The Prostitute and the Jewish Question." In *Sex, Politics, and Science in the Nineteenth-Century Novel,* ed. Ruth Bernard Yeazell, pp. 39–62. Baltimore: Johns Hopkins Univ. Press, 1986.

Gay, Peter. *The Bourgeois Experience: Victoria to Freud: The Cultivation of Hatred.* Vol. 3. New York: W. W. Norton, 1993.

The Gentlewoman's in Memoriam of Victoria the Good. In Memoriam Number. Jan. 1901.

Gernsheim, Helmut, and Alison Gernsheim. *Queen Victoria: A Biography in Word and Picture.* London: Longmans, 1959.

Gilbert, Elliot L. "The Female King: Tennyson's Arthurian Apocalypse." *PMLA* 98, no. 5 (1983): 863–78.

Gilman, Charlotte Perkins. *The Charlotte Perkins Gilman Reader.* Ed. Ann J. Lane. New York: Pantheon, 1980.

Greenblatt, Stephen, ed. *Representing the English Renaissance.* Berkeley: Univ. of California Press, 1988.

Grey, C. *The Early Years of His Royal Highness the Prince Consort. Compiled under the Direction of Her Majesty the Queen.* New York: Harper, 1867.

Haggard, H. Rider. *She.* Oxford: Oxford Univ. Press, 1991.

Heller, Tamar. *Dead Secrets: Wilkie Collins and the Female Gothic.* New Haven: Yale Univ. Press, 1992.

Helsinger, Elizabeth K., Robin Lauterbach Sheets, and William Veeder, eds. "Queen Victoria and 'The Shadow Side.'" In *The Woman Question: Society and Literature in Britain and America.* Vol. 1, *Defining Voices, 1837–1883,* pp. 63–76. Chicago: Univ. of Chicago Press, 1983.

Henderson, Philip. *Swinburne: The Portrait of a Poet.* London: Routledge and Kegan Paul, 1974.

Hobsbawm, Eric J., and Terence O. Ranger, eds. *The Invention of Tradition.* Cambridge: Cambridge Univ. Press, 1983.

Homans, Margaret. "The Powers of Powerlessness: The Courtships of Elizabeth Barrett and Queen Victoria." In *Feminist Measures: Soundings in Poetry and Theory,* ed. Lynn Keller and Cristanne Miller, pp. 237–59. Ann Arbor: Univ. of Michigan Press, 1994.

——. "Queen Victoria's Highland Journal: The Self-Construction of a Domesticated

Monarch." Paper presented at the annual Modern Language Association Conference, New York, N.Y., Dec. 1992.

———. "'To the Queen's Private Apartments': Royal Family Portraiture and the Construction of Victoria's Sovereign Obedience." *Victorian Studies* 37, no. 1 (1993): 1–41.

Homans, Margaret, and Adrienne Munich, eds. *Remaking Queen Victoria.* Cambridge: Cambridge Univ. Press, 1997.

Houston, Gail Turley. *Consuming Fictions: Gender, Class, and Hunger in Dickens's Novels.* Carbondale: Southern Illinois Univ. Press, 1994.

———. "Gender Construction and the *Kunstlerroman: David Copperfield* and *Aurora Leigh.*" *Philological Quarterly* 72, no. 2 (1993): 213–36.

The Illustrated London News. 26 Jan. 1901.

International Magazine (New York) 2, no. 2, 1 Jan. 1850.

Jay, Elisabeth. "Freed by Necessity, Trapped by the Market: The Editing of Oliphant's *Autobiography.*" In *Margaret Oliphant: Critical Essays on a Gentle Subversive,* ed. D. J. Trela, pp. 135–46. Selinsgrove: Susquehanna Univ. Press, 1995.

———. *Mrs. Oliphant: "A Fiction to Herself."* Oxford: Clarendon Press, 1995.

Jewett, Sarah Orne. "The Queen's Twin." In *The Country of the Pointed Firs and Other Stories,* pp. 141–167. New York: Modern Library, 1995.

Jones, Michael Wynn. *A Cartoon History of the Monarchy.* London: Macmillan, 1978.

Kaplan, Fred. *Dickens.* New York: William Morrow, 1988.

Keller, Lynn, and Cristanne Miller, eds. *Feminist Measures: Soundings in Poetry and Theory.* Ann Arbor: Univ. of Michigan Press, 1994.

Killham, John. *Tennyson and "The Princess": Reflections of an Age.* London: Athlone Press, 1958.

Knoepflmacher, U. C. "From Outrage to Rage: Dickens's Bruised Femininity." In *Dickens and Other Victorians: Essays in Honour of Philip Collins,* ed. Joanne Shattock, pp. 75–96. London: Macmillan, 1988.

Langland, Elizabeth. "Nation and Nationality: Queen Victoria in the Developing Narrative of Englishness." In *Remaking Queen Victoria,* ed. Margaret Homans and Adrienne Munich. Cambridge: Cambridge Univ. Press, 1997.

———. *Nobody's Angels: Middle-Class Women and Domestic Ideology in Victorian Culture.* Ithaca: Cornell Univ. Press, 1995.

Laqueur, Thomas. *Making Sex: Body and Gender from the Greeks to Freud.* Cambridge: Harvard Univ. Press, 1990.

Lenard, Mary. *Preaching Pity: Sentimentalism and the Victorian Cultural Discourse of Social Reform.* New York: Peter Lang. Forthcoming.

L'Estrange, A. G. K., ed. *The Life of Mary Russell Mitford.* 2 vols. New York: Harper, 1870.

Longford, Elizabeth. *Victoria R. I.* London: Weidenfeld and Nicolson, 1964.

Maitland, Frederic William. *The Collected Papers of Frederic William Maitland.* Ed. H. A. L. Fisher. Vol. 3. Cambridge: Cambridge Univ. Press, 1911. Reprint, Buffalo: William S. Hein, 1981.

Martin, Kingsley. *The Crown and the Establishment.* London: Hutchinson, 1962.

Martin, Theodore. Letter to Margaret Oliphant. 30 Jan. 1868. National Library of Scotland MS 23210.

McClintock, Anne. *Imperial Leather.* New York: Routledge, 1995.

Miller, Andrew H., and James Eli Adams, eds. *Sexualities in Victorian Britain.* Bloomington: Indiana Univ. Press, 1996.

Montrose, Louis Adrian. "'Shaping Fantasies': Figurations of Gender and Power in Eliza-
bethan Culture." In *Representing the English Renaissance,* ed. Stephen Greenblatt,
pp. 31–64. Berkeley: Univ. of California Press, 1988.

More, Thomas. *The Latin Epigrams of Thomas More.* Trans. and ed. Leicester Bradner and
Charles A. Lynch. Chicago: Univ. of Chicago Press, 1953.

Moore, Thomas. "Sovereign Woman." Quoted in Peter Gay, *The Bourgeois Experience:
Victoria to Freud: The Cultivation of Hatred.* Vol. 3. New York: W. W. Norton, 1993.

Munich, Adrienne Auslander. "'Capture the Heart of a Queen': Gilbert and Sullivan's
Rites of Conquest." *The Centennial Review* 28, no. 1 (1984): 23–44.

———. "Queen Victoria, Empire, and Excess." *Tulsa Studies in Women's Literature* 6,
no. 2 (1987): 265–81.

———. *Queen Victoria's Secrets.* New York: Columbia Univ. Press, 1996.

Myers, Margaret. "The Lost Self: Gender in *David Copperfield.*" In *Gender Studies: New
Directions in Feminist Criticism,* ed. Judith Spector, pp. 75–96. Bowling Green, Ohio:
Bowling Green State Univ. Press, 1986.

Nabholtz, John R., ed. *Prose of the British Romantic Movement.* New York: Macmillan, 1974.

Nadel, Ira B. "Portraits of the Queen." *Victorian Poetry* 25, nos. 3–4 (1987): 169–191.

National Memorial to His Royal Highness the Prince Consort. London: John Murray, 1873.

Nevill, Barry St. John, ed. *Life at the Court of Queen Victoria, 1861–1901.* Exeter, England:
Webb and Bower, 1984.

The New York Times. 4 April 1860.

O'Doherty, Morgan. "On Prince Albert's Birthday." *Fraser's Magazine* 22, no. 129. (Sept.
1840): 382.

Old England. "This Country Must Be Governed." London: James Fraser, 1841. National
Library of Scotland MS 3.1139.

Oliphant, Margaret. *Miss Marjoribanks.* 1866. Reprint, London: Virago Press, 1988.

———. "The Queen of the Highlands." *Blackwoods Magazine* (Feb. 1868): 242–50.

———. *Historical Sketches of the Reign of George Second.* 2d ed. Edinburgh: William Blackwood, 1870.

———. Letter to Sir Henry Ponsonby. 9 Nov. 1881. Royal Archives PPVic. 1881/11773.

———. Letter to W. Blackwood. 13 Mar. 1886. National Library of Scotland. MS 23209.

———. *The Victorian Age of English Literature.* London: Percival, 1892.

———. *Historical Sketches of the Reign of Queen Anne.* London: Macmillan, 1894.

———. Letter to Sir Fleetwood Edwards. 20 Mar. 1896. Royal Archives PPVic. 1896/
14345.

———. *Annals of a Publishing House: William Blackwood and His Sons: Their Magazine and
Friends.* Vol. 2. Edinburgh: William Blackwood and Sons, 1897.

———. *Autobiography and Letters of Mrs. Margaret Oliphant,* ed. Mrs. Harry Coghill. 1899.
Reprint, New York: Humanities Press, 1974.

———. *Queen Victoria: A Personal Sketch.* London: Cassell, 1900.

———. Lines upon her impending death. National Library of Scotland MS 23210,
no. 217, n.d.

One of Her Majesty's Most Loyal Subjects. "Letter to the Queen, On Her Retirement
from Public Life." London: Samuel Tinsley, 1875. National Library of Scotland MS
1875.

One of Her Majesty's Servants. *The Private Life of the Queen.* London: C. Arthur Pearson,
1897.

One of the people. "The Queen of Queens." Salisbury: Brown, 1897.

One of Themselves. "An Address to the People; Occasioned by 'A letter to the Queen' from 'A friend of the People.'" London: James Fraser, 1839. National Library of Scotland MS 3.1137.

O'Toole, Patricius. "A Full, True, and Particular Account of Her Majesty's Marriage with His Royal Highness Prince Albert." *Fraser's Magazine* 21, no. 125 (May 1840): 589–93.

The Pall Mall Gazette. 28 June 1897. National Library of Scotland MS 23211.

Parrinder, Patrick. *Authors and Authority: A Study of English Literary Criticism and Its Relation to Culture, 1750–1900.* London: Routledge and Kegan Paul, 1977.

Parton, James. *Eminent Women of the Age.* Hartford, Conn.: Park Publishing, 1868.

Partridge, Eric. *The Macmillan Dictionary of Historical Slang.* London: Routledge and Kegan Paul, 1961. Abridged by Jacqueline Simpson, New York: Macmillan, 1974.

Patten, Robert L. "George's Hive and the Georgian Hinge." *Browning Institute Studies* 14 (1986): 37–69.

"A Physician's Dreams." *All the Year Round* 2, no. 32 (3 Dec. 1859): 135–40.

Platt, Smith H. *Queenly Womanhood: A Private Treatise for Females Only, on the Sexual Instinct as Related to Moral and Christian Life.* Brooklyn: S. Harrison, 1875.

Ponsonby, Arthur. Letter to Margaret Oliphant. 13 Nov. 1881. Royal Archives PPVic. 1881/11773.

———. Letter to Margaret Oliphant. 28 Feb. 1886. National Library of Scotland MS 23210.

———. Letter to Margaret Oliphant. 5 Sept. 1887. National Library of Scotland MS 23194.

Poovey, Mary. *Making a Social Body: British Cultural Formation, 1830–1864.* Chicago: Univ. of Chicago Press, 1995.

———. *Uneven Developments: The Ideological Work of Gender in Mid-Victorian England.* Chicago: Univ. of Chicago Press, 1988.

Pratt, Mary Louise. "Women, Literature, and National Brotherhood." *Nineteenth-Century Contexts* 18, no. 1 (1994): 27–47.

The Queen, The Lady's Newspaper. 6 Apr. 1867, 5 Jan. 1867.

"Queen's Address to the Volunteer Army: Given at Holyrood Palace, 25 Aug. 1881." National Library of Scotland MS 1942.

Richards, Thomas. *The Commodity Culture of Victorian England: Advertising and Spectacle, 1851–1914.* Stanford: Stanford Univ. Press, 1990.

Ricks, Christopher. "The Princess and the Queen." *Victorian Poetry* 25, nos. 3–4 (1987): 133–139.

Rossetti, Christina. *The Complete Poems of Christina Rossetti, A Variorium Edition.* Ed. R. W. Crump. Vol 3. Baton Rouge: Louisiana State Univ. Press, 1979.

Royal Archives (RA), Windsor Castle, Journals and Letters of Victoria. RA QVJ: 25 May 1880, 9 June 1842, 24–25 June 1837, 1 July 1837, 22 June 1838, 20 June 1845, 18 Dec. 1839; RA PPVic. 1896/14345: 20 Mar. 1896; RA PPVic. 1881/11773: 9 Nov. 1881, 13 Nov. 1881; RA Y190/10, RA L13/159: 28 Jan. 1874; RA Vic. Add. MSS. U32.

Ruskin, John. "Of King's Treasures." In *Sesame and the Lilies,* pp. 33–123. Philadelphia: David McKay, 1900.

———. "Of Queen's Gardens." In *Sesame and the Lilies,* pp. 127–85. Philadelphia: David McKay, 1900.

Said, Edward W. *Beginnings: Intention and Method.* New York: Basic Books, 1975.

Sanders, C. R. "Carlyle's Pen Portraits of Queen Victoria and Prince Albert." In *Carlyle Past and Present: A Collection of New Essays,* ed. K. J. Fielding and Rodger L. Tarr. London: Vision, 1976.

St. Aubyn, Giles. "Queen Victoria as an Author." *Essays by Divers Hands* 38 (1975): 127–42. Transactions of the Royal Society of Literature, new ser. ed. John Guest. London: Oxford Univ. Press.

Saturday Review. 1857.

Scott, Bonnie Kime, ed. *New Alliances in Joyce Studies: When It's Aped to Foul a Delfian.* Newark, Del.: Univ. of Delaware Press, 1988.

Scribner's Monthly Magazine 1, no. 2 (Dec. 1871): 185–88.

Shattock, Joanne, ed. *Dickens and Other Victorians: Essays in Honour of Philip Collins.* London: Macmillan, 1988.

Shelley, Percy Bysshe. "A Defence of Poetry." In *Prose of the British Romantic Movement,* ed. John R. Nabholtz, pp. 724–38. New York: Macmillan, 1974.

Smith, W. Anderson. Quoted in John Killham, *Tennyson and "The Princess": Reflections of an Age.* London: Athlone Press, 1958.

Spector, Judith, ed. *Gender Studies: New Directions in Feminist Criticism.* Bowling Green, Ohio: Bowling Green State Univ. Press, 1986.

Staker, Susan, ed. *Waiting for World's End: The Diaries of Wilford Woodruff.* Salt Lake City: Signature Books, 1993.

The Star. 28 June 1897. National Library of Scotland MS 23211.

Stewart, Susan. *Crimes of Writing: Problems in the Containment of Representation.* New York: Oxford Univ. Press, 1991.

Strachey, Lytton. *Queen Victoria.* New York: Harcourt, Brace, 1921.

Sutherland, J. A. *Victorian Novelists and Publishers.* London: Athlone Press, 1976.

Swiney, Frances. *The Cosmic Procession or The Feminine Principle in Evolution: Essays of Illumination.* London: Ernest Bell, 1906.

Tennyson, Alfred Lord. *The Princess.* In *The Works of Alfred Lord Tennyson,* ed. William J. Rolfe. Vol. 3. Boston: Colonial Press, 1895.

———. "To the Queen." In *The Works of Alfred Lord Tennyson,* ed. William J. Rolfe. Vol. 1. New York: Macmillan, 1899.

Thompson, Dorothy. *Queen Victoria: The Woman, the Monarchy, and the People.* New York: Pantheon, 1998. Originally published as *Queen Victoria: Gender and Power.* London: Virago, 1990.

Translations of Extracts of Letters from Albert, Prince Consort to Princess Victoria of Prussia, 1858–1862. Royal Archives Y190/10.

Trela, D. J., ed. *Margaret Oliphant: Critical Essays on a Gentle Subversive.* Selinsgrove: Susquehanna Univ. Press, 1995.

Trimmer, Mrs. *Fabulous Histories, Designed for the Amusement and Instruction of Young Persons.* Philadelphia: William Gibbons, 1794.

Tulloch, W. W. "The Reader: Mrs. Oliphant." *The Bookman* (Aug. 1897). National Library of Scotland MS 23211.

Vaihinger, Hans. *The Philosophy of "As If": A System of the Theoretical, Practical and Religious Fictions of Mankind.* Trans. C. K. Ogden. N.p., 1924. Reprint, London: Routledge and Kegan Paul, 1952.

Vallone, Lynne. "The Princess and the Authoress: Queen Victoria's Childhood Imitation of Maria Edgeworth." Paper presented at the 7th annual 18th and 19th Century British Women Writers Conference, Chapel Hill, Mar. 1998.

Victoria, Queen. Letter to Margaret Oliphant. 2 Mar. 1886. National Library of Scotland MS 23210.

————. Letter to Margaret Oliphant. 28 June 1887. National Library of Scotland MS 23210.

————. *The Letters of Queen Victoria to her eldest daughter the Princess Royal*. Royal Archives Vic. Add. MSS. U32. Kronberg Letters.

————. *Queen Victoria in Her Letters and Journals*, ed. Christopher Hibbert. London: John Murray, 1984.

Walkowitz, Judith R. *Prostitution and Victorian Society: Women, Class, and the State*. Cambridge: Cambridge Univ. Press, 1980.

Ward, F. W. Orde. "Song for the Jubilee." In *The Queen's Resolve: And Her "Doubly Royal" Reign*, ed. Charles Bullock. London: Home Words Publishing Office, 1901. National Library of Scotland MS S.146.L.

Whiting, Mary Bradford. "LILIES." *Social Pioneer* 1, no. 4 (April 1890): 173–175.

Williams, Merryn. *Margaret Oliphant: A Critical Biography*. New York: Macmillan, 1986.

Wilson, Robert. *The Life and Times of Queen Victoria, Illustrated with Numerous Portraits, Views, and Historical Pictures*. Vol. 3. London: Cassell, 1905.

Wolff, Robert Lee. *Sensational Victorian: The Life and Fiction of Mary Elizabeth Braddon*. New York: Garland, 1979.

Yeazell, Ruth Bernard, ed. *Sex, Politics, and Science in the Nineteenth-Century Novel*. Baltimore: Johns Hopkins Univ. Press, 1986.

Index

Victorian Literature and Culture Series

———··✦··———

DANIEL ALBRIGHT
Tennyson: The Muses' Tug-of-War

DAVID G. RIEDE
Matthew Arnold and the Betrayal of Language

ANTHONY WINNER
Culture and Irony: Studies in Joseph Conrad's Major Novels

JAMES RICHARDSON
Vanishing Lives: Style and Self in Tennyson, D. G. Rossetti, Swinburne, and Yeats

JEROME J. MCGANN, EDITOR
Victorian Connections

ANTONY H. HARRISON
Victorian Poets and Romantic Poems: Intertextuality and Ideology

E. WARWICK SLINN
The Discourse of Self in Victorian Poetry

LINDA K. HUGHES AND MICHAEL LUND
The Victorian Serial

ANNA LEONOWENS
The Romance of the Harem
Edited by Susan Morgan

ALAN FISCHLER
Modified Rapture: Comedy in W. S. Gilbert's Savoy Operas

EMILY SHORE
Journal of Emily Shore
Edited by Barbara Timm Gates

RICHARD MAXWELL
The Mysteries of Paris and London

FELICIA BONAPARTE
The Gypsy-Bachelor of Manchester: The Life of Mrs. Gaskell's Demon

PETER L. SHILLINGSBURG
Pegasus in Harness: Victorian Publishing and W. M. Thackeray

ANGELA LEIGHTON
Victorian Women Poets: Writing against the Heart

ALLAN C. DOOLEY
Author and Printer in Victorian England

SIMON GATRELL
Thomas Hardy and the Proper Study of Mankind

JEFFREY SKOBLOW
Paradise Dislocated: Morris, Politics, Art

MATTHEW ROWLINSON
Tennyson's Fixations: Psychoanalysis and the Topics of the Early Poetry

BEVERLY SEATON
The Language of Flowers: A History

BARRY MILLIGAN
Pleasures and Pains: Opium and the Orient in Nineteenth-Century British Culture

GINGER S. FROST
Promises Broken: Courtship, Class, and Gender in Victorian England

LINDA DOWLING
The Vulgarization of Art: The Victorians and Aesthetic Democracy

TRICIA LOOTENS
Lost Saints: Silence, Gender, and Victorian Literary Canonization

MATTHEW ARNOLD
The Letters of Matthew Arnold, vols. 1–3
Edited by Cecil Y. Lang

EDWARD FITZGERALD
Edward FitzGerald, Rubáiyát of Omar Khayyám: *A Critical Edition*
Edited by Christopher Decker

CHRISTINA ROSSETTI
The Letters of Christina Rossetti, vols. 1–2
Edited by Antony H. Harrison

BARBARA LEAH HARMAN
The Feminine Political Novel in Victorian England

JOHN RUSKIN
The Genius of John Ruskin: Selections from His Writings
Edited by John D. Rosenberg

ANTONY H. HARRISON
Victorian Poets and the Politics of Culture: Discourse and Ideology

JUDITH STODDART
Negotiating a Nation: Ruskin's Fors Calvigera *in the Late Victorian Culture Wars*

LINDA K. HUGHES AND MICHAEL LUND
Victorian Publishing and Mrs. Gaskell's Work

GAIL TURLEY HOUSTON
Royalties: The Queen and Victorian Writers

DATE DUE